Oil Crisis in Iran

Focusing on the turbulent twenty-eight months between April 1951 and August 1953, this book, based on recently declassified CIA and US State Department documents from the Mossadeq administration, tells the story of the Iranian oil crisis, which would culminate in the coup of August 1953. Throwing fresh light on US involvement in Iran, Ervand Abrahamian reveals exactly how immersed the USA was in internal Iranian politics long before the 1953 coup, in parliamentary politics, and even in saving the monarchy in 1952. By weighing rival explanations for the coup, from internal discontent, a fear of communism, and oil nationalization, Abrahamian shows how the Truman and Eisenhower administrations did not differ significantly in their policies towards Mossadeq, and how the surprising main obstacle to an earlier coup was the shah himself. In tracing the key involvement of the USA and the CIA in Iran, this study shows how the 1953 coup would eventually pave the way to the 1979 Iranian revolution, two of the most significant and widely studied episodes of modern Iranian history.

ERVAND ABRAHAMIAN was Distinguished Professor of History at Baruch College and Graduate Center, City University of New York. He is the author of several books including *Iran Between Two Revolutions* (1982) and *A History of Modern Iran* (2018). He was elected in 2010 to the American Academy of Arts and Sciences.

Oil Crisis in Iran

From Nationalism to Coup d'Etat

ERVAND ABRAHAMIAN
City University of New York

CAMBRIDGE
UNIVERSITY PRESS

CAMBRIDGE
UNIVERSITY PRESS

University Printing House, Cambridge CB2 8BS, United Kingdom

One Liberty Plaza, 20th Floor, New York, NY 10006, USA

477 Williamstown Road, Port Melbourne, VIC 3207, Australia

314–321, 3rd Floor, Plot 3, Splendor Forum, Jasola District Centre,
New Delhi – 110025, India

79 Anson Road, #06–04/06, Singapore 079906

Cambridge University Press is part of the University of Cambridge.

It furthers the University's mission by disseminating knowledge in the pursuit of
education, learning, and research at the highest international levels of excellence.

www.cambridge.org
Information on this title: www.cambridge.org/9781108837491
DOI: 10.1017/9781108946278

First published 2021

A catalogue record for this publication is available from the British Library.

ISBN 978-1-108-83749-1 Hardback

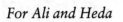

For Ali and Heda

Contents

Preface

People will say, or even write, the most fantastic nonsense about their own thoughts and intentions, to say nothing of deliberate lies.
Lewis Namier on Diplomatic Documents

This book was prompted by the recent publication of US government documents on Iran for the Mossadeq period – the turbulent twenty-eight months from April 1951 to August 1953. Declassified in November 2017 – long beyond the thirty-year rule, these documents were published in the annual State Department series entitled *Foreign Relations of the United States* – better known as the *FRUS*. Even as late as 1978, the UK had sought US assurances that such documents would not implicate Britain in the "removal of Musaddiq in 1953." "In the current situation," the British warned, "there is a good chance that public opinion will once again focus on that chapter of Iranian history. We hope therefore that the US administration would agree on a joint approach to minimize the damage which could be done to our interests by the release of US records."[1]

This new *FRUS* volume contains 375 documents totaling some 1,000 pages. It includes extensive cables, reports, notes, minutes, and memoranda not only from the State Department and the US Embassy, but also from the US Cabinet, the Central Intelligence Agency (CIA), and the National Security Council (NSC) – especially its annual and periodic National Intelligence Estimates (NIEs). Not surprisingly, the volume provides a wealth of information on the politics of this period – especially on the US involvement in Iran.

---

[1] R. Graham, Letter to R. Muir (16 and 19 November 1978), and Mr. R. Muir, Iran: Release of Confidential Records (22 December 1978), *FOC 8/3216*.

The book, therefore, focuses primarily on what these documents reveal about American policies in Iran during these controversial months. It will not digress either into the role of the oil crisis in the Cold War nor into the details of the August 1953 coup d´état. The former has been examined extensively elsewhere; nothing new on the subject is likely to be uncovered until Soviet archives are opened up. The coup has also been examined in detail by historians of Iran. Instead of rehashing the narrative of the coup and the Cold War, the book will focus on what new information the recent documents reveal about US policies in Iran leading to the eventual coup. In doing so, the book will keep in mind Lewis Namier's advice that diplomatic papers should be taken with a pinch of salt and "what is unsaid or unexplained" may often be more important than what is written down.[2]

Transliteration requires some explanation since few agree on a standard system. The name Mossadeq is a case in point. The State Department tended to spell his name sometimes as Mossadeq, sometimes as Mossadegh, sometimes as Musaddiq, and sometimes as Mosadeq. The British Foreign Office preferred Musaddiq; the *New York Times* Mossadegh; *Time* Mosadeq; and the London *Times* Moussadek. They were not always consistent. Throughout the book I have modified the systems developed by the Library of Congress and the International Journal of Middle East Studies. I have dispensed with diacritical marks; substituted o and e for equivalent sounds in English; used the backwards apostrophe (') for the letter *eyn*, and –e rather than –i for *ezafeh*; and, most important, adopted spelling that has become standardized through the mainstream media – Tehran, rather than Teheran, Mashed rather than Mashhad, Isfahan rather than Esfehan, Hussein rather than Husayn; and Khomeini rather Khomeyni. Hopefully, readers will read this preface before nit picking.

I would like to thank Alice Stoakley for editing the manuscript, as well as Maria Marsh, Daniel Brown, Natasha Whelan, Atifa Jiwa, and Raghavi Govindane for guiding it through the production process at Cambridge University Press.

[2] D. Hayton, *Conservative Revolutionary: The Lives of Lewis Namier* (Manchester: Manchester University Press, 2019), 289.

Chronology

1951

April 27	Majles elects Mossadeq premier
April 30	National Iranian Oil Company (NIOC) established
May 1	Oil Nationalization Law finalized
May 9	Allen Dulles recommends Mossadeq's removal
May 25	UK submits case to The Hague
June 10	AIOC delegation in Tehran
June 15	Iranian flag raised over AIOC's Khorramshahr offices
June 26	British oil technicians resign
July 14	Harriman arrives in Tehran
	Street clashes in Tehran
July 26	Harriman leaves for London
August 3–23	British delegation in Tehran
August 22	Majles gives Mossadeq vote of confidence
September 9	Bank of England restricts Iran transactions
September 21	Henderson arrives as ambassador
September 24	Mossadeq declares, "True Majles resides in the People"
September 27	UK submits case to UN Security Council
October 3	Last British oil technicians leave
October 6	Mossadeq leaves for UN
October 15–19	Mossadeq at UN
October 23	Mossadeq at White House
October 25	General Elections in UK
November 22	Mossadeq returns
November 25	Majles gives Mossadeq vote of confidence
December 5	Street clashes in Tehran

| December 18 | Seventeenth Majles elections start |
| December 23 | World Bank delegation in Tehran |

1952

January 21	British consulates closed
January 27	Ambassador Shepherd leaves
February 11	World Bank delegation arrives
February 14	Fatemi shot
February 18	Sixteenth Majles ends
April 27	Seventeenth Majles opens
May 1	Italian tanker *Rose Marie* in Abadan
May 9	Henderson reports oil problem cannot be solved with Mossadeq
May 16	Washington meeting to replace Mossadeq
May 19	Majles elections stopped
May 24	Henderson repeats problem cannot be solved with Mossadeq
May 28–24 June	Mossadeq at The Hague
June 6–10	Henderson sees Qavam twice
June 17	Italian tanker *Rose Marie* impounded in Aden
July 6	Majles reelects Mossadeq premier
July 16	Mossadeq resigns
July 17	Majles elects Qavam premier
July 20–21	July Uprising Majles reelects Mossadeq premier
July 22	Hague issues verdict
July 29	US asks UK for joint action to replace Mossadeq
August 3	Majles votes Mossadeq Special Powers
August 27	Truman-Churchill Proposal
September 9	Schacht arrives in Tehran
September 19	CIA meets with US Joints Chiefs on Iran "War-Game Plans"
October 16	Iran breaks diplomatic relations with UK
October 23	Senate dissolved

1953

| February 17–25 | Bakhtiyari revolt |
| February 20 | Eisenhower-Churchill Proposal |

July 14	Government deputies announce intention to resign
	Government calls for referendum and new electoral law
July 16	Fifty-two deputies resign
July 21	Rallies on anniversary of July Uprising
July 25	Princess Ashraf returns to Tehran
July 27	Mossadeq addresses nation on need for referendum
July 28	Foster Dulles expresses concern about Tudeh
August 1	Schwarzkopf arrives in Tehran
August 3	Referendum in Tehran
August 4	Kashani supports dissolving majles
August 5	Eisenhower expresses concern on Tudeh
August 9	Shah-Roosevelt secret meeting
August 10	Allen Dulles expresses open concern on Tudeh
	Referendum in the provinces
August 11	Pan-Iranists demonstrate outside Kashani's home
August 13	Soviet delegation in Tehran
August 15	Nasseri tries to remove Mossadeq
August 16	Shah flees to Bagdad
	Government dissolves Seventeenth Majles
	Government rallies in Tehran
August 17	Anti-Shah demonstrations
	Henderson returns to Tehran
	Shah in Rome
August 18	Government calls for Regency Council
	Henderson sees Mossadeq
	Street clashes
August 19	
8:15 a.m.	Crowd gathers in southern Tehran
9:40	Crowd moves into central Tehran
10:10	Offices of Iran Party attacked
10:30	Offices of Pan-Iranist Party and Third Force pillages
10:35	Offices of *Shabaz and Shuresh* burnt down
10:45	Offices of *Bakhtar-e Emruz* burnt down
11:30	Tanks in Tehran

1:00 p.m.	Two other publishing houses pillaged
2:30	Tanks occupy police HQ
2:45	Prisoners released
3:00	Telephone-telegraph HQ occupied
3:30	Sherman tanks begin bombarding Mossadeq's home
5:20	Zahedi speaks on Radio Tehran
6:15	Mossadeq's home pillaged

List of Notable Persons

Acheson, Dean. US Secretary of State.
Afshartous, General Mahmud. Chief of Police.
Akhavi, Ali. Minister of Economy.
Akhavi, Colonel Hassan. Former head of Iranian G-2.
Ala, Hussein. Minister of Court and former prime minister.
Alemi, Ibrahim. Minister of Labor.
Allen, George. US ambassador.
Amini, Abdul Qassem. Minister of Court.
Arfa, General Hassan. Former Chief of Staff.
Ashrafi, Colonel Hussein. Military Governor of Tehran.
Azar, Dr. Mehdi. Minister of Education.
Baqai, Mozaffar. Leader of Toilers Party.
Behbehani, Ayatollah Mohammad. A cleric close to the royal court.
Boroujerdi, Hussein Tabatabai. The paramount grand ayatollah.
Browne, Nicholas. Author of the British postmortem on the 1979 revolution.
Bullard, Sir Reader. British ambassador.
Butler, Rohan. Author of British postmortem on the 1951 Oil Crisis.
Daftari, General Mohammad. Commander of Custom Guards.
Dulles, Allen. CIA director.
Dulles, Foster. US Secretary of State.
Falle, Sam. British Embassy counsellor.
Faramarzi, Abdul Rahman. Majles deputy.
Farmanfarmayan, Saber. Minister of Health.
Fatemi, Hussein. Mossadeq's deputy prime minister.
Grady, Dr. Henry. US ambassador.
Haerizadeh, Abdul Hussein. Majles deputy.
Harriman, Averell. Special US envoy to oil negotiations in Tehran.
Hassibi, Kazem. Mossadeq's adviser on oil.
Helms, Richard. Member of CIA's Near East Division.

Henderson, Loy. US ambassador.

Imami, Hassan. Majles president.

Kashani, Ayatollah Abul Qassem. Cleric prominent in the nationalization campaign.

Kazemi, Baqer. Minister of Foreign Affairs.

Lofti, Abdol Ali. Minister of Justice.

Makki, Hussein. Prominent spokesman for the National Front.

McGhee, George. US Under Secretary of State.

Matin-Daftari, Dr. Ahmad. Senator and former prime minister.

Middleton, Sir George. British chargé d'affaires.

Mir Ashrafi, Mehdi. Cashiered army officer and majles deputy.

Moazemi, Abdollah. A leader of the Iran Party.

Moazemi, Sheifollah. A leader of the Iran Party and Minister of Post and Telegraph.

Nariman, Mahmud. Mossadeq's main adviser on financial matters.

Perron, Ernest. Shah's friend and courtier.

Polk, William. Consultant to the National Security Council.

Pyman, Lancelot. British Embassy counsellor.

Qavam, Ahmad. Veteran aristocratic politician.

Qonatabadi, Shams al-Din. Majles deputy.

Riyahi, General Mohammad Taqi. Mossadeq's military chief of staff.

Roosevelt, Kermit. Chief of CIA's Near East Division.

Sadeqi, Ghulam-Hussein. Minister of Interior.

Saleh, Allayar. Iran's ambassador to the US.

Sha'aban Brainless (*Beymogh*). Prominent gang leader in Tehran.

Shayegan, Dr. Ali. Majles deputy and Mossadeq's legal adviser.

Shepherd, Sir Francis. British ambassador.

Tayyeb, Hajj Rezai. The main gang leader in Tehran.

Waller, John. Chief of the CIA's Iran Branch.

Wilber, Donald. Author of the CIA's 1954 study on the coup.

Wisner, Frank. The CIA's Deputy Director of Plans.

Zaehner, Robin. Fellow of All Souls and British Embassy counsellor.

Zahedi, General Fazlollah. Nominal head of the 1953 coup.

Zaheri, Ali. A leader of the Toilers Party and editor of *Shahed*.

Zirakzadeh, Ahmad. A leader of the Iran Party.

Introduction

History is about arguments.

Christopher Hill

The new edition of the declassified documents throws invaluable light on how deeply the United States was involved in the internal politics of Iran from the very beginning of the oil crisis – an involvement previously overlooked by both historians and informed observers. A cursory comparison between the 2017 version of *Foreign Relations of the United States, 1952–54*, Vol. X, *Iran, 1951–54 (FRUS)* with the 1989 version with the same title indicates that these documents were withheld for so long precisely because the State Department was reluctant to admit to such deep involvement.[1] The 2017 version reveals that the 1989 version had "redacted" – euphemism for deleted and censored – the following two short, but significant, phrases from a long 1951 National Security Council document: US "conduct special political operations" in Iran; and US "coordinated US-UK support for pro-Western Iranian elements."[2] Similarly, the old version reported that Foster Dulles, the Secretary of State, immediately after the successful 1953 coup, profusely thanked " .... ." The new version fills the blank with "the CIA, State, and FOA [Foreign Affairs Operations]."[3] The main function of FOA was to funnel money into covert CIA operations.

---

[1] State Department, *Foreign Relations of the United States, 1952–54*, Vol. X, *Iran, 1951–54* (ed. William Slany) (Washington, DC: US Government Printing Office, 1989), 1–1092; State Department, *Foreign Relations of the United States, 1952–54, Iran, 1951–54* (ed. William Van Hook) (Washington, DC: US Government Printing House, 2017), 1–970.

[2] NSC, 27 June 1951, *FRUS* (1989), 75. Compare it with *FRUS* (2017), 109.

[3] NSC, Memo of Meeting (27 August 1953), *FRUS* (1989), 773. Compare it with *FRUS* (2017), 720. The document gives no precise definition for FOA. It could be a variation of OPC (Office of Policy Coordination) – a bland name for secret operations including assassinations, bribery, rumormongering, and financing noncommunist front organizations. See Tim Weiner, *Legacy of Ashes: The History of the CIA* (New York: Random House, 2008), 33.

The new volume, thus, is less meticulous in keeping up the pretense that American diplomats did not interfere in the internal affairs of their host countries.

The previous volume, although 1,000 pages long, had nothing on the actual coup itself, and remarkably little for periods of heightened crises in the previous twenty-eight months. It was hard to believe that the Tehran embassy had not been communicating with Washington, particularly during those critical days and weeks. Not surprisingly, when the earlier version was first released, the American Historical Association raised an "outcry" and some leading members dismissed the volume as a total "fraud." Consequently, Congress passed the Foreign Relations Statute instructing the government to release after thirty years all documents – not just State Department ones – relevant to the understanding of American foreign policy.[4] This thirty-year rule was soon reduced to twenty-five years. In 1996 the State Department announced it would soon release a new version of the Iran volume for the years 1951–4.[5] After a series of delays and false starts, the long-promised volume eventually saw the light of day in late 2017.

The editor describes the new volume as a "retrospective supplement" to the earlier one that, he claims, provided "a thorough accurate, and reliable account of the role the United States played in mediating" the dispute between Iran and the United Kingdom. The new one, he further claims, placed the whole crisis solidly within the "context of the Cold War." In other words, the first depicts America as an "honest broker" in the oil crisis; the second revealed America as being mainly concerned with the communist danger – both from the Tudeh Party and the Soviet Union. These claims are not always borne out by the contents. The editor, in passing, admits that the new volume still withholds ten full documents, excises a paragraph or more from thirty-eight others, and

---

[4] Historical Advisory Committee to the State Department, "Report of the
     Committee," *Perspectives*, September 2012.
[5] Warren Kimball, "Classified!" *Perspectives*, February 1997, 9–10, 22–4; Stephen
     Weissman, "Censoring American Diplomatic History," *Perspectives*,
     September 2011, 48–9; Weissman, "Why Is US Withholding Documents . . . ?"
     Christian Science Monitor, 25 March 2011; Richard Immerman (Chair),
     "Report on Diplomatic Documentation," *Perspectives*, January 2013. See also
     National Security Archive, "Have the British Been Meddling with the FRUS
     Retrospective Volume?" www2.gwu.edu/~nsarchiv/NSAEBB/NSAEBB435/; and
     "CIA Stalling State Department Histories," www2.gwu.edu/~nsarchiv/NSAEBB/
     NSAEBB52/.

makes minor cuts in another eighty-two. He adds that many CIA cables for the 1953 "covert action" had apparently been "destroyed" during routine "office relocations" in 1961–2. The CIA itself admits destroying nine-year-old cables deemed "unimportant" in order to "house clean" and "gain space."[6]

Our knowledge of US relations with the Mossadeq administration has been further enriched in recent years by the opening up of a number of other sources. First, the CIA has been pressured – probably because of the Freedom of Information Act – to release reams of relevant telegrams, reports, and memos on its Electronic Reading Room.[7] They are readily available on the Internet. Second, the National Security Archive in Washington has performed the Herculean task of persuading the CIA to declassify two in-depth internal studies – *The Battle for Iran* and *"Zendebad Shah!" The CIA and the Fall of the Iranian Prime Minister Mohammed Mossadeq, August 1953.*[8] *Zendebad* means "Long Live."

Third, the Internet provides easy access to important Iranian sources, particularly to the proceedings of the turbulent majles and senate – the country's lower and upper Houses of Parliament. It also provides ready access to *Ettela'at (Information)* – a daily which in those years served as the "paper of record." It not only reported fairly objectively on political events, but also carried an unsigned column, "Day's Events," written by a correspondent who visited the prime minister every morning and conveyed his views to the readers.[9] One senior senator – who happened to be a highly regarded historian – described *Ettela'at* as required reading for anyone interested in national and international politics.[10] He read the paper from cover to cover every day during lunch or dinner. What is more, during these months, Iran had a lively press

---

[6] Scott Koch, *"Zendebad Shah!": The CIA and the Fall of the Iranian Prime Minister Mohammed Mossadeq, August 1953* (Washington, DC: CIA History Staff, 1963) (declassified in 2018), 1–93, iv.

[7] The CIA posted them on www.cia.gov/library/readingroom/search/site/iran%2C%201951–79.

[8] Koch, *"Zendebad Shah!": The CIA and the Fall of the Iranian Prime Minister Mohammed Mossadeq, August 1953*; and CIA History Staff, *The Battle for Iran* (Washington, DC: Near East Division, n.d.).

[9] Anonymous (Ahmad Shahidi), "Dar Mohafel-e Tehran" (Day's Events), *Ettela'at*, 21 March–18 August 1953.

[10] Mehdi Malekzadeh, *Muzakerat-e Majles-e Sena* (Senate Debates) (Tehran: Majles Publishing House, 1951), 1st Senate, 11 May 1951.

with most political groups publishing their newspapers and stressing the importance of the "Fourth Estate."

Finally, the famous Wilber Report – leaked to the *New York Times* in 2000 – provides a down-to-earth and in-depth study of the mechanisms used in the eventual 1953 coup. Dr. Donald Wilber, one of the coup planners, was assigned to write it immediately after the event by the CIA itself. The report can be taken to be a reliable primary source. Designed for internal use only, it cannot be dismissed as simple propaganda even though it contains some expected self-promotion and self-censorship. Since it was designed as a practical self-help book for future CIA coups, it remains our best source for the overthrow of Mossadeq.[11]

In fact, the Wilber report is so thorough that scholars eager for fresh information on the actual coup hastily dismissed the new *FRUS* volume as worthless on the grounds that it "contained no new revelations."[12] Andrew Bacevich, the eminent historian of American foreign policy, argued that the tome reads "like the Book of Genesis describing the Garden of Eden but leaving out the bit about Eve and the Serpent."[13] Malcolm Byrne of the National Security Archive declared the "big news about the much anticipated volume was that it contained nothing new about the coup."[14] These American specialists, eager for new information on the coup itself, have overlooked the goldmine of information that the new volume provides on Iran – especially on US involvement in internal Iranian politics. The main aim of the present book is to examine this new information.

This book contains five essays, one in each chapter. The first explores US involvement in Iran during 1951–2 – the period before the coup. The new documents reveal for the very first time that the US

---

[11] Donald Wilber, *Overthrow of Premier Mossadeq of Iran, November 1952–August 1953* (Washington, DC: CIA Historical Division, 1954), 1–95, plus Appendices A–E. See http://cryptome.org/cia-iran-all.htm. This is the best source. A shorter version – with many names erased – was published as *Regime Change in Iran: Overthrow of Premier Mossadeq of Iran* (London: Russell Press, 2006).

[12] Mark Gasiorowski, "New Details on the 1953 Coup in Iran," www.lobelog.com /7/12/2017.

[13] Andrew Bacevich, "A Prize from Fairyland," *London Review of Books*, 2 November 2017.

[14] Roland Brown, "The 1953 Coup: What Secrets Remain?" https://iranwire.com /en/features/4169.

tried unsuccessfully in July 1952 to replace Mossadeq with Qavam – triggering the July Uprising. It also intervened – this time successfully – in February 1953 in persuading the shah not to leave the country, and, thereby, in the shah's own words "saving the monarchy." The second essay examines the new documents, trying to answer the question whether US policy was shaped by fear of communism or concern about "contagion of oil nationalization." The third looks at the various attempts made to bring down Mossadeq through parliamentary means. The new documents reveal, again for the first time, that the United States was deeply involved in majles elections and thus in majles politics. The fourth traces the road to the coup once the parliament path had been blocked. The new documents also reveal an ongoing debate within the US government, even within the CIA, on the pros and cons of a military coup. This debate took place under Truman long before the advent of the Eisenhower administration. The final essay explores the legacy of the 1953 coup, especially the wide gap between on one hand, Iranian memory, and on the other hand, American-induced amnesia – especially through official documents.

The new sources will hopefully clarify questions raised by historians of modern Iran: how far was the United States an "honest broker" in the oil dispute; could negotiations have resolved the oil crisis; did the USA-United Kingdom offer Iran a "fair compromise"; did the Eisenhower and Truman administrations differ significantly in their policies towards Iran; how much was Mossadeq's overthrow due to external or internal forces; how significant were economic difficulties in the overthrow; and is there a close link between the 1953 coup and the 1979 revolution?

These questions have loomed even larger in recent years as revisionist historians in Iran, as well as in America and Britain, have mounted a concerted assault on previous answers and assumptions. Ironically, the new *FRUS* volume appeared at the very same time that Americans were becoming familiar with three novel terms: "fake news," "deep state," and "electoral collusion." These terms may not have been current in America of the early 1950s, but the documents show that the United States, in its dealing with Mossadeq, readily relied on a toolbox that contained these very same three instruments.

1 | US Involvement

The Shah wished the Ambassador to know that he believed if it had not been for the actions of the Ambassador at that time [28 February 1953] the institution of monarchy in Iran would have been overthrown.

Memorandum for National Security Council (14 May 1953)

According to conventional wisdom America's deepening involvement in Iran began with the 1953 coup – with the firm installation of Mohammad Reza Shah on the throne. The new documents, however, show that the involvement began much earlier – as early as the nationalization of the oil industry in April 1951. It was most intrusive at three separate junctions: at the initial point of oil nationalization; in the July 1952 Uprising famous as *Siyeh-e Tir* (30th Tir) (21 July); and in the open confrontation between the shah and Mossadeq on 28 February 1953 – known as the February Incident (*Vaq'eh-e Esfand*).

Oil Nationalization

The whole oil crisis began on 27 April 1951 when parliament elected Mossadeq as prime minister with the mandate to form a cabinet and implement the recently enacted bill nationalizing the British-owned Anglo-Iranian Oil Company (AIOC). Mossadeq later revealed that Hussein Ala, the court minister and previous premier, had privately beseeched him to take the premiership in part because of concern about the forthcoming May Day, and in part because the majles was convinced he was the only person capable of implementing the nationalization law.[1]

Mossadeq presented his cabinet and program to the majles at the very end of April. Endorsed by another overwhelming vote, he received the automatic *farman* (royal decree) to head the new government. The

[1] Mohammad Mossadeq, Address to Senate, *Muzakerat-e Majles-e Sena Aval* (*1st Senate Debates*) (Tehran: Senate Printing House, 1953), 4 September 1951.

shah also placed his pro forma signature onto the nationalization law on 1 May. In his May Day address to the nation, Mossadeq confessed he never expected in his old age and ill health to become prime minister, but nevertheless promised to implement fully the nationalization law. Congratulating workers on their day, he beseeched the nation, including journalists, to be "moderate," "orderly," and "not abuse their freedoms."[2] The British embassy remarked that Mossadeq permitted public celebration of May Day because he was committed to the constitution and the rule of law – especially the right of citizens to speak, organize, and assemble.[3] The CIA reported Mossadeq's "first official act was to instruct the police not to ban the May Day demonstration." It added, "his willingness to permit the May Day demonstration is indication of his rather unreliable political philosophy."[4]

The CIA also reported that oil nationalization enjoyed "almost universal support" and was seen as a "fight for national independence from foreign interference in the internal affairs of Iran." It added "for the first time a government in Iran had come to power with popular backing."[5] The US chargé d'affaires later noted that Mossadeq had been elected in a wave of unprecedented popularity:[6]

There seems to be no question of the broad base of popular support for Dr. Mosadeq at the time he first took office as Prime Minister. As leader of the struggle against the Anglo-Iranian Oil Company in a country where resentment and even hatred of the British is deep-rooted, Mosadeq could count upon the support of the people from all levels of society with but few exceptions. For many months after oil nationalization, the Prime Minister's popularity continually mounted. To the common people, Mosadeq was looked upon almost as a demigod. The phenomenon of Mosadeq was almost unique in Iran. The figure of a frail, old man, in an Oriental country where age of itself commands respect, who appeared to be successfully winning a battle against tremendous odds, aroused the sympathy of almost all Iranians. In a country where political corruption

[2] Mossadeq, May Day Speech, *Ettela'at*, 2 May 1951.
[3] British Embassy, Activities and Development of Tudeh Party, *FO 416/Persia 1951/104*.
[4] CIA, Daily Digest (30 April 1951), CIA Electronic Library, www.cia.gov/readingroom/search/site/Iran.
[5] CIA, Current Outlook in Iran (25 September 1951), www.cia.gov/readingroom/search/site/Iran.
[6] Roy Melbourne, Popularity and Prestige of Prime Minister Mohamed Mosadeq (1 July 1953), *FRUS* (2017), 612–15.

had been the accepted norm, there now appeared a man whose patriotism and financial honesty was unassailable.

Similarly, Sam Falle, a Persian-speaking British counsellor – the Foreign Office term for political attaché – later admitted that Mossadeq come to power "loved by the people" and with "tremendous popular support" in most part because he was a "brilliant" speaker, as well as a "sincere," "honest," "non-violent," and "sort of an Iranian Mahatma Gandhi."[7] When Sir Francis Shepherd, the British ambassador, tried to persuade the shah to forestall Mossadeq's election by dissolving the majles, declaring martial law, and appointing a more pliable prime minister, the shah declined on the grounds that any future government would still have to deal with overwhelming public opinion. Moreover, he was "not sure whether soldiers would obey orders if they were told to fire on crowds."[8] Thus began a breathtaking roller-coaster crisis that shook the international community as well as Iran for the next two years. It came to an abrupt end only with the military coup of August 1953.

Even before the nationalization bill had been finalized, George McGhee, President Truman's assistant secretary of state, rushed to Tehran to persuade the shah not to sign the bill into law. He harbored the false notion that the shah had such constitutional prerogatives. Dr. Henry Grady, the US ambassador, had earlier warned that the only way to forestall the danger of nationalization was for the AIOC to offer Iran an agreement similar to that of Aramco – one based on the "principle" of 50/50 sharing of profits.[9] An Iranian senator raised the not-so-rhetorical question why a dispute between Iran and a private British company was attracting so much American attention.[10] McGhee, himself a Texan oil man, continued to serve as President Truman's point man on Iran throughout the forthcoming crisis.

When McGhee arrived in Tehran he found the public mood such that "no one could persuade Iranians not to nationalize the AIOC."[11] In the previous months, Mossadeq's National Front had held mass meetings

---

[7] Sam Falle, *My Lucky Life* (London: Book Guild, 1996), 75.
[8] Sir Francis Shepherd, Letter to Foreign Office (6 May 1951), *FO 248/Persia 1951/1514*.
[9] Editorial Note, Note on Grady's Report (7 March 1951), *FRUS* (2017), 15.
[10] Baqer Kazemi, Speech, *1st Senate*, 15 April 1951.
[11] George McGhee, *Envoy to the Middle East* (New York: Harper and Row, 1983), 327.

demanding nationalization. At the same time, the Tudeh Party – the outlawed communist party – and its main front organizations, the Peace Partisans and the Society against the Imperialist Oil Company, had organized petitions, protests, and a general strike throughout the oil industry. They had also organized "sympathy strikes," some violent, in other industries – especially in the textile factories in Isfahan. The senior senator from Isfahan described these strikes as a national *qeyam* (uprising) and praised nationalization as culmination of the country's two-centuries-long struggle for unity, sovereignty, freedom, and "national independence" (*isteqlal-e melli*).[12]

As Grady begrudgingly admitted to the State Department: "Mosadeq has the backing of 95 to 98 percent of the people of this country. It is folly to try to push him out."[13] Although Grady persisted in opposing nationalization, he retained great respect for Mossadeq, describing him as: "A man of great ability, a popular leader and regarded by even his critics as thoroughly honest. He is also a man of great intelligence, wit, and education – a cultured Persian gentleman reminiscent of the late Gandhi."[14] Some in the CIA concurred – at least in these early days. They stressed that Iranians regarded the oil struggle as a "fight for national independence," and, therefore, would rather suffer full revolution than see the British return to Iran.[15]

Nationalization received overwhelming support not only in the majles but also in the conservative upper house. Even senators wary of Mossadeq voted for nationalization. Hassan Taqizadeh, the senate president and veteran politician, who had negotiated the 1932–3 AIOC concession, privately told the *Manchester Guardian* reporter, whom he knew from the days of the Constitutional Revolution, that he "did not believe his ears" in 1933 when he heard Reza Shah had abruptly accepted the bad offer made by the oil company. He attributed the shah's unexpected about-turn either to AIOC pressure or to perhaps a "private deal."[16] He left others to figure out what he meant by "private deal."

---

[12] Mehdi Malekzadeh, Speech, *1st Senate*, 19 April 1951 and 18 May 1951.
[13] Dr. Henry Grady, Telegram (1 July 1951), *FRUS* (1989), 78.
[14] Grady, "What Went Wrong in Iran?" *Saturday Evening Post*. This is preserved in the British Petroleum Archives in Warwick University. See *BP/10624*.
[15] CIA, Current Strength of the Tudeh Party (13 September 1951), *FRUS* (2017), 133.
[16] Arthur Moore, Letter (22 October 1951), *FO 371/Persia 1951/34–91606*.

The National Security Council (NSC) in Washington rushed a National Intelligence Estimate (NIE) – known internally as an "Estimate." It argued that Mossadeq, despite the opposition of the shah and the ruling elite, had "radically transformed" Iranian politics. He had done so by obtaining the support of the vast majority including "peasants, laborers, and tradesmen." It concluded:

The most significant aspect of Mossadeq's advent to power is that moderate elements in Iran's government class appear to have lost control of the situation. Many deputies in the Majlis supported Musaddiq for Prime Minister in the hope that the oil crisis for which he is largely responsible, would result in his own downfall. In view of his strong popular backing, however, he will not be easily replaced.[17]

A follow-up estimate elaborated that Mossadeq had "come to power as leader of a nationalist movement"; that he had "aroused intense popular support"; that he "could not be removed from power as long as the oil question remains"; and that an "attempt to set up a non-parliamentary regime would involve grave risks which the Shah is not willing to take."[18] A more detailed NIE for 1952 reemphasized the conclusion the shah "cannot risk the danger of attempting to remove the premier because of the almost universal support on the oil issue." It speculated that there was as an "outside chance that under British pressure he [the shah] would arrest him and his extreme supporters, but this would certainly risk a certain civil war."[19] The US embassy concurred.[20]

McGhee, in his memoirs, is candid about his rushed trip to Tehran. He writes that he made it crystal clear to the shah that his administration was dead against nationalization since such a measure "would jeopardize oil concessions held by the USA, United Kingdom, and other firms around the world."[21] Loy Henderson, the incoming American ambassador, in a detailed report to the State Department listed reasons why the shah refused to heed

[17] Office of National Estimates, Memo for the NSC (1 May 1951), *FRUS* (2017), 73–5.

[18] NCS, Special Estimate: Current Developments in Iran (22 May 1951), *FRUS* (2017), 91–6.

[19] NSC, NIE-46 (19 December 1951) www.cia.gov/readingroom/search/site/Iran.

[20] US Embassy, Popularity and Prestige of Prime Minister Musaddiq (1 July 1953), in *FO 371/Persia 1953/34–104568*.

[21] McGhee, *Envoy to the Middle East*, 327.

McGhee's advice.[22] The shah felt "helpless": politicians were unwilling to "speak up" or "lift a finger" against Mossadeq; "national sentiment" had rallied behind the premier against Britain; and religious leaders, headed by Grand Ayatollah Hajj Aqa Hussein Boroujerdi – the paramount *marja'-e taqled* (source of religious imitation) – had openly come out in full support of nationalization. The shah, in Henderson's words, pleaded:

Brits tell me I should be strong man and take resolute action, but these so-called strong men like my father, Hitler, Stalin, etc. took resolute and bold action when they knew national sentiment was behind them. They never moved against the basic feelings of their peoples. In this case, national feelings in Iran are against Britain in oil matters; these feelings have been inflamed by demagogues; no matter how strong and resolute I may wish to be, I cannot take unconstitutional move against strong current of national feelings. What slogans do I have? Can appeals to balanced budgets and increased national income have much effect when deep national passions have been aroused? I know that Mosadeq's policies are leading Iran towards ruin ... I am convinced that attempt on my part to remove Mosadeq just now would give his friends and my enemies opportunity (to) convince Iran public that Crown has degenerated into mere Brit tool and such prestige as Crown has would disappear. Only hope as I can see is for Mosadeq either to become more sober and reasonable or for him to make so many mistakes that responsible leaders of Iran will overthrown him in Majlis.

In early September 1951 the shah conveyed to Robin Zaehner, the British counsellor, via Ernest Perron, his personal emissary, that however much he favored Mossadeq's removal he was afraid of the consequences. He would instead wait for an opportune moment.[23] Henderson assured the CIA that "an organized plan was underway in the majles to force" Mossadeq's resignation.[24] The shah, meanwhile, doggedly held on to his original position through thick and thin during the whole course of the twenty-eight month crisis. He proved more consistent, realistic, down-to-earth, and prescient than most of his advisers and foreign ambassadors. He did not like Mossadeq; he would be more than happy to have him gone; but he did not want to jeopardize the monarchy and carry the stigma of appearing to oppose

[22] Loy Henderson, Telegram to the State Department (30 September 1951), *FRUS* (1989), 185–8.

[23] Shepherd, Telegram (26 September 1951), *FO 371/Persia 1951/91464*.

[24] CIA, Bulletin (8 September 1951), www.cia.gov/readingroom/search/site/Iran.

him and the national movement. In other words, he preferred to have others, preferably the majles deputies, carry the onus of removing him. In May 1953 – just three months before the coup, Henderson again spelled out for Washington the shah's position:[25]

The emissary wished to make clear to the Ambassador certain fundamental features of the Shah's policy toward Dr. Mosadeq. The latter had come to power as a result of careful planning over a period of several years before actually assuming power. He had stirred the emotions of the Iranian people when he took office, and he had had public and Majlis support. The Shah had not willingly agreed to make Mosadeq Prime Minister, but he had bowed to the forces behind him and now believed that the only way to obtain Mossadeq's eventual dismissal from office was through the same parliamentary means which had granted him the premiership. ... The Shah preferred Mosadeq's removal in a legal way to the others, such as a military coup, and arbitrary move of the Shah removing Mossadeq and appointing another prime minister, the imprisonment of Mosadeq, his exile, or even his death at the hands of a Tehran mob. In all these alternatives Mosadeq would be made a martyr or a source of serious future trouble. It was the Shah's policy towards Dr. Mosadeq to bow slowly to Mosadeq's pressure, but at the same time to regain as much ground as possible through taking advantage of shifting conditions. If the Shah had rigidly opposed Mosadeq, the Shah would have been completely eliminated, like a tree which would have crashed through the force of a violent wind. Such explanations were made by the emissary to depict the Shah's policy, which he understood had caused a certain dissatisfaction on the part of American officials who wished the Shah to take a much stronger stand toward Mosadeq.

The CIA seconded Henderson's assessment. It argued:

The Shah is increasingly aware of the strength of the "street," and fears the "street" at present more than the British. No other Prime Minister prior to Mossadeq could claim such sponsorship. The Shah does not talk back or step out of line. He is fully aware that the political wave which brought Mossadeq into power was in great part an anti-court wave.[26]

Even in late spring of 1953, the US embassy reported: "The Shah insists that it would be unwise for him to openly oppose Mossadeq before the myth of his greatness has been exposed. The Shah prefers to wait until it

[25] Henderson, Memorandum on Conversation (14 May 1953), *FRUS* (2017), 557.
[26] CIA, Telegram (12 October 1951), *FRUS* (2017), 147.

is quite clear that Mossadeq is bankrupt, both economically and in ideas, before taking any action."[27]

McGhee, having failed initially to forestall nationalization, soon came up with an ingenious "compromise" formula. The USA would urge the United Kingdom to accept the principle of nationalization, but with the important caveat that actual "control" of the oil industry – sometimes the term "management" was substituted for "control" – would remain firmly in the hands of either the AIOC or a consortium of western companies including the AIOC. McGhee admits that his "alternative" plan paid "lip-service to nationalization," but cut so thin that it could be workable for the AIOC and Iran, and "would not upset concessionary arrangements elsewhere."[28] The American ambassador in London emphasized to the Foreign Office the clear message that to "help the Iranians save face it is tactically important to give unequivocal lip service to nationalization."[29]

The British initially protested that "nationalization" was tantamount to "confiscation," and as such would threaten "all foreign oil concessions in the Middle East."[30] They objected that such "surrender" would have "catastrophic" worldwide consequences.[31] At a top-level meeting in Washington, the British initially recommended joint action with the Americans to induce the shah to remove Mossadeq and if need be carry out a coup d'état.[32] But under US pressure, the British soon came round to accepting McGhee's formula. They announced they "favoured accepting the principle of nationalization" so long as it caused no "serious harm to British interests."[33] The British ambassador in Washington claimed that the US and UK positions were not very different since the two "had a joint interest in the matter." "Mr. McGhee," he reported, "suggested accepting the pretence and the

---

[27] Foreign Office, US Report on Iran (19 March 1953), *FO 371*/Persia 1953/ 104564.

[28] McGhee, *Envoy to the Middle East*, 327.

[29] CIA, Intelligence Bulletin (8 May 1951), www.cia.gov/readingroom/search/site/ Iran.

[30] State Department, Memorandum of Conversation with British Foreign Secretary (4 November 1951), *FRUS* (1989), 257.

[31] State Department, Memo of Foreign Ministers Meeting (2 January 1952), *FRUS* (1989), 320.

[32] Rohan Butler, *British Policy in the Relinquishing of Abadan in 1951* (London: Foreign Office, 1962), 1–324, in *FO 370*/2694.

[33] Foreign Office, Note on Phone Conversation with Sir Oliver Frank, *FO 371*/ Persia 1951/91471.

'façade' of nationalization while retaining effective control."[34] At times the terms "pretence" and "façade" were replaced with "cloak" and "flavor."

Averell Harriman, President Truman's later troubleshooter sent to Tehran, explained that for Iranians "nationalization" meant control over exploration, production, and exploitation. But, he added, it could also mean "under the authority of."[35] Years later the Foreign Office claimed – without evidence – that Shepherd, the British ambassador, even before McGhee's arrival had let the Iranian government know the United Kingdom "did not see any objection to the endorsement of the principle of nationalisation so long as it was rejected in practice."[36] The CIA concurred that it was "tactically important to give unequivocal lip service to the principle of nationalization."[37] The British ambassador in Washington explained that McGhee felt strongly that the "essence of the problem was how to concede something to this emotional concept of 'nationalization' while retaining actual control over oil operations."[38]

This policy was admitted in the postmortem on the crisis commissioned by the Foreign Office. Authored by Rohan Butler, a senior MI6 official, this 324-page investigation claimed the British government did not object to the principle of nationalization so long as actual operations were not run by Iran.[39] Known as the Butler report, this document was circulated in limited numbers only within the Foreign Office. It took the AIOC to task for failing to offer timely concessions, and the embassy for not taking nationalism seriously. Its harshest criticisms were directed at the Americans: for signing a new Saudi contract without consulting the AIOC; for preventing the United Kingdom from occupying Khuzestan; for pressuring the United Kingdom to take the case to the UN where it suffered a "humiliating defeat"; and, more seriously, for "ruthlessly" and "abruptly" cutting off Lend-Lease

---

[34] British Ambassador (in Washington), Anglo-US Talks in Washington, *BP*/Persia 1951/00043859. See also State Department, Memo on Conversation (18 April 1951), *FRUS* (1989), 37–42.

[35] Shepherd, Oil Problem in Persia (18 October 1951), *FO 248/1529.*

[36] Butler, *British Policy in the Relinquishing of Abadan in 1951.*

[37] CIA, Intelligence Bulletin (8 May 1951), www.cia.gov/readingroom/search/site/Iran.

[38] British Ambassador (in Washington), Memos to the Foreign Office, 2–11 April 1951, *FO 371/34–91470.*

[39] Butler, *British Policy in the Relinquishing of Abadan in 1951.*

to Britain. It quoted a senior official complaining the "Americans at the early stage of the dispute urged us to make a deep bow in the direction of nationalization." It quoted another complaining the "only constructive idea the Americans made was the possibility on one hand of accepting the Persian thesis on nationalization, but on the other hand insisting that the management of oil production and refinery in Persia should be carried out by a British company – either AIOC under another name or a subsidiary of it." It noted that McGhee's main aim was to "preserve the 50–50 arrangement for fear that anything beyond that would jeopardize the position of all companies in the area." The report was restricted for eyes only so as not to "revive strong anti-American feelings in the country (Britain)." It concluded that the "real winner was the American *tertius gauden.*" John Le Carré of MI6 was probably thinking of the Iran crisis when he put the following words into the mouth of his famous spy Smiley:[40]

The sad answer is, I'm afraid, that the Cold War produced in us a kind of vicarious colonialism. On one hand we abandoned practically every article of our national identity to American foreign policy. On the other hand we brought ourselves a stay of execution for our vision of our colonial selves. Worse still, we encouraged the Americans to behave in the same way. Not that they needed our encouragement, but they were pleased to have it naturally.

Not surprisingly, the main newspapers in America echoed the State Department on how the US had embraced the principle of nationalization. The *New York Times, Wall Street Journal,* and *Washington Post* all published reams of articles proclaiming that nationalization had to be accepted and could not be "reversed." But only in passing did they mention that it would be best if the actual management of the industry remained with the United Kingdom – or, at least, with Western companies.[41]

The Foreign Office convened a Working Party on Persian Oil. It was given two major tasks: keep effective "control" of the oil facilities out of Iranian hands; and "discourage other concessionary countries from following the Persian example."[42] Similarly, a series of top-level State

---

[40] John Le Carré, *The Secret Pilgrim* (New York: Ballantine Books, 1990), 229.
[41] British Embassy in Washington, Dispatch on American Newspapers (4 April 1951), FO 371/Persia 1951/34–91471.
[42] Working Party, Final Draft (23 June 1951), FO 371/Persia 1951/34–91409.

Department-Foreign Office meetings in London and Washington concluded the "most important consideration was that a settlement in Iran should not destroy concessionary arrangements in other areas or foreign investments generally."[43]

Although the AIOC, like the British government, had initially abhorred the word "nationalization," it gradually came round to accepting McGhee's formula after some prodding from the Foreign Office. It agreed the settlement could involve some form of "nationalization" so long as actual "control of future operations" remained out of Iranian hands.[44] It even claimed nationalization had never been an issue since according to ancient Iranian traditions sovereignty over minerals, resources, and underground treasures had always belonged to the crown. This type of woolly thinking – or double-talk – eventually became an integral part of the official narrative. Years later the State Department claimed in its standard history of the crisis: "For Iran, the most important objective in this crisis was to establish title to her own resources, and in this aim she was eventually successful."[45]

Double-talk was blatant in a memorandum entitled "Department's Thinking on AIOC Nationalization" sent by Dean Acheson, the Secretary of State, to the Tehran embassy:[46]

(1) While in general US does not favor nationalization, US recognized right of sovereign states to nationalize provided prompt payment just compensation made. However, this policy not publicized abroad as it might encourage foreign states to nationalize.

(2) Dept. not at present opposing AIOC nationalization because of (1) and because such opposition would in present circumstances jeopardize politically US and West in Iran ...

(3) Therefore, only Dept statement at this time is expression of hope Iran and AIOC will work out satisfactory arrangement ...

The NSC proposed the US should "urge further efforts be made to find a formula that would square with the principle of nationalization

---

[43] Foreign Office, Memorandum of Conversation (14 February 1952), *FO 371/ Persia 1952/34–98608.*

[44] F. J. Hopwood, Letter to Ministry of Fuel (5 June 1951), *BP/00043859.*

[45] Yonah Alexander and Allan Nanes (eds.), *The United States and Iran: A Documentary History* (Maryland: University Publications of America, 1980), 213.

[46] Dean Acheson, Memorandum to the Embassy, *FRUS* (1989), 25–6.

without serious detriment to effective British control."[47] Acheson, in his memoirs, while depicting Mossadeq as a "demagogue who sowed the wind and reaped the whirlwind," admitted the main US interest lay in "the implications this controversy held for everyone's interest in the Near East" and how the crisis could "upset relations with the oil-producing states."[48]

The various parties to the crisis formulated their basic positions early on and retained them throughout the whole crisis – through negotiations first in Tehran, then in London, and eventually in Washington, especially at the World Bank known then as the International Bank for Reconstruction and Development. The USA did its best to persuade Mossadeq to accept the formula of nationalization without actual control. It tried to "educate" him on the intricate complexities of the international market: the supposed hurdles in finding competent technicians; the technical difficulties of exploration and production; and the differences between crude and refined oil, between various forms of refined, and between posted prices in the Mexican Gulf and the Persian Gulf.

Mossadeq, for his part, refused to be overwhelmed by such complexities. Instead he cut through the details straight to the core issues: who would determine the level of production, the technicians to be hired, the extent of new explorations, the price of the product, and the destination of the exports? In a rare moment of candor, the British Minister of Fuel admitted: "Although something might be done to put more of a Persian façade on the setup we must not forget that the Persians are not so far wrong when they say that all our proposals are, in fact, merely dressing up AIOC control in other clothing ... Any real concession on this point is impossible."[49] Candor also occasionally seeped into the State Department. Acheson, early in the crisis, admitted:

We are convinced that the primary concern of the nationalist elements is that Iran must gain control of her natural resources and end foreign interference in the internal affairs of Iran which they attribute to the AIOC. There is widespread fear that, if an agreement is made with the British relating to the

---

[47] James Webb, Progress Report for the NSC, *FRUS* (2017), 76–8.
[48] Dean Acheson, *Present at the Creation* (New York: Norton, 1969), 506.
[49] Sir Donald Fergusson, Letter to Sir William Strong (5 September 1951), FO 371/ Persia 1951/34–91587.

operation of the oil industry with Iran, the AIOC would simply be continued under a new name.[50]

Mossadeq's insistence on real nationalization exasperated the Foreign Office. It responded by describing him as "obstinate," "stubborn," "impossible," "irrational," "unstable," "unreasonable," "verbose," "theatrical," "wild," "mad," "crazy," "tragic," "erratic," "eccentric," "imperious," "unbalanced," "unscrupulous," "bizarre," "old and short-sighted," "extremist," "fanatical," "Robespierre," "Frankenstein," "hysterical," "abnormal," "demagogic," "xenophobic," "megalomaniacal," and, to top it all, "effeminate" and a "wily Oriental." Shepherd set the tone after his first failed attempt to dilute Mossadeq's definition of nationalization:

Cunning, slippery, and completely unscrupulous. He does not make a pleasant impression. He is rather tall but has short and rather bandy legs so that he shambles like a bear. He looks rather like a cab horse and is slightly deaf.... What is more, he refuses to be called Excellency and does not use his ministerial motor car.[51]

Such depictions were readily picked up by American diplomats as well as by prominent journalists in both the USA and the United Kingdom. The famous Alsop brothers – Stewart and Joseph – of the *New York Herald Tribune* led the way. They insisted, "all educated and political elements in Iran, not just Mossadeq, are lacking in realism and understanding." The venerable Joseph Alsop claimed Mossadeq was "impervious to reason" and had done nothing "for forty years but listen to his own voice."[52] Likewise, the London *Observer* described Mossadeq as "impervious to common sense" and "a confused, bewildered and desperately short-sighted man with only one political idea in his gigantic head."[53] *Time* gave him a backhanded compliment naming him "Man of the Year" but at the same time depicting him as a "Dervish in Pin-Striped Suit."[54] Describing him as "an austere old man consumed by illness and by strange fires of faith," it claimed that

---

[50] Acheson, Memorandum to the Embassy (28 September 1951), *FRUS* (1989), 182.
[51] Shepherd, On Government Resignation, *FO 371/Persia* 1951/34–91459.
[52] Foreign Office, Notes (5 May 1951), *FO 371/Persia* 1951/34–91533.
[53] Anonymous, "Profile of Muhammed Mossadek," *Observer*, 20 May 1951.
[54] Anonymous, "Dervish in Pin-Striped Suit," *Time*, 4 June 1951.

imprisonment under Reza Shah had left him permanently "psychologically damaged."

The British press attaché in Tehran informed the Foreign Office that he was dispatching direct to Washington "poison" usable in America but "too venomous for the BBC."[55] This included such fake "information" as that Mossadeq was an "opium addict" and his associates had long criminal records. Drew Pearson, another doyen of American journalism, claimed that Hussein Fatemi, the assistant premier and later foreign minister, had been convicted on four counts of embezzlement but had managed to suppress the information. "Yet," exclaimed Pearson, "he is the man who will eventually decide whether the US has gas rationing or possibly, whether the American people go into World War III."[56]

In London *The Times* was more sophisticated but no less dismissive of Iranian nationalism. In a series of articles an unnamed "special correspondent" – perhaps Elizabeth Monroe, lecturer of Middle East politics, or possibly Ann Lambton, professor of Persian, both at London University – claimed the whole crisis had been generated by "social disequilibrium" and by the "projection of inner conflicts" onto the external arena. Iranian society, the articles expounded, was sharply divided. On one side were the "stupid and greedy ruling class" formed of "landlords, merchants, and contractors" and backed by the central government with its army of civil servants. On the other side were the "exploited" provincial masses, formed of peasants, tribesmen, and laborers. "The inner tension of Persian society," the articles argued, "has now become such that it can be met only by an acceleration of the drive against the external scapegoats. This is the real explanation of the present crisis."[57] Karl Marx would have enjoyed reading *The Times*.

Less sophisticated explanations, however, prevailed in the US media – even after the coup. For example, *Encounter* – the well-known CIA journal for intellectuals in the English-speaking world – published a long article in 1954 entitled "Persia: Land of Unrealities."[58] It claimed

---

[55] British Embassy, Letter to Information Policy Dept. (4 September 1951), *FO 248/* Persia 1951/1528.

[56] Drew Pearson, "USSR Wants Long Peace Parley," *Washington Post*, 11 July 1951.

[57] Special Correspondent, "The Crisis in Persia," *The Times*, 22 March 1951; "Persia's Oil Claim," *The Times*, 23 March 1951.

[58] F. R. Allemann, "Persia: Land of Unrealities," *Encounter*, January 1954, 49–56.

that Mossadeq had led the country into economic ruin by refusing to "compromise" on oil, by "exploiting" his own rare reputation of "indisputable personal integrity," by taking advantage of his "opium-smoking" country, by resorting to demonstrations to threaten opponents, and by acting like a possessed *illumine* – a sort of secular mystic. "This makes an impression on the people who have no understanding of rational European thinking and are thoroughly imbued with mysticism."

Henderson resorted to similar terminology – especially after unsuccessful meetings to water down Mossadeq's meaning of nationalization. After one such session, he informed the State Department that the prime minister was "irrational," "paranoid," "lacking stability," "dominated by prejudices," and "declining in mental stability." Henderson was not always consistent. He privately admitted he was "exceedingly fond" of Mossadeq and considered him "one of the greatest men of the Middle East."[59] In an interview two decades later, he remembered Mossadeq as "charming," "sympathetic," "decent," and endowed with a "high sense of humor." "We decided," he explained, "to have good relations with him but not at the price of our approving the cancellation of the British oil concession. We did not believe that such an expropriation was in the basic interest of Iran, GB, or the US. Acts of this kind tend to undermine the mutual trust that was necessary if international trade was to flourish."[60] When Mossadeq visited the White House in late 1951, a State Department memorandum for President Truman described the visitor as "honest," "alert," "witty," and "well-informed."[61] The President was advised to steer the conversation away from oil to generalities on "dangers of international communism." The US-UK reactions contain some inner logic. If their formula for solving the crisis was "generous" then Mossadeq's refusal must be "irrational."

Although the Foreign Office in public embraced the McGhee formula, in private it insisted that Mossadeq would never accept the empty formula. Instead, it marked time expecting his early demise – after all, the average tenure of recent premiers in Iran has been less than seven

[59] Henderson, Conversation with Court Minister (4 May 1953), *FRUS* (2017), 549.

[60] Don North, "Interview with Ambassador Loy Henderson (December 1979)," *Oral History Research Office* (New York: Columbia University, 1979).

[61] State Department, Memorandum for the President in Meeting Prime Minister Mossadeq, *Declassified US Documents*/1979/78D.

months.[62] In September 1951 – a mere five months into the crisis, Shepherd told Taqizadeh, the senate president, that the United Kingdom – as well as the USA – hoped and expected "soon a change of government" and had reached the conclusion that it was impossible to "deal with the present prime minister."[63] Taqizadeh retorted that it was a mistake to seek the removal of the premier. He added that as longtime ambassador to London he would have never contemplated similar intervention in internal British politics.[64]

The shah, for his part, held doggedly onto his original position. The State Department reported in late 1951:

The Shah has made it clear it would be a mistake for him or a foreign power to try to remove Mossadeq at this time ... Our analysis confirms that the Shah's own position would be seriously endangered if he should endeavor to bring this about until the widespread support for Prime Minister has considerably diminished. The Shah has, however, been made aware of the fact that we would encourage him to move if he should feel his position sufficiently strong to do so.[65]

Similarly, the British ambassador in Washington reiterated his earlier warning to the State Department that the shah feared Mossadeq "more in opposition than in power."[66] The British embassy in Tehran reaffirmed this warning: "The Shah had told us Musaddiq must go, but must go quietly and must be overthrown by parliamentary means ... He is afraid to take any action to bring about his fall so long as the people are behind him."[67] Acheson, together with McGhee and other NSC members, drafted the following cable to the embassy:[68]

One of the fundamental difficulties in deciding upon what course of action wld be most effective is the improbability of arriving at a satisfactory settlement under existing circumstances. It obviously wld be much easier to find a

[62] British Ambassador, Telegram (1 May), *FO 248/1526*.
[63] Shepherd, Interview with Mr. Taqizadeh (22 September 1951), *FO 248/1951–1529*.
[64] Robin Zaehner, Interview with Mr. Taqizadeh (September 1951), *FO 248/1529*.
[65] State Department, The Current Situation in Iran (10 October 1951), *FRUS* (2017), 140–4.
[66] British Ambassador in Washington, Telegram (17 December 1951), *FO 371/Persia 1951/34–91466*.
[67] Middleton, Telegram (13 July 1952), *FO 248/1539*.
[68] Acheson, Telegram to the Embassy (28 September 1951), *FRUS* (1989), 181.

solution if a more reasonable govt cld come to power under conditions which wld permit the Brit to undertake negotiations on a realistic basis. The Shah recognizes this fact, but it is extremely difficult or impossible for him to assume responsibility of installing a new govt before this can be brought about by natural political changes in Iran. If this shld be done prematurely, there is great danger that the Shah himself wold be overthrown.

The State Department firmly held onto this position for at least a year. Even in mid-1952, it hoped to persuade Mossadeq to accept the McGhee formula. In a detailed memo on Mossadeq, it argued that because he enjoyed "popular support" and the "backing of the majority" he was the only person who could "settle the oil dispute."[69] The same memo explained: "By developing cooperation with Musaddiq we may be able to guide him towards working out an equitable settlement on the oil question. Our assistance and advice can surely help him to gain a clearer understanding of present issues and their complications ... Its quite conceivable that if we play our cards right we may exert real influence over him."

The CIA, however, from the very beginning harbored different ideas – ones more in tune with those of the British Foreign Office. Allen Dulles, the CIA deputy director since early 1951, was adamant from the very start that "only one thing could save the situation – namely the Shah throw out Mosadeq, close the Majles, and temporarily rule by decree." "New premier," he added expansively, "could be installed with our help at a later date."[70] He took the shah for granted – a problem the State Department quickly pointed out. The CIA director instructed Dulles to consult the State Department and asked the NSC for a new advisory. Dulles expounded on his theme at a follow-up meeting with the State Department arguing the shah would soon have to choose between exile and fighting for his throne. If he chose the latter he would have to dissolve the majles, replace Mossadeq, and rule like his father. He suggested an American trusted by the shah should be sent immediately to Tehran to "stiffen" his will.[71] This suggestion came not on the eve of the coup but early in May 1951 – a mere one month into Mossadeq's administration.

---

[69] US Embassy, The Political Strength of the Mossadeq Government, FRUS (2017), 80–5.
[70] CIA, Meeting of the Director of the CIA (9 May 1951), FRUS (2017), 87.
[71] CIA, Memo of Meeting (10 May 1951), FRUS (2017), 88.

Kermit Roosevelt, Dulles' chief assistant, similarly argued the "extreme" and "paranoid" nature of Iranian nationalism had created a serious economic and political situation. Favoring "vigorous action," he echoed the British claim that any compromise offered would be refused by the "xenophobic majles."[72] He remarked that the CIA could be underestimating the communist danger since it lacked information on the Tudeh. This was a surprising remark since the main avowed purpose of the large CIA station in Iran ever since 1948 had been precisely to monitor the same Tudeh. Well before Mossadeq's election, the CIA had drawn up an elaborate blueprint for a "psychological campaign" – fancy jargon for propaganda – to bolster the shah, support candidates for the majles and the premiership, extend subsidies and "guidance" to newspaper editors and politicians (ten lines of names remain classified), buy off clerical figures, sow division within Mossadeq's supporters, and spread false rumors that some of his supporters had clandestine ties to the Tudeh and the Soviet Union. "Mossadeq," the blueprint noted, "is too widely admired to be the subject of successful attacks." It proposed distributing "forged" Tudeh hand sheets attacking Islam, advocating violent revolution, and naming the clerics to be "liquidated." It also proposed establishing links between army commanders and southern tribes, especially the Qashqayis, and "providing amenable groups with money, arms, material, food, and possibly personnel."[73] It noted that Mossadeq in early May 1951 had to take sanctuary in the majles because the Fedayan-e Islam had threatened to kill him for refusing to implement the shari'a and release the assassin of former premier General Razmara.[74] The Fedayan had also recently shot and injured Hussein Fatemi, Mossadeq's adviser and assistant premier.

Dulles and his close colleagues – Roosevelt, Frank Wisner, Richard Helms, John Waller, and Donald Wilber – manned the CIA's Iran section throughout the oil crisis, beginning as early as April 1951. They, in fact, constituted a "deep state" promoting policies in variance with those of the State Department and White House. They began calling for a coup long before the end of the Truman administration

---

[72] Roosevelt, Memorandum to Allen Dulles (15 March 1951), *FRUS* (2017), 36–8.
[73] CIA, Paper Prepared in the Directorate of Plans (March 1951), *FRUS* (2017), 19–20. See also CIA, CIA's Role in Iran, *FRUS* (2017), 47–50.
[74] CIA, Digest (17 May 1951), www.cia.gov/readingroom/search/site/Iran.

and the advent of the Eisenhower presidency in January 1953.[75] Allen
Dulles and his elder brother Foster, Eisenhower's Secretary of State,
had long-standing ties with Iran and the oil companies. They were
veteran members of the law firm of Sullivan and Cromwell, which,
over the years, had represented major oil companies including AIOC.
Allen Dulles himself had crossed paths with Mossadeq in 1949 in the
royal gardens in Tehran. He had been there to negotiate on behalf of
Overseas Consultants, the world's largest "development project."
Mossadeq had been there to protest the rigging of majles elections.
He had taken the opportunity to criticize Overseas Consultants for
undermining Iran's policy of "negative equilibrium" – his way of
defining neutralism and keeping distant from all major powers including the USA, United Kingdom, and the USSR.[76]

Although the State Department resisted the idea of a coup, it fine-
tuned policy once it concluded that Mossadeq could not be persuaded
to settle for the McGhee formula. It started looking around for a new
prime minister – one who would accept such a formula. Henderson,
after a long discussion with Ala, the court minister, reported it was now
obvious that Mossadeq would not "yield his attitude," and, therefore,
no settlement was possible so long as he remained prime minister. The
two discussed possible replacements.[77] Henderson later claimed he had
reached such a decision only after Mossadeq had rejected many "reasonable" proposals offered by the World Bank and the Eisenhower
administration in 1953. This long discussion with Ala, however, had
come in May 1952.

A high-level US-UK meeting was convened in Washington on 16
May 1952 to examine the credentials of possible premiers to "settle
the oil issue."[78] Lancelot Pyman, the UK representative, played a key
role in the meeting since he spoke Persian and knew the ins-and-outs of
Iranian politics having served as Tehran embassy counsellor for over a
decade. The meeting scrutinized a short list of eighteen candidates.

---

[75] The CIA had tried to overthrow the Guatemalan government in 1951 but had
    been thwarted by the State Department. See Stephen Kinzer and Stephen
    Schlesinger, *Bitter Fruit: The Story of the American Coup in Guatemala*
    (Cambridge: Harvard University Press, 1999), 92, 102.
[76] Stephen Kinzer, *The Brothers: John Foster Dulles, Allen Dulles, and Their Secret
    World War* (New York: Times Books, 2013), 119–20.
[77] Henderson, Telegram (24 May 1952), *FRUS* (2017), 239.
[78] William Rountree, Memorandum of Conversation (16 May 1952), *FRUS*
    (2017), 232–8.

They were grouped into three categories: establishment politicians labeled "normal-types"; military figures; and National Front leaders. Henderson described the roster as "Pyman's list of possible candidates."[79]

The first group was headed by Ahmad Qavam. Although described as "old," "feeble," "decrepit," "sick," and tarnished with "corruption and nepotism," Qavam was deemed "a strong opportunistic man prepared to settle the oil dispute along any basis he felt he could get away with." The shah, however, "feared" him as an aristocratic "threat." As premier in 1922–3, in 1942–3, and again in 1946–7, he had clashed with the royal family – especially over royal interference in politics. In 1946, the shah had bestowed on him the title of Jenab-e Ashraf (Noble Excellency) for successfully negotiating the Soviet withdrawal from northern Iran. But three years later the shah had stripped him of the title for opposing his bid to enhance royal prerogatives. Qavam saw this bid as the "violating the fundamental laws."[80] Accused of "treason" (*khiyanat*), he was forced into intermittent exile from 1949 until 1951.[81] One royalist senator argued that Qavam should be kept busy in Riviera casinos on the grounds he was worse than Mossadeq, who, with all his shortcomings, at least was not grossly corrupt.[82] Henderson soon came to favor Qavam mainly because he would be the "most effective of all the possible candidates in reviving the oil industry."[83] The shah, however, initially resisted on the grounds that "it is all very well bringing Qavam to power but how are we going to get rid of him when we want to do so."[84] Unbeknown to Henderson, Qavam in one of his recent trips to Paris had quietly offered the Tudeh the removal of the ban on the party if the latter supported him. The Tudeh did not trust him enough to pursue the bait.[85]

The Washington meeting dismissed the other establishment politicians as either too old, too weak, too petulant, too opportunistic, or even too pro-British. Sayyed Ziya Tabatabai, the maverick politician

---

79 Henderson, Telegram (20 June 1952), *FRUS* (2017), 258–9.
80 Ahmad Qavam, Letter to the Shah, *Bakhtar-e Emruz*, 31 December 1949.
81 Court Minister, Letter to Qavam, *Bakhtar-e Emruz*, 31 December 1949.
82 Mehdi Farrukh, Speech, *1st Senate*, 13 November 1951.
83 Henderson, Telegram (1 April 1952), *FRUS* (2017), 225.
84 Falle, Telegram (21 June 1952), *FO* 248/1531.
85 Iraj Iskandari, *Yadnameh-ha va Yaddasht-ha-ye Parakandeh* (Scattered Notes and Reminiscences) (Germany: Mard-e Emruz Publication, 1986), 78.

exiled by Reza Shah, was eliminated both because he had the reputation of being too much of a "British tool" and because he had criticized
the Pahlavi shahs for their unconstitutional behavior. Dr. Ahmad
Matin-Daftari, a former prime minister who happened to be
Mossadeq's nephew, was eliminated from the list because he championed not only oil nationalization but also a strict neutralist foreign
policy. He was dubbed "Neutralist Joe" for supposedly espousing the
maxim "Say nothing, do nothing, and the Soviets will not know Iran is
there." He argued that Soviet actions in Iran could be explained as
reactions to Western-initiated ones. The motto "neutralism is as bad as
communism" was already current in the Truman administration –
especially in Henderson's thinking.

The military list featured Generals Fazlollah Zahedi, Hassan Arfa,
and Amir Ahmadi. Zahedi was favored; he was "unscrupulous,"
"energetic," "ambitious," and, most important of all, "opportunistic
enough to settle the oil controversy." He came with additional advantages. He was a senator. And he could not be tarred with the British
brush having been interned during the war for having clandestine ties to
the Third Reich. The British described Zahedi as interested mainly in
money and "more of a politician than a soldier."[86] Henderson later
added the meeting had overestimated Zahedi's supposed popularity.[87]

The meeting dismissed General Arfa, a former chief of staff, as
"wild" and "unstable." Descendant of an aristocratic Tsarist family,
he was a self-avowed monarchist and full supporter of the White
Russians. Although a staunch Anglophile, the British embassy ridiculed
him for searching for communists under every bed and for "constantly
spy-hunting mania for plots against the life of himself and the Shah."[88]
He owned a village near Tehran, which he had turned into a barrack
with peasants wearing uniforms, insignias, and being woken up in the
morning with bugle calls.[89] In his memoirs he presents himself as a
liberal aristocrat, but inadvertently admits he worked closely with the
Arya Party – one of the two Nazi organizations. Ahmadi, last of the
three generals, was dismissed by the meeting as having a "low level of

[86] Foreign Office, Biographical Notes: Leading Personalities in Persia, FO 416/
    105.
[87] Henderson, Telegram (20 June 1952), FRUS (2017), 258.
[88] British Military Attaché, Weekly Report (11–17 February 1948), India Office,
    L/P&S/12–3505.
[89] Hassan Arfa, Under Five Shahs (New York: William Morrow, 1965), 400.

intelligence" and being more interested in "collecting rent from his estates."

The list named the following National Front figures: Hussein Makki, Ayatollah Sayyed Abul Qassem Kashani, Dr. Mozaffar Baqai, and Allahyar Saleh. Each came with advantages and disadvantages. Makki, an orator and former air force sergeant, had been Mossadeq's majles spokesman in 1948–50. He had originally been a Qavam protégée, but was now a "newspaper hack" and "moderate" pretending to be a "firebrand." The meeting speculated he would "not be a bad replacement" since he was "an opportunist willing to settle the oil issue." The Foreign Office depicted him as: "A loud-mouthed man with no ideas of his own; an extremist and irresponsible . . . an unprincipled adventurer . . . but being an opportunist he would undoubtedly desert Musaddiq."[90]

Kashani, on the other hand, had let it be known he was not interested in the premiership for himself even though he was the most prominent cleric in the oil nationalization campaign. He merely wanted to "influence development behind the scenes" by placing his nominees in the majles and the cabinet. His Foreign Office biography claimed "he and his sons are so venal that they could be detached from Musaddiq by any rival who was prepared to pay enough." He also happened to be friendly with Zahedi; both had been interned during the war because of their German contacts. The CIA, in its early blueprint on "psychological warfare," had suggested: "Efforts should be made to buy off Kashani. It would appear that at heart Kashani is primarily interested in himself rather than being inspired by a crusading zeal, and he has indicated that his attitude toward the US can be influenced by money."[91] The CIA described him as "unique in so far as he avoids couching remarks in flowery politeness," uses blunt "sometimes rude candid language," and is "definitely megalomaniacal with aspirations greater than Iran."[92] It went on to describe him as "ambitious," "bombastic," "opportunistic," "fanatical," and "psychopathic." He had survived Reza Shah by "keeping out of his way." The CIA biography noted he carried "little respect among colleagues" and could be bribed since "he has at least on one occasion made overtures to the

---

[90] Foreign Office, Biographical Notes: Leading Personalities in Persia, *FO 416/ 105.*

[91] CIA, Paper Prepared for the Directorate (13 March 1951), *FRUS* (2017), 20.

[92] CIA, Personality Sketches (5 January 1951), *FRUS* (2017), 173.

American embassy for financial support."[93] The State Department later explained his break with Mossadeq as caused by the latter's refusal to place his favorites and relatives in high positions. The State Department added that Kashani was intensely "jealous" of Mossadeq's "reputation for integrity."[94]

Baqai, a French-educated professor of philosophy, was another former Qavam protégé who now headed his own organization named the Toilers Party (Hezb-e Zahmatkeshan). Playing on words, critics dubbed it the Hezbe-e Mardomkeshan (People-Killers Party). It used ultra-radical rhetoric and claimed to be a Titoist organization opposed to the Soviet Union. Baqai had little support outside his hometown, Kerman. The British embassy suspected he received funds from the shah as well as the Americans even though his party was "not much more than a gang of thugs."[95] The British embassy years later reiterated its earlier assessment of Baqai as "receiving financial support from the Americans and his followers being a gang of hooligans."[96] The CIA reported that Baqai had "contacted" them and deemed him a "very valuable asset to control."[97] The State Department depicted him as an "opium smoking alcoholic."[98] Henderson described him as "lacking in intelligence and popular support."[99] Despite these assessments, the American labor attaché, as well as Henderson, had regular meetings with him throughout the crisis.[100] Henderson endured with much patience Baqai's long pontifications on the "philosophy of the sublime," on the "dirty game of politics," and on the "psychology of despair" supposedly prevalent throughout Iranian society.[101]

Saleh, the last on the list, was in many ways by far the strongest candidate. He was "honest," "intelligent," a "man of integrity," and, most important of all, a diplomat's diplomat. A graduate of the American College in Tehran, he had served for years as special

---

[93] Arthur Richards, Biography of Ayatollah Kashani, *FRUS* (2017), 128–30.
[94] State Department, Character of Kashani (31 March 1953), *FRUS* (2017), 506.
[95] Middleton, Memo (28 January 1952), *FO 248/1541.*
[96] British Embassy, Leading Personalities in Iran (1979), *FCO 8/3349.*
[97] CIA, Monthly Report (September 1952), *FRUS* (2017), 359.
[98] Melbourne, The Workers Party of Iran (5 June 1953), in *FO 371/Persia 1953/ 104567.*
[99] Henderson, Estimate of Iranian Situation (3 August 1952), *FRUS* (2017), 12.
[100] Melbourne, Labor Attaché's Conversations with Baqai (27 October 1952), *FRUS* (2017), 382.
[101] Henderson, Conversations with Baqai, *FRUS* (2017), 857.

secretary to the American Legation, and later gained the reputation of being a respected ambassador in Washington. He was soft-spoken, succinct, and, unlike Mossadeq, avoided oratory. Equally important, Saleh – again unlike Mossadeq – had avoided entanglements with the shah over constitutional issues during the many spells he had served in the cabinet. The shah was "particularly impressed by him." Saleh received support even from Wilber in the CIA on the grounds that as an Iran Party leader he could effectively split the National Front.[102] Henderson, however, promptly nixed Saleh from the list. He stated in no uncertain terms that Saleh was "even more stubborn than Musaddiq in matter of the oil dispute."[103] He later described him as a "demagogue," and repeated his claim he was "even more irreconcilable than Mossadeq on the oil issue."[104] The State Department instructed Henderson to delicately inform the shah that while the USA "did not want to name" prime ministers the appointment of Saleh would "constitute a serious danger to Iran."[105] No irony was intended. Henderson continued to raise precisely the same objection to Saleh whenever his name came up in the following months.[106] This should provide food for thought to those who insist that the coup had absolutely nothing to do with oil.

This Washington meeting shows clearly that the Truman administration began contemplating Mossadeq's "replacement" as early as spring 1952. Henderson, in a cable from Tehran on 24 May 1952, stressed that Mossadeq's "retirement" was a prerequisite since "no (oil) settlement was possible so long as he remained prime minister."[107] The British embassy in Tehran echoed this and reaffirmed that the American ambassador was now more than ever "convinced" that "it was impossible to do business" with Mossadeq.[108]

Two weeks after the Washington meeting, Henderson made "arrangements" to come across Qavam at a Turkish embassy

[102] Donald Wilber, Memorandum for the Record (23 September 1952), *FRUS* (2017), 356.
[103] Henderson, Telegram (24 May 1952), *FRUS* (2017), 240.
[104] Henderson, Telegram (13 June 1952), *FRUS* (2017), 256.
[105] State Department, Telegram (9 June 1952), *FRUS* (2017), 246.
[106] Henderson, Telegram (6 June 1952), *FRUS* (2017), 243; Henderson, Telegram (20 June 1952), *FRUS* (2017), 254.
[107] Henderson, Telegram (24 May 1952), *FRUS* (1989), 382.
[108] Falle, Dispatch (16 April 1952), FO 248/1052–1531.

reception.[109] Qavam – on a recent "medical visit" to Paris – had already met local American emissaries. He had reassured them he was strong willed – unlike the shah – "unwaveringly pro-American," and, most important of all, more than eager to "settle the oil problem."[110] Henderson arranged to have a "quiet dinner" with Qavam on 10 June. After the dinner, Henderson reported back that Qavam, despite his age, was "alert," "energetic," "humorous," and willing to form a cabinet of responsible ministers eager to settle the oil issue. He had sounded out the possibility of emergency American aid in anticipation of an oil agreement. He had agreed to meet as soon as possible George Middleton, the British chargé d'affaires who had replaced Shepherd as his country's main representative in Iran.[111] The British embassy reported that Henderson had been impressed by Qavam and had come away from the three-hour meeting with the strong feeling that he would be the best choice – and Saleh the worst.[112]

Henderson went to the palace on 12 June to tell the shah that Mossadeq was "leading the country to ruin," and that he – the shah – had to take drastic action to preserve his "throne and prestige." He reassured the monarch that Qavam was "too old to have personal ambitions," would take on the heavy responsibility of heading the government only if he had the monarch's confidence, and would not remain in office for a "single moment" if he lost that confidence. Henderson explained he was merely giving voice to "his own thoughts" and in no way "venturing to press advice upon the shah." Middleton reported that "his American colleague had spoken to His Majesty in the frankest terms" about the need to replace Mossadeq with Qavam.[113] The shah privately complained to Sayyed Ziya – the lead Anglophile politician – that he had always made it clear to the British and American embassies that he would support the removal of Mossadeq – but only through the majles and the senate. He also complained that the British blocked his favored candidate, Saleh, who could in no way be "labeled a foreign

[109] Henderson, Telegram (6 June 1952), *FRUS* (2017), 243.
[110] US Embassy in Paris, Telegram (28 March 1952), *FRUS* (2017), 223.
[111] Henderson, Telegram (12 June 1952), *FRUS* (2017), 246–8; Henderson, Telegram (13 June 1952), *FRUS* (2017), 258.
[112] Zaehner, Memo (11 June 1952), *FO 248/531*.
[113] Middleton, Development in the Persian Internal Situation (12 June 1952), *FO 416/105*.

stooge."[114] The shah obviously had not figured out that the main objection to Saleh came from Henderson.

Henderson's activities subsequent to his palace visit remain shrouded. The new US documents, as well as the old ones, strangely contain no Tehran dispatches for a full month – from 12 June until 16–18 July.[115] Henderson may have hidden his dealings, but we know from British sources that an array of influential figures, some of whom had opposed Qavam in the past, now lobbied vigorously on his behalf. They included the Queen Mother and Princess Ashraf, the shah's twin sister; Sayyed Ziya himself; Ayatollah Mohammad Behbehani, the main cleric in the royal court and son of one of the two religious figures who had led the 1906 Constitutional Revolution – the British embassy depicted Behbehani as "corrupt," "unscrupulous," and the recipient of regular payments from the Shah;[116] Sayyed Mohammad Sadeq Tabatabai, son of the other famous ayatollah from the Constitutional Revolution – the British dismissed him as an "incorrigible intriguer" with grandiose notion of becoming premier himself;[117] and, last but not least, Hassan Imami, the Imam Jum'eh of Tehran, who, because of his image, was dubbed Imam Jum'eh-e Landan (London).[118] Trained in seminaries, Imami had discarded his turban to become a high court state judge. He had recently been stabbed by an unknown assailant after accusing Mossadeq of "enflaming passions." After the coup, he lobbied hard for Mossadeq's execution.[119] The British embassy reported the "opposition finally realized they have to unite behind one individual – Qavam."[120] A Foreign Office official in London

[114] Zaehner, Confidential Report (13 July 1952), *FO 248/1539*.

[115] These dispatches remained classified probably because they implicate the British. Zaehner, a personal friend of Qavam, was most likely to have been heavily involved in the latter's election. Soon after the fiasco, Zaehner left Iran for All Soul's College and apparently was not involved in the 1953 coup.

[116] Foreign Office, Bibliographical Notes: Leading Personalities in Persia, *FO 416/105*.

[117] Foreign Office, Bibliographical Notes: Leading Personalities in Persia, *FO 416/1952–105*. Sadeq Tabatabai claimed that Mossadeq was "an epileptic suffering syphilitic deterioration of the brain." He had presented himself to the British embassy as suitable for the premiership on the grounds he possessed the suitable attributes: "courage, sincerity, and directness." George Micklethwail, 24 May 1952, *FO 248/1531*.

[118] Hussein Makki, *Vaqa'-e Seyum-e Tir* (The Events of 21 July) (Tehran: Nashr Publications, 1985), 60.

[119] CIA, Report (4 October 1953), *FRUS* (2017), 785.

[120] Middleton, Telegram (13 July 1952), *FO 248/1539*.

scribbled: "I tend to the view that Musaddiq still enjoys public support, more than some of our close friends (in Tehran) would have us believe ... A coup d'état may well be the only answer."[121]

The July Uprising

Mossadeq, long before taking up the oil issue, had championed the constitutional cause – the need to restrict royal powers and implement fully the fundamental laws. He had formulated the mantra "The shah must reign, not rule." He often pleaded that he had great regard for the young monarch but his regard for the constitution was greater.[122] For Mossadeq, the royal title of "commander-in-chief of the armed forces" was merely symbolic. The armed forces, he argued, were supposed to be under the authority of the war minister; and the war minister, like the prime minister and the rest of the cabinet, were all supposed to be responsible only to the majles.

Aware of the behind-the-scenes politicking on behalf of Qavam, Mossadeq pulled a fast one. Suddenly on 16 July he brought the whole constitutional issue to the fore by reshuffling his cabinet and retaining for himself the portfolio for the war minister. The shah not surprisingly balked. He had named – as his father had done – all war ministers since coming to the throne. Middleton noted the shah could not risk relinquishing the war ministry since control of the armed forces was the main source of power he had inherited from his father.[123] To distance himself from the inevitable crisis, Middleton went on a fishing trip in a remote region with no telephone connections.[124]

Mossadeq promptly resigned the very same night, releasing next morning his resignation letter to the shah: "I will not be able to bring to successful fruition the struggle the nation has embarked on unless I take charge of the war ministry. Since your Majesty objects, it is better that the next government be headed by some one who fully enjoys your confidence and will carry out your royal orders."[125] With one bold stroke Mossadeq had merged the oil issue with the constitutional one, and forced the shah into the position he had consistently dreaded: that

---

[121] Anonymous, Handwritten comment (28 May 1952), FO 208/1531.
[122] Mossadeq, Speech in Parliament, Rahbar, 16 October 1944.
[123] Middleton, Telegram (28 July 1952), FO 248/1541.
[124] Peter Avery, Modern Iran (London: Benn Limited, 1965), 427.
[125] British Embassy, Telegram (18 July 1952), FO 248/1539.

of appearing to stand in the way of the country's struggle for oil nationalization and full sovereignty. Mostafa Fateh, a leading Iranian historian of the oil crisis, writes the resignation letter landed on the country like a "bomb."[126]

The majles, in a closed session late on the night of 18 July, chose Qavam to become prime minister. His majority was slim. The shah, following constitutional procedures, issued the pro forma decree inviting Qavam to present to the majles both a cabinet and a program. The decree surprisingly addressed Qavam as Jenab-e Ashraf. Qavam wasted no time. He sought a one-to-one meeting with Henderson reassuring him that he planned to be "flexible and prudent" in settling the oil problem. Henderson promptly advised Washington to offer Qavam "a lump sum of aid not loan" and promise him "further assistance if progress was soon made on the oil dispute."[127] Acheson immediately approved $26 million in aid.[128]

At the scheduled meeting the very next morning, Qavam sounded out Henderson on what would be the US attitude if he dissolved the majles and ruled through martial law. Claiming many "unqualified" deputies were sheltering behind "parliamentary immunity," he argued "strong action" was needed to protect "democracy."[129] Henderson, after congratulating him on his election, replied that the "world could not tolerate the continuation of political paralysis" and that the dissolution of the troublesome majles could be "justified" but hoped it could be accomplished by "constitutional means." He added that the USA had "no desire to interfere" in the selection of ministers but public opinion at home would be "more favorable" if they were all men of "integrity and ability." He ended the meeting by drawing attention to the fact that large numbers of workmen had been mobilized in the oil regions to "create disorder." Qavam reassured him that measures were being taken to preserve law and order.

Qavam followed up the meeting with a nationwide broadcast. He began boasting he had initiated the nationalization campaign by ending

---

[126] Mostafa Fateh, *Panjah Saleh-e Naft* (Fifty Years of Oil) (Tehran: Kavesh Publication, 1979), 605.
[127] Henderson, Telegram (18 July 1952), *FRUS* (2017), 266–8.
[128] Acheson, Telephone Conversation with President Truman, *FRUS* (2017), 304.
[129] Henderson, Telegrams (19 July 1952), *FRUS* (2017), 274–7. Henderson sent two separate telegrams that day describing his same meeting with Qavam. The first, sent at 2 p.m., dealt with internal politics. The second, sent at 3 p.m., dealt with emergency aid.

the oil crisis with the Soviet Union. He promised to bring the oil dispute
to a fruitful conclusion, and criticized Mossadeq for "inflexibility,"
"lack of prudence," and "sacrificing ends for means." He went on to
claim that the country suffered from a "mortal sickness," and needed to
rally behind him to find the right cure – namely by separating religion
from politics. He ended by denouncing "demagogues," "street politicians," "red extremists," and "black reactionaries." "I condemn," he
insisted, "political demagogy as much as religious hypocrisy. Those
who pretend to be fighting red extremists are actually strengthening
reaction. They are striking blows against freedom and destroying the
work initiated by the constitutional revolution. I shall put an end to the
spread of outdated superstitions."[130] He even talked of resorting to
"revolutionary executions." It was rumored he had issued an arrest
warrant for Kashani.

Henderson reported that Qavam requested the shah to dissolve the
majles so that deputies could then be arrested.[131] Hassan Arsanjani, a
young but close adviser to Qavam, admitted in a later book on the July
Uprising that this provocative radio speech had been a major blunder.
He blamed an "unknown" scriptwriter.[132] Makki, who published his
own account of the July Uprising, concurred that the speech – especially
the attack on Kashani – had inevitably unified the whole opposition
against Qavam.[133]

On 20 July, the National Front proclaimed Mossadeq the only
acceptable prime minister, and called for peaceful protests and a
nationwide general strike for the following day. Kashani, meanwhile,
denounced Qavam as a "British tool" and a *mofsad fey al-araz* (sower
of corruption on earth) – a crime punishable with death according to
shari'a. Sayyed Shams al-Din Qonatabadi, a vociferous cleric close to
Kashani, called for Qavam's "revolutionary execution." The Society of
Merchants, Guilds and Craftsmen, the main bazaar organization,
joined the National Front in calling for a general strike. The Tudeh
Party seconded the call by instructing supporters, including in provincial towns, to denounce Qavam for plotting with imperialists to undo
oil nationalization. Male supporters were urged to protest wearing

---

[130] Middleton, Qavam's Address (19 July 1952), *FO 248/1539*.
[131] Henderson, Telegram (19 July 1952), *FRUS* (2017), 274.
[132] Hassan Arsanjani, *Yaddashtha-ye Siyasi-e Man: Seyum Tir* (My Political
       Memoires: 21 July) (Tehran: Atesh Publications, 1956), 29.
[133] Makki, *The Events of 21 July*, 64.

their usual Tudeh attire of white shirts and grey trousers.[134] Immediately after the uprising, Kashani issued an open letter to the Tudeh declaring that the "unity of workers and the Iranian people had brought us victory over British imperialism."[135]

Mass protests broke out on 21 July. In Tehran the whole economy came to a standstill as angry crowds from the university and the bazaar as well as from the working class neighborhoods near the railway station converged on Parliament Square.[136] They set fire to army jeeps and trucks, and immobilized tanks that had been rushed into the inner city. One tank officer was seriously injured. Another tank officer joined the demonstrators. The main slogans were "Long Live Mossadeq" and "Down with Qavam." The shah's brother, Shahpour Ali Reza, was lucky to escape uninjured when his car inadvertently drove near protestors. A deputy, who tried to calm the crowd outside the majles, was promptly pelted with stones. A middle-aged woman, sitting on the shoulders of a colleague, urged the crowd on. The military detained over 600 people and used tear gas as well as live bullets in trying to disperse the crowds. The worst clashes took place outside the majles and the bazaar. Lesser ones occurred in northern Tehran, especially near the university, the municipal building, and Qavam's private residence. Henderson reported Tehran was on the verge of "civil war" and even a "revolution."[137] He complained no one was eager to "beat the drum" for Qavam, and no newspaper was willing to reprint a *New York Times* editorial praising him as a "harbinger of change for the better."[138]

Protests also broke out in a number of other cities – Isfahan, Shiraz, Tabriz, Kermanshah, Rasht, Zanjan, Hamadan, Arak, and Mashed. The most serious were in the oil regions – in Abadan, Ahwaz, Khorramshahr, and Masjed-e Suleiman. Makki recounts that protestors in Khuzestan put on white shrouds to show they were willing to march onto Tehran and die there. The crisis climaxed at 2 p.m., when the shah – increasingly concerned by the emergence of anti-monarchist slogans – refused Qavam's request to dissolve the majles. Instead he ordered the troops back to their barracks. Qavam handed in

---

[134] Makki, *The Events of 21 July*, 65.   [135] *New York Times*, 23 July 1952.
[136] Anonymous, "Either Death or Mossadeq," *Salnameh-e Donya*, Vol. 9 (1953), 187–8.
[137] Henderson, Telegrams (20–1 July 1952), *FRUS* (2017), 281–5.
[138] Henderson, Telegram (21 July 1952), *FRUS* (2017), 285.

his resignation at 4 p.m. *Kayhan,* the second major daily, reported that
the death count totaled sixty-three – twenty-nine in Tehran, twenty-
seven in Abadan, five in Kermanshah, one in Isfahan, and one in
Hamadan.[139]

Middleton recounted that he and Henderson had done their very best
to "stiffen the shah's will" but the "rioting had destroyed the last shred
of his courage."[140] He added: "The Shah and indeed the whole Court
appear to be paralysed with fear. Ala insisted that only [the] resignation
of Qavam would satisfy public opinion. I replied if the mob were
allowed to dictate terms the whole authority of the State including
the position of the monarchy would be fatally impaired."[141]
Middleton later reported: "The Shah was in the grip of fear: fear of
taking a decision, and fear of taking a decision that might expose him to
the fury of the populace."[142] He depicted the shah's "lamentable"
behavior as lacking "moral courage" and permitting a vital state
issue to be "settled by the large street crowds." He complained the
BBC gave too much coverage to the protests and requested the corpor-
ation to "tone down" its broadcasts.[143] In a printed report for the
Foreign Office, he added the riots had "cowed" the shah, forced him
to accept Qavam's resignation, and thereby handed over to Mossadeq
a "crowning triumph."[144] He was even more dramatic in an
internal memo:[145]

July 21st was a turning point in Persian history. The old system has always
been, with certain variations, that the small ruling class in fact nominates
successive Prime Ministers with the throne acting more or less as umpire.
Since yesterday I doubt whether this pattern can ever be repeated. The mob
successfully defied the security forces and from now on the consent of the
mob will be the decisive factor in judging the acceptability of any future
government.

[139] Mohammad-Hussein Khusrupanha, "The July 21st Uprising," *Negah-e Now,*
       No. 94 (Summer 2012), 16–25.
[140] Middleton, Telegrams (28–30 July 1952), *FO 248/1541; FO 416/105.*
[141] Middleton, Telegram (21 July 1952), *FO 248/1539.*
[142] Middleton, Review of the Recent Crisis in Persia, *FO 371/Persia 1952/34-*
       98602.
[143] US Embassy in London, Telegram (21 July 1952), *FRUS* (2017), 287.
[144] Middleton, Summary of Events in Persia 1952 (31 December 1952), *FO 416/*
       106.
[145] Middleton, Memo from Tehran (22 July 1952), *FO 248/1531.*

Similarly, Henderson reported he had conveyed to the shah via Ala that "drastic action" had to be taken since rioters were milling through the streets shouting "Death to American and British Imperialists."[146] He seconded Middleton's opinion that "no prime minister could succeed unless the shah gave him the necessary powers to establish law and order." Acheson informed Eisenhower that the "Shah's vacillation and refusal to give support to Qavam had led to general disintegration of authority in Iran."[147]

The consensus in the American and British embassies was that if the shah had taken their advice and stood firm behind Qavam he would have weathered the storm. Zaehner later exclaimed it was "difficult for the Western mind to understand the Shah."[148] A year later, Henderson told the NSC: "In March 1952 we didn't see how the Government of Mossadeq would last out the summer ... As a matter of fact, the government did fall in July and Qavam became Prime Minister. But the Shah did not back Qavam and the mobs forced him out in two days."[149] Falle likewise reminisced later that both Henderson and Middleton had concurred that Qavam could have survived if only the shah had backed him up.[150]

The shah obviously disagreed. He was convinced the crisis threatened not only Qavam but more importantly himself. He was probably right. Royal statues had been toppled. General Morteza Yazdanpanha, a court confidant, had reported that soldiers were reluctant to fire on demonstrators.[151] What is more, Middleton admitted later that the protests had been "much more severe than we suspected," that as many as 200 may have lost their lives, and that protestors had taken over cities such as Isfahan.[152] In his annual report, he admitted that Mossadeq "was still the idol of the Tehran mobs and able to use this popularity to cow all the politicians opposed to him."[153] Years later, he reminisced that if the bloodshed had continued the uprising could have turned easily into "another 1917."[154] He even wrote that Qavam must

---

[146] Henderson, Telegram (21 July 1952), *FRUS* (2017), 282.
[147] Acheson, Memo to the President (21 July 1952), *FRUS* (2017), 288.
[148] Zaehner, Notes, *FO 248/1541*.
[149] Henderson, Notes to the NSC (25 June 1953), *FRUS* (2017), 599.
[150] Falle, *My Lucky Life*, 79.   [151] Makki, *The Events of 21 July*, 283.
[152] Middleton, Telegram (28 July 1952), *FO 371/Persia 1952/34–98602*.
[153] Middleton, Summary of Events – Persia 1952, *FO 416/106*.
[154] Habib Ladjevardi, Interview with Sir George Middleton, *Iranian Oral History Project* (Cambridge: Harvard University, 1993).

have been "quiet mad" to think he could survive the crisis. The British military attaché, whose job was to keep close tabs on the armed forces, reported that army personnel had become so unpopular that officers advised their men not to wear uniforms in public.[155]

In a rushed analysis of the uprising, the State Department concluded that the heavy casualties had brought the country to the verge of "civil war"; that the shah was now "discredited"; that the protests had expressed "deep national feelings"; that there was no prospect of an oil settlement; and that Mossadeq was "stronger than any time since April 1951."[156] The State Department concluded the USA had to abandon the long-held British "thesis" that Mossadeq "could easily be replaced." It urged immediate discussions with the British over a whole range of issues, especially finding an alternative policy. The CIA concurred and concluded that Mossadeq had consolidated power, that his position was now stronger than ever, and that the influence of Kashani, as well as of the shah, had weakened.[157]

Henderson's own assessment – explicitly restricted to the Near Eastern department – was equally bleak. He described the situation as "depressing," military morale as "shattered," the shah as a "negligible factor in future politics," and the "Americans as much of a target as Qavam, the British, and the Shah."[158] He proposed that at his next meeting with Mossadeq

if his manner should be sufficiently friendly to permit me to talk to him frankly as I have in a number of occasions in the past I might try to convince him that since the National Front has crushed all opposition and has unchallenged control of the country ... he can now afford to approach the oil problem in a more conciliatory manner.

When a week later the meeting took place, Mossadeq accused Henderson of intriguing with Qavam and "interfering" in internal politics.[159] Henderson vehemently denied this, insisting he had met Qavam

---

[155] Military Attaché, Annual Report on the Persian Army for 1952, FO 371/Persia 1952/98638.
[156] Bureau of Near Eastern Affairs, Position Paper on Iranian Situation (22 July 1952), FRUS (2017), 289–94.
[157] CIA, Current Situation in Iran (28 October 1952), www.cia.gov/readingroom/search/site/Iran.
[158] Henderson, Telegram (24 July 1952), FRUS (2017), 294–6.
[159] Henderson, Memo to the State Department (28 July 1952), FRUS (1989), 416–21.

casually and in "pursuance of US government instructions had never directly or indirectly endeavored (to) support Qavam or other Iranian as Prime Minister." "Such ridiculous stories," Henderson insisted, "were being circulated by people who had completely lost their ability to reason. I told Mosadeq that US was in many ways trying to help Iran. He laughed and said if we were really trying (to) assist by other than words, we were certainly succeeding in hiding our helpful activities." Mossadeq complained the USA was working in cahoots with the United Kingdom to prevent the spread of oil nationalization. Henderson retorted that America's policy toward Iran was not governed by oil and that its interests in international oil were only of "secondary nature."

Mossadeq also complained about America's reluctance to provide emergency aid so he could deal with financial difficulties created by the British embargo. Henderson replied it would be hard to persuade the US congress to provide such aid when the country was oil rich. Mossadeq would have known – from his Foreign Office minutes – that only two days earlier Henderson had offered Qavam $26 million. The two-hour conversation left Henderson "exhausted" and "depressed." He was now more than ever convinced that Mossadeq "lacked stability," was "not quite sane," and was "dominated by emotions and prejudices." Mossadeq, nevertheless, refrained from publicly implicating Henderson in the crisis, and instructed Saleh, his Washington ambassador, to do the same.[160] He wanted to keep lines open to the USA and instead place all the blame on the United Kingdom.

Middleton reported that he and Henderson were now "convinced that the only remedy was a coup d'état."[161] He added: "Musaddiq has so flattered the mob as the source of his power that he has, I fear, made it impossible for a successor to oust him by normal constitutional means."[162] He concurred with the State Department's request for a US-UK meeting to hammer out a joint policy towards Iran. The State Department request had explicitly sought future course of action "*including recommendation on the possible alternative to Mosadeq, methods of bring about such a government to power, and the type of encouragement and support that would be*

---

[160] Makki, *The Events of 21 July*, 311.
[161] Middleton, Telegram (28 July 1952), *FO 371/Persia 1952/34–98602*.
[162] Middleton, Review of the Recent Crisis in Persia, *FO 371/Persia 1952/ 34–98602*.

necessary.[163] It concluded: "We are considering, in some cases in conjunction with CIA, every possible alternative to save Iran. This includes the probable position of the British and ourselves with the local tribes, which could be a big factor in any coup d'état type of action."

The British War Office promptly sent urgent instructions to its military attaché in Tehran requesting him to assess the "loyalty of the armed forces," their potential for pulling off "a successful coup," and their likelihood of producing a suitable Naguib – the general who had recently taken over Egypt.[164] The Foreign Office passed on to the British ambassador in Washington the information that the Americans were now actively looking for a Naguib.[165] The attaché suggested a number of possible candidates including Generals Zahedi and Arfa, but added that a "coup would have to be in the name of the Shah."[166] The CIA reported that the US G-2 had "canvassed through the entire list of moderately senior officers to find a possible alternative leadership along the lines of Naguib and found no individual appearing to possess the required drive and following." It warned that even if such a leader emerged the "situation was very different from Egypt" – the Iranian army was "unpopular" and the National Front had "great prestige."[167]

Henderson and Middleton met on 29 July to discuss the dire situation. They came to the following conclusions: only a military coup could remove Mossadeq; no obvious figure had emerged to head such a coup – Zahedi was still deemed by the Americans to have a "weak character"; a coup would require the full participation of the commander of the Tehran garrison; it would have to be carried out "in the name of the shah"; and, most troublesome, the shah would be extremely reluctant to lend his name to such a risky proposition.[168] The CIA Tehran station offered suggestions on how to prepare the

---

[163] Near Eastern Department, Memo to Dean Acheson (29 July 1952), *FRUS* (2017), 299 (emphasis in the original).

[164] War Office, Letter to the Military Attaché (29 July 1952), *FO 371/Persia 1952/ 34–98602.*

[165] Foreign Office, Letter to the Ambassador in Washington (29 July 1952), *FO 371/ Persia 1952/34–98602.*

[166] British Embassy, Memo to the War Office (4 August 1952), *FO 371/Persia 1952/34–98602.*

[167] CIA, Memorandum for Mr. Dulles (17 November 1952), www.cia.gov/read ingroom/search/site/Iran.

[168] Henderson, Meeting with Middleton (31 July 1952), *FRUS* (2017), 305–6.

ground for an eventual government that would among other things "accept a reasonable oil settlement."[169] The station suggested that the CIA should "establish contact with influential army leaders" and encourage the shah to increase his popularity by publicly opposing Britain, supporting Mossadeq ("at least initially"), and "cultivating relations with conservative religious and political." The station also urged the shah to "use constitutional prerogatives to establish a new government"; and, if he failed to act, urged "military leaders to carry out a coup in the shah's name, even if they do not have his authority." The CIA stressed the "US and UK should scrupulously avoid giving any indication that they had anything to do with the coup."

Falle, the new British counsellor, wrote that immediately after the July Uprising, Middleton began to actively explore "contingency plans, fair or foul," to remove Mossadeq.[170] Falle himself planted a full-blown alarmist article in the *Washington Star* entitled "The Mob in Iran."

One of the more depressing aspects of Mr. Mossadegh's quick return to power is that the return has been made possible by the mob spirit. Although his policies have brought Iran to the brink of ruin – to the point when a coup by the Communist Tudeh is quite conceivable – he seems, at least in Tehran, to have most of the people behind him, and they are people who have acted in the past few days as if they were psychoneurotics hysterically intent upon promoting the destruction of both themselves and their country. Never has a majority looked less wise, never has popular passions looked uglier. This mob – for it must be called that – does not appear to have been motivated by the slightest semblance of common sense. Led by homicidal fanatics of every type ... Iran has become a place of gravest uncertainties.[171]

It is hard to believe that colleagues had nicknamed Sam Falle "Sam the Red" because he harbored sympathy for the "natives."

The February Crisis

Henderson had failed in the July Uprising – so much so that rumors spread he had offered to resign.[172] He was to have more success in the

---

[169] John Leavitt, Program to Support the Shah (22 September 1952), *FRUS* (2017), 351–5.

[170] Falle, *My Lucky Life*, 81.

[171] Falle, *Washington Star*, FO 248/1531. Falle noted the paper had accepted all his suggestions and amendments.

[172] Henderson, Estimate of Iranian Situation, *FRUS* (2017), 310–15.

forthcoming 28 February crisis. Earlier that month Bakhtiyari tribes-men had ambushed an army column killing some forty officers and conscripts. Although the declassified documents again retain long gaps for the preceding weeks, later dispatches indicate that in the previous months MI6 had been arming southern tribes – most especially the Bakhtiyaris, but also the Lurs, Khamseh, Boir Ahmadis, and Ka'abs. The CIA had done the same with the nearby Qashqayis.[173] Two very different senators – Matin-Daftari, a government supporter, and Mehdi Farrukh (Mu'tasem al-Saltaneh), a staunch opponent – both had raised the rhetorical question who is arming the southern tribes? They praised Reza Shah for disarming the tribes and insisted that only soldiers should bear arms.[174]

On 20 February, Mossadeq confronted the shah with a "brusque message" threatening to go public with hard information linking the British-instigated Bakhtiyari revolt with members of the royal court – especially with Ali Reza, the shah's brother, as well as with the queen mother, princess Ashraf, and some retired army officers. Queen Soraya also happened to be related to Abul Qassem Bakhtiyari – the rebel leader.[175] Mossadeq demanded a prompt official and public investiga-tion into the Bakhtiyari ambush of the army column.

Ala, the court minister, "obviously distressed" rushed in "utmost secrecy" to tell Henderson that the shah had "lost his nerve," was on the "verge of a nervous breakdown," and had offered to take an extended vacation abroad. The queen had implored him to do so. Perron, shah's personal emissary, informed the British embassy that the "atmosphere at court resembled hell."[176] The shah had agreed to depart quietly on 28 February together with the queen, master of ceremonies, two servants, and several guards. Ala saw an Egyptian-style "disaster coming," but failed to dissuade the "hysterical" shah from packing to leave. Henderson agreed that the shah's "departure may be first step in the direction of the abolition of the monarchy."[177] The CIA concluded the shah had "capitulated" completely, and had

[173] CIA, Memorandum from Directorate of Plans (25 February 1953), *FRUS* (2017), 456.
[174] Matin-Daftari, Speech, *1st Senate*, 9 March 1952; Mehdi Farrukh, Speech, *1st Senate*, 24 February 1952.
[175] CIA, Prime Minister Mossadeq's Threat to Resign (24 February 1952), *FRUS* (2017), 450–2.
[176] Zaehner, Court Gossip, FO 248/Persia 1953/1541.
[177] Henderson, Telegram (25 February 1952), *FRUS* (2017), 456–7.

relinquished all "control to the prime minister."[178] Henderson was less pessimistic:[179]

I dislike remaining inactive at time when monarchical institution which we have in the past regarded as stabilizing influence in the country is in grave danger .... Members of Embassy and other American agencies here are endeavoring to ascertain whether any political or other forces exist which might at least in name of Shah oppose this latest Musaddiq move. Story of Shah's imminent departure may leak prior his departure ... I have no objection the British government being informed but would prefer details not be furnished.

The predicted "leak" came on the eve of the scheduled departure. The following morning, some 300 angry protestors, mostly retired officers and gang leaders, gathered outside the palace to denounce the prime minister for hounding their monarch into exile. The military officers – led by General Hedayatollah Gilanshah, the former air force chief with CIA connections – blamed Mossadeq for their early retirement even though many had been laid off by a previous administration.

The gang leaders – the same ones who reappear in the eventual coup – were known politely as *lutis*, *javanmards*, and *pahlavans*; less politely as *chaqukeshan* (knife-wielders), *lumpen* (lumpen), *lats* (sodomites), *jahels* (foolish youngsters), and *gardan kolofts* (rough necks). They frequented bodybuilding gyms known as *zurkhanehs* (houses of strength), and "protected" small stands outside the large, covered bazaar in southern Tehran. Not surprisingly, diplomats described them as "mobsters" and "racketeers." Soon after the coup the British chargé d'affaires wrote an in-depth study of their role in the southern Tehran slums.[180] He reported that by far the most dominant gang leader was Tayyeb Hajj Rezai – famous simply as Tayyeb. He described him as "part gangster, part labour racketeer, part police nark, part tribune of the Plebs." He controlled two important retail markets – greengrocers and general produce; levied protection money; set daily prices; enjoyed the undeviating loyalty of the porters; and recruited strongmen from the local *zurkhaneh*. His right-hand man was Sha'aban Ja'afari, known sometimes as *Beymogh* (Brainless), sometimes as *Timsar* (General), and later as Taj Bakhsh

[178] CIA, Briefing for the Director (undated), *FRUS* (2017), 452–3.
[179] Henderson, Telegram (26 February 1953), *FRUS* (2017), 458–9.
[180] John Russell, "Moharram in Tehran (August 1957)," *FO 371/127139*.

(Kingmaker or Crown Bestower).[181] The CIA estimated that Tayyeb's and Sha'aban's followers totaled no more than one hundred. The lesser known *lutis* included Hassan the Arab, Hussein Ramazun Yakhi (Icemaker), Ahmad Eshqi, Mahmud Mesgar, and Buik Saber nicknamed after his favorite car. The British chargé depicted the *zurkhanehs* as "recruiting grounds for the toughs and hatchet-men who act as runners for their labour bosses. The dirtiest jobs, which sometimes include the disposing of inconvenient opponents for unscrupulous politicians, are usually left to the lower echelons of the chaqukeshan."

The February protest was augmented by two small organizations: Sumka (National Socialist Workers Party) and the Arya Party. Sumka, modeled on the Nazi Party, was founded and led by Davoud Munshizadeh, a German-trained philologist enamored by racial theory and Aryan mythology. He had lost a leg in Europe during World War II. Arya had been created by Hadi Sephr, a blind intellectual interned during the war for his ties to the Third Reich. Arya and Sumka tried to outdo each other with their anti-Semitism. The CIA suspected Ala and the shah were financing Arya.[182] *Ettela'at* reported that the army further augmented the palace protest by trucking in some rural "protestors."[183]

The protest was also supported by Ayatollah Behbehani, Ayatollah Kashani, and such lesser clerics as Sheikh Beharaldin Nouri, Hajj Mirza Tehrani, and Mohammad Taqi Falsafi – the government had declined to renew a substantial loan to the latter to buy a modern printing press.[184] They became known as the '*Uluma-e Novum-e Esfand* (The 28 February Clergy). Mossadeq had alienated some by refusing to launch a campaign against the Bahais; he had explicitly stated he did not distinguish between Muslims and Bahais since they were all equal citizens of Iran.[185] The CIA credited Kashani for playing a "key role" in this palace protest.[186] Makki later claimed

---

181 Masoud Noqrehkar, *Naqsheh-e Siyas-ye va Ejtema'ye Jahal va Lat dar Tarekh-e Mo'aser-e Iran* (The Political and Social Role of Street Thugs and Ruffians in Contemporary Iran) (Cologne: Forough Publications, 2016).

182 British Embassy, Report on Arya Party, FO 371/Persia 1953/104569.

183 Ali Rahnema, *Neruha-ye Mazhabi* (Religious Forces) (Tehran: Gam Now Press, 1985), 826.

184 Falle, Telegram (6 June 1952), FO 248/Persia 1952/1531.

185 Mina Yazdani, "The Persecution of Bahais: Before and After the Coup," www.bbc.co.uk/Persian/iran/2013/08/130820_144_coup_bahai_shtml.

186 CIA, Memo for the Directorate (1 March 1953), *FRUS* (2017), 468.

he warned the shah not to make the mistake of thinking that a few hundred protestors represented the whole nation.[187] The British embassy cautioned that such a "manufactured" crowd should not be seen as an "expression of spontaneous loyalty for the crown."[188] The 28 February, however, turned out to be a small dress rehearsal for the 19 August coup.

Henderson later reported he "decided he was free to try to effect cancellation of the departure." He conveyed this message to the shah first indirectly through his military attaché, and then directly through a secure phone call to the royal palace. "I told Ala," he reported,

that even though I might later be charged with interference in Iranian affairs, I would welcome the offer to assure the Shah that the US government would consider him leaving not in the best interest of his country. I added that a very important personage for whom he had most friendly feeling has also expressed sincere hope he would not leave.[189]

The "important personage" was too important to be named. A very similar message came from Eden explicitly discouraging the shah from leaving the country.[190]

Henderson also rushed to Mossadeq's residence – which happened to be near the royal palace – to warn the prime minister that the shah's departure would seriously harm the country. He urged resolution of their differences behind closed doors without public airing. When Mossadeq pointed out that this was blatant interference, Henderson replied he had learnt from experience that it was better to suffer such a charge than to fail to "advance the interests of a friendly country." On leaving Mossadeq's residence, Henderson saw "surly" demonstrators outside. A separate embassy dispatch reported that this surly "mob" had moved from the palace to the prime minister's residence and then

---

187 Morteza Rasuli, "Conversation with Hussein Makki," *Tarekh-e Mo'aser-e Iran*, Vol. I, No. 1 (Spring 1997), 176–216.
188 British Embassy, Report to the Foreign Office (3 March 1953), *FO 371/Persia 1953/104562.*
189 Henderson, Telegram (28 February 1953), *FRUS* (2017), 462–6.
190 See footnote page 463 in *FRUS* (2017). It states: "The Department relayed a message from the Embassy in London that reads in Part: 'Foreign Office this afternoon informed us of receipt message from Eden from Queen Elizabeth expressing concern at latest developments re Shah and strong hope we can find some means of dissuading him from leaving country'."

tried to break in by crashing a jeep through the gates. Mossadeq, in a later radio broadcast, claimed a "foreign power" had hired thugs to kill him.[191] He also named the shah's brother, Shahpour Hamid Reza, as the main instigator of the assault on his home. The US embassy relished Mossadeq being administered some of his own medicine, and, thereby, "developing a healthy fear of angry crowds."[192] The Secretary of State promptly cabled Henderson that the administration fully "concurred with his decision to take energetic measures to discourage the Shah's departure."[193]

At the end of the day, the shah announced he would not be leaving the country. The CIA reported the "mob" disbanded, but Sha'aban Brainless as well as sixty-five officers, including General Gilanshah, were all arrested.[194] Allen Dulles informed Eisenhower that the February crisis had increased Mossadeq's strength and his hostility towards the shah. "He might," Dulles added, "resent Henderson's activities during the crisis."[195] This last short phrase was redacted from the 1989 version of the same document.[196]

Three months later the shah privately but profusely thanked Henderson for having dissuaded him from leaving: "He wished the Ambassador to know he believed if it had not been for the actions of the Ambassador at that time the institution of monarchy would have been overthrown."[197] He could not have been more categorical. Henderson, in a personal presentation to the NSC, reiterated his own role in the February crisis as well as the shah's heartfelt acknowledgment. Henderson ended his NSC presentation by repeating his long-standing conviction that "there is no hope of settling the oil

[191] Mossadeq, Radio Address to the Nation, *Ettela'at*, 6 April 1953; Mossadeq, "Report on the 28th February Conspiracy," *Musaddiq's Memoirs* (ed. Homa Katouzian) (London: Jeb'eh Publications, 1988), 296–305. See also US Embassy, Prime Minister Radio Speech (6 April 1953), FO 371/Persia 1953/ 104567.

[192] CIA in Tehran, Telegram to CIA (12 April 1953), *FRUS* (2017), 519.

[193] Secretary of State, Telegram (28 February 1953), *FRUS* (2017), 467.

[194] CIA, The Iranian Situation (3 March 1953), www.cia.gov/libraryroom/search/ site/Iran.

[195] CIA, Memo from CIA Director to President Eisenhower (1 March 1953), *FRUS* (2017), 470.

[196] CIA, Memo from CIA Director to President Eisenhower (1 March 1953), *FRUS* (1989), 690.

[197] NSC, Memorandum (14 May 1953), *FRUS* (2017), 556–67.

problem so long as Musaddiq remained in power."[198] The CIA later revealed that immediately after the February crisis a senior Iranian officer – whose name remains redacted – sounded out the embassy about the possibility of a military coup d'état.[199]

[198] NSC, Remarks to the NSC (25 June 1953), *FRUS* (2017), 599.
[199] Foreign Office, Leading Personalities in Persia (1952), *FO 416/105*.

2 | *US Concerns: Oil or Communism?*

If this, the largest British overseas investment, is destroyed by violence or expropriated under duress, every other oil concession in the Middle East will be threatened with a similar fate. Production and selling of oil will be at the mercy of political passions and the economic and strategic plans of the western world will be deeply affected, for oil is perhaps the most vital of all raw materials. If only for this reason the Unites States, too, is vitally affected by the dispute ...

Editorial, "Persia's Road to Ruin," *The Economist*, 5 May 1951

My Dear Compatriot Mr. Sho'aiyan, I will not attend to the details of your article, as certain points are in need of revision – a task discordant with my life in this prison. I will comment only briefly and in general terms on the reason for our defeat ... The Colonial Powers would not accept Iran controlling its oil resources and were concerned that our success would ignite similar movements in the oil rich countries of the region.

Dr. Mohammad Mossadeq

Oil

The conventional explanation for US involvement in the coup tends to underplay the concern about oil nationalization. Instead, it stresses the importance of the Cold War and fear of communism – both from the Soviet Union and the Tudeh Party. This explanation is shared by American as well as British historians, by leftists as well as centrists and rightists, by monarchists as well as some Mossadeq supporters. Roger Louis, the preeminent historian of the decline of the British Empire, writes that the coup was seen at the time as "saving the country from communism." He adds this was ironic since Mossadeq was a "nationalist and an anti-Communist."[1] Mark Gasiorowski, the lead

---

[1] Wm. Roger Louis, "How Mussadeq Was Ousted," *Times Literary Supplement*, 29 June 2001.

expert on the mechanics of the coup, insists that the driving force was not oil, but the Cold War and the mortal fear that "Iran was in danger of falling behind the Iron Curtain."[2] He dismisses those who think otherwise as "blind to stark facts" and deniers of hard reality.[3] Similarly, Mohammad Movahhed, an avowed nationalists and lead expert in Iran on the oil crisis, subscribes to the view that American policy was primarily driven by the ever-present fear of communism.[4]

Madeleine Albright, the former Secretary of State, expressed regret in 2000 for the overthrow of the "popular prime minister," but went on to explain that "President Eisenhower had felt it was justified for strategic reasons."[5] This was the very first time a senior official had admitted the USA had been involved in the coup. Likewise, President Obama in 2009 admitted that the "United Sates had played a role in the overthrow of the democratically elected Iranian government," but again placed the event squarely within the "context of the Cold War."[6] As of 2020, no serving senior official in the British government has acknowledged any UK role in the coup.

Although US and UK public pronouncements emphasize that their policies had little to do with oil and much to do with the Cold War, their internal documents reveal deep and abiding concern that nationalization posed serious dangers to international business, including American companies. The released State Department documents make this clear. It is true that Middle East counties eventually nationalize their oil industries. But it is equally true that in the early 1950s nationalization was seen as an imminent threat that would drastically shift economic power away from the developed world towards the developing countries. Some saw it as the end of civilization as they knew it.

Middleton, the British chargé d'affaires, put it succinctly: "There was considerable fear that a bad example would have repercussions elsewhere. We had already had Mexico. We didn't want to see it

---

[2] Mark Gasiorowski, "The Truth about the 1953 Coup," *Le Monde Diplomatique*, October 2000.

[3] Mark Gasiorowski, "Refusal to Accept Facts," *Andisheh-e Pouya* (Autumn 2013), 147.

[4] Mohammad Movahhed, *Khavb-e Ashufteh-e Naft* (The Oil Nightmare) (Tehran: Karnameh Publications, 1999), Vol. I, 108, 188, 440.

[5] Madeleine Albright, Speech to the American Iranian Council, *C-Span*, 17 March 2000.

[6] President Obama, Speech in Cairo, *ABC-CBN News*, 5 June 2009.

happen ten more times."[7] Similarly, the British embassy conveyed to the American ambassador the clear message: "Britain would *never* agree to an oil solution unfavorable to British interests in Iran. This was fundamental because it would jeopardize favourable contracts Britain had in other parts of the Middle East and the world. It was as simple as that."[8] The British Foreign Secretary reported that chairmen of major American companies had visited him, and expressed "grave concern," especially since countries such as Venezuela, Kuwait, Iraq were showing "unhealthy interest in developments in Persia."[9]

The British government consistently warned – but only in confidential reports – that a settlement favorable to Iran would set a highly dangerous precedent. It insisted:

The main point here is that Persia should not get more than other countries have done. In fact it would be greatly to our advantage if she got less in order to show that intransigence does not pay ... The general damage which oil companies operating in other areas would suffer if Persia is seen to get by intransigence more than they have got by being reasonable is not susceptible of mathematical evaluation and might be very great indeed.[10]

One executive from a major American oil company bluntly told Acheson that it would be better to lose Iran behind the Iron Curtain than to have it succeed.[11] Another stressed that nationalization in Iran "breached international law" and undermined "other oil concessions throughout the Middle East."[12] Acheson himself cabled the ambassador in Tehran: "American companies have expressed fear that soft American position with respect to unilateral cancellation of concession might weaken their own position in Middle East and elsewhere."[13] The British Defense Ministry assured the AIOC:

[7] Habib Ladjevardi, Interview with Sir George Middleton, *Iranian Oral History Project* (Cambridge, MA: Harvard University, 1993).

[8] Eric Pollard (Military Attaché), Memorandum to the Ambassador (28 August 1953), Declassified Doc No. 532934 (emphasis in original).

[9] Foreign Office, Notes (7 May 1951), FO 371/Persia 1951/34–91533.

[10] Ministry of Fuel, Persia (October 1951), FO 371/Persia 1951/34–91607.

[11] Acheson, Princeton Seminar Papers, cited by James Goode, *The United States and Iran: In the Shadow of Musaddiq* (New York: St. Martin's Press, 1997), 29–30, 195.

[12] British Middle East Office (Cairo), Letter to the Foreign Office (4 April 1951), FO 371/Persia 1951/34–91525.

[13] Acheson, Telegram (11 May 1951), *FRUS* (1989), 53.

The other companies, including the Americans, were becoming increasingly apprehensive of the effects in other Middle East countries. They say that what had been sauce for the AIOC goose might well become sauce for their own gander. It was not only the oil companies which might be effected; the Egyptians for instance might think that this gave them a lead to nationalise the Suez Canal.[14]

Early in the crisis, the State Department summarized a meeting McGhee had with the chief oil executives:[15]

Representatives of the (oil) group emphasized the very grave consequences of giving the Iranians terms more favorable than those received by other counties. They expressed the opinion that if this were done the entire international oil industry would be seriously threatened. The opinion was offered that even the loss of Iran would be preferable to the instability which would be created by making too favorable an agreement with Iran. Other representatives pointed out that not just the oil industry was involved but indeed all American investments overseas and the concept of the sanctity of contractual relations.

Herbert Hoover, Jr., an oilman himself, who in the midst of World War II had provoked a crisis by trying to obtain a concession for Standard Oil on Russia's doorstep in Iran, was adamant that nationalization would have a domino effect spreading as far afield as Venezuela and Saudi Arabia.[16] David Painter, a leading expert on American oil companies, writes that the five majors (Gulf, Texas, as well as Standard Oil of New Jersey, New York, and California) were unanimous in opposing appeasement of Iran. "In their opinion," he writes, "losing Iran to the Soviets would be preferable to the instability successful nationalization would create."[17] The five, together with seventeen

---

[14] Ministry of Defence, Meeting with Sir William Fraser (23 May 1951), *FO 71/ Persia 1951/34–91537*.

[15] State Department, Memorandum of Conversation on Iranian Oil Problem (16 October 1951), Harry Truman Library. Cited by James Bill, *The Eagle and the Lion* (New Haven: Yale University Press, 1988), 429, 507. The meeting included representatives from Standard Oil of New Jersey, Standard Oil of California, Gulf Oil, Texas, and Socony-Vacuum.

[16] Goode, *The United States and Iran*, 128.

[17] David Painter, *Oil and the American Century* (London: John Hopkins University Press, 1986), 181. See also "The United States, Great Britain, and Mossadegh" (Instructors Copy A and B), Institute of Diplomacy, School of Foreign Service, Georgetown University, 1–22. http://data.georgetown.edu/sfs/programs/isd.

minor American companies, soon set up a Foreign Petroleum Supply Committee to "make it difficult for Iran to find tankers and customers."[18] In short, they enabled Britain to implement its embargo on Iran.

Press releases from the US and UK governments repeated endlessly that they were more than ready to reach a "fair compromise" that would include the "principle of nationalization." At the same time, their internal memos, discussions, and position papers all stressed the overriding danger posed by the possible spread of nationalization. Their priority remained consistent before, during, and after the crisis. It was to "safeguard sanctity of contracts and international agreements."

Even before the nationalization law had been finalized, the Bank of England warned the Foreign Office that an "intense inflammatory" mood had completely taken over Iran, including senior oil company staff, and now posed a serious threat to other oil concessions in the Middle East. "Anything," it warned, "might now happen."[19] The bank also reported that the American ambassador had confided to his British counterpart that the "only hope for Persia was the emergence of a dictator."[20] The Foreign Office argued that Mossadeq must be compelled to accept an arrangement, and that an unsatisfactory one would have "catastrophic effects" elsewhere.[21] It also insisted it was "better to have no agreement than one that would have dangerous repercussions on our foreign interests not only in the oil industry."[22] The British motto soon became – especially under Foreign Secretary Anthony Eden – "Better no agreement than a bad one." The British embassy reported to London: "It is extremely difficult for any Ambassador to tell the reigning monarch to get rid of his Prime Minister. This, however, in no way altered the fact that we did want to get rid of Musaddiq."[23]

---

[18] William Langer, Memorandum to CIA Director (6 July 1951), *FRUS* (2017), 112.
[19] Claude Loombe, Visit to Persia (April 1951), *FO 371/Persia 1951/34–91531*; Foreign Office, Discussion with Mr. Loombe from the Bank of England (1 May 1951), *FO 371/Persia 1951/34–91530*.
[20] Foreign Office, Minutes (1 May 1951), *FO 371/Persia 1951/34–91530*.
[21] State Department, Meeting of UK Foreign Minister and Secretary of State (9 January 1952), *FRUS* (1989), 311–20.
[22] Foreign Office, Telegram to Washington (15 January 1952), *FO 371/Persia 1952/34–104606*.
[23] Zaehner, Conversation with Perron (29 August 1951), *FO 248/1514*.

Clement Attlee, the British prime minister, in accepting McGhee's formula, sent the following convoluted message to his ambassador in Washington: "We have to agree on principle of nationalization ... like Dominion status. It might well be that in negotiating an agreement in such a context a number of modifications would be introduced that the resulting agreement would confer something that was, in fact, a good deal less than domination status."[24] The very first task of the Persian Oil Working Party set up in the Foreign Office was to list the major enterprises inside and outside the Commonwealth that could be affected by the nationalization contagion. These included not only the obvious oil ones and the Suez Canal, but also companies involved in copper, rubber, tin, iron ore, nickel, and nitrates in such far afield places as Spain, Portugal, Greece, Burma, Bolivia, Chile, India, Pakistan, and Indonesia.[25] The Foreign Office made sure the elaborate list reached the State Department.

The Americans did not need such lists. The chief executive of Standard Oil of New Jersey assured the British that "nationalization" was tantamount to "abrogation," and such bad behavior directly threatened "international investments," "civilized society," and the "well-being of the peoples of the world."[26] Even before Iran had implemented the nationalization law, the CIA warned: "Developments in Iran are bound to have continuing effect not only on Iraq, but also upon other countries in the Middle East."[27] It added: "Unrest in Iran can readily spread to other Middle East countries or Eastern hemisphere oil centers with concomitant jeopardy to supplies ... It is a matter of common knowledge that Iraq, another source of strategic importance, is dissatisfied with current arrangements. Likewise Indonesia ... "[28]

As soon as the crisis erupted, the NSC declared:[29]

---

[24] Prime Minister, Letter to the British Ambassador in Washington, *FO 371*/Persia 1951/34–91533.

[25] Persian Oil Working Party, Consequences of Nationalization (6 July 1951), *FO 371*/ Persia 1951/34–91544.

[26] AIOC, Persian Oil: The American View (14 June 1951), *BP*/00003565.

[27] CIA, Daily Digest (30 March 1951), CIA Electronic Library, www.cia.gov/library/readingroom/search/Iran.

[28] CIA, Current World Petroleum Situation (1 June 1951), CIA Electronic Library, www.cia.gov/library/readingroom/search/Iran.

[29] NSC, Memorandum for the Record (16 May 1951), *FRUS* (2017), 89.

We agree that we could not afford to be neutral with respect to the controversy between Britain and Iran. We should indeed give vigorous support to Britain. The Iranian Prime Minister and Government have unilaterally broken contract and such a breach of contract was not only wrong in itself, but was likely to set an example and precedent which would induce Iraq and other countries to suppose they could undertake similar actions. This was a highly contagious situation which we should do all we can to check.

In a follow-up report, the NSC added: "It (US Government) has stressed its strong opposition to unilateral cancellation of valid contracts and attempts by the Iranian Government to settle a serious international controversy unilaterally."[30]

Acheson, early in the negotiations, stressed: "Oil concessions throughout the world are in trouble as a result of the situation that had been created in Iran."[31] In his memoirs, Acheson mentions – but only in passing – that Mossadeq "upset relations with other oil-producing countries."[32] Henderson, in conveying an early offer, privately reiterated that any agreement must "not have unfavorable effect elsewhere," and "should preserve the sanctity of international contracts, in particular the position of the oil firms which have contracts with various countries for the exploitation of oil products and other raw materials." He summarized the whole crisis as being "all about the importance of the sanctity of international contracts."[33] He had been appointed ambassador to Iran precisely because he had experience negotiating petroleum issues with oil states such as Iraq and Indonesia. The Butler report, the British postmortem on the crisis, gave the Foreign Office high marks for persistence in protecting national interests and the sanctity of international contracts.[34] "These principles," it stressed, "were maintained throughout negotiations."

The concern for the sanctity of contracts continued throughout the crisis. Late in the day and close to the coup, President Eisenhower, who liked to keep his hands out of dirty dealings, at a select NSC meeting

---

[30] James Webb, Progress Report for NSC (31 May 1951), *FRUS* (2017), 99–100.

[31] State Department, Meeting of UK Foreign Minister and Secretary of State (9 January 1952), *FRUS* (1989), 315.

[32] Acheson, *Present at Creation*, 504.

[33] Henderson, Memo to the State Department (28 August 1953), National Archives, Declassified Document 832984. I would like to thank Kambiz Fattahi of the BBC for locating this document.

[34] Butler, *British Policy in the Relinquishing of Abadan in 1951*, FO 370/2694.

expressed his personal sentiment that "we should respect the enormous investments the British had made in Iran," and that a bad "example might have grave effects on US oil concessions in other parts of the world." His Defense Secretary echoed him: "We should not risk destroying what was left of the idea of sanctity of contracts."[35] The Pentagon chief seems to have had an inordinate concern about the sanctity of private property. A later CIA history described Eisenhower as a president who "kept his distance" and avoided participating in coup plans, but, nevertheless, was kept informed by Foster Dulles over cocktails.[36]

Once Mossadeq had been overthrown, the USA sent Herbert Hoover to negotiate a new concession. He was instructed to work with Henderson to produce a concession that would not have adverse repercussions elsewhere. The NSC gave him explicit instructions that "settlement must not establish precedent adversely affecting the presently established international oil industry in a way inimical to US interests."[37] According to Sir Dennis Wright, the new British chargé d'affaires and soon to be ambassador, he and Henderson reached a satisfactory "formula" by which Iran "appeared to keep sovereignty" while the consortium retained the "control it considered essential for the running of operations."[38] Henderson was told that the "Iranian government could not be completely frank with its people on the necessity for and the reasons behind an oil agreement."[39] The Butler report described the new concession as a "public opinion camouflage" which accepted nationalization but kept "effective control of the refinery and oil fields in the hands of the Consortium."[40] McGhee's formula had won hands down. Years later, Falle reminisced that Mossadeq's main mistake had been to not realize that the Americans "could not afford to

---

[35] NSC, Memoranda on Discussions (4 and 11 March 1953), *FRUS* (2017), 474–84, 489–93. The meeting was taken up mostly with Iran but began with the announcement that Stalin was fatally ill. This was a day before the official announcement of his death.

[36] Koch, *"Zendebad Shah!": The Central Intelligence Agency and the Fall of Iranian Prime Minister Mohammed Mossadeq, August 1953*, 20.

[37] NSC, Certain Problems Relating to Iran (1954), *FRUS* (2017), 880.

[38] Sir Dennis Wright, Annual for Persia (1954), *FO 371/Persia 1954/34–114805*.

[39] Henderson, Memorandum of Conversation (23 October 1953), *FRUS* (2017), 819.

[40] Butler, *British Policy in the Relinquishing of Abadan in 1951*.

conclude an agreement that would start a vast series of re-negotiations with all the world's oil producers."[41]

This concern for the sanctity of contracts was implicit in the two most important offers made: that of the World Bank in early 1952 (the bank was known then as the International Bank for Reconstruction and Development); and that of Truman-Churchill in the summer of 1952, which soon became the Eisenhower-Churchill "letter" of February 1953. Many, including some Iranian nationalists, claim that Mossadeq made a serious mistake in not accepting these "reasonable compromises." One high official from the shah's regime praises Mossadeq for being a "great patriot" in nationalizing the oil industry, but then argues he made a terrible mistake in not accepting the best offer – the Truman-Churchill of February 1953.[42] He probably means the final Eisenhower-Churchill letter.

The World Bank offer was drawn up by its president, Eugene Black, a prominent Republican with considerable influence in Washington.[43] He ran his proposals first through the Foreign Office and the State Department before presenting them to Iran.[44] The British ambassador in Washington made it clear that "the Bank must be certain that the terms of the arrangement it proposes must not encourage the governments of a score of other oil producing countries to confiscate the properties of the oil companies."[45] The bank gave assurances that it would not offer "anything that would endanger other agreements."[46] Its proposal contained one central core: that the bank would run the industry "on behalf" of both Iran and the AIOC for at most two years until the International Court of Justice at The Hague arbitrated the final settlement.

Mossadeq, not surprisingly, was reluctant to accept. The proposal implicitly undercut nationalization since it handed control to a non-Iranian entity. Saleh privately told the British embassy that Mossadeq

---

[41] Falle, *My Lucky Life*, 83.

[42] Parviz Mina, "The Nationalization of the Oil Industry in Iran," *Rahavard*, No. 110 (Spring 2015), 152–60.

[43] Foreign Office, Meeting with Mr. Black (18 November 1952), *FO 371*/Persia 1952/34–98652.

[44] Foreign Minister, Conversation with Eugene Black (13 December 1951), *FO 371*/Persia 1951/34–91617.

[45] Sir Oliver Franks, Telegram on International Bank Negotiations, *FO 371*/Persia 1952/34–98650.

[46] Franks, Memorandum (14 March 1952), *FO 371*/Persia 1952/34–98650.

would never accept such a proposal.[47] What is more, it was intended as only an interim solution. Mossadeq, well aware that the British were eager to remove him, had no guarantees of still being around in two years' time. Despite his reluctance, Mossadeq asked Makki and Dr. Hjalmar Schacht – the famous German finance expert – to travel to Washington to further explore the World Bank proposal. The State Department refused Schacht entry on the grounds that he had served the Third Reich. Of course, so had many other prominent Germans working closely with NATO. Without Schacht's presence, Makki's discussions in Washington fizzled out. Mossadeq never officially rejected the bank's proposal, but Falle and others claim the Americans came round to the idea of a coup only after the World Bank offer had been turned down.[48]

One prolific and prominent National Front historian has argued that if Mossadeq had seized the World Bank offer there would have been no coup, and, thus, the whole course of Iranian history would have been different. He blames "intransigent advisers" for the "greatest missed opportunity in the whole of the Anglo-Iranian Oil dispute."[49] Of course, if Mossadeq had not nationalized oil in the first place, and had accepted the hollow form of nationalization then there would have been no reason for the coup. Henderson was more realistic. Well aware that Mossadeq took nationalization seriously, he had been pessimistic about the bank's proposals from the very first. Despite his awareness, he still claimed that Mossadeq rejected it because "Iran is a sick country and the Prime Minister is one of its most sick leaders."[50]

The final Eisenhower (Truman)-Churchill letter seemed to go further in meeting Mossadeq's terms. Henderson described it as the "most liberal."[51] It avowedly accepted nationalization, but insisted that The Hague court should determine how much Iran should pay the AIOC as "fair compensation." The drafters of the letter had been fully aware that the vague terminology would be unacceptable in Iran. As the letter

---

[47] Falle, Conversation with Saleh (28 May 1952), *FO 248/1531.*
[48] Falle, *My Lucky Life*, 76.
[49] Homa Katouzian, *Khalil Maleki: The Human Face of Iranian Socialism* (London: Oneworld Academic Press, 2018), 111, 143.
[50] Henderson, Telegram to State Department (4 January 1952), *FRUS* (1989), 302.
[51] Henderson, Notes to the NSC (25 June 1953), *FRUS* (2017), 599–601.

was being drafted, an Iranian legal adviser – who happened to be
Mossadeq's distant cousin – had privately warned the State
Department that the prime minister would never agree to a vague
definition of "compensation." He would agree if the amount was
specified or based on the current value of the oil installations. The
nationalization law itself had left room for payment of
compensation.[52] The legal adviser explained that Mossadeq was fearful of putting Iran "forever in debt" by inadvertently agreeing to an
"astronomical sum" that would be based not on current value, but on
projected profits extended to 1993 – to the very end of the original
AIOC contract. He calculated that if the British expected compensation
based on high 1950 profits multiplied by 42 years, they were thinking
of a huge sum – perhaps over $2.8 billion. He was not far wrong; in
fact, the AIOC was thinking of $1.3 billion.[53] The legal adviser
concluded:

Mossadeq has declared he would submit to the International Court if the
British first set the maximum sum they would claim. Mossadeq has two
reasons for doing so. First, to reduce the astronomical figure of future profits.
Second, to guard against a possible fall of his government or his own death.
He is afraid that in either event the following government may lack the will to
continue to fight in the Court, thus submitting to the extraordinary demands
of the British Government. Those who are familiar with the position in Iran
agree that these fears are well founded ... One cannot but sympathize with
the position taken by Iran.

Kazem Hassibi, one of Mossadeq's oil advisers, expressed similar
concerns to the majles. He argued that such vaguely worded clause
could be worse than the previous 1933 agreement. It could drown the
country in debt lasting more than forty years.[54]

Henderson conceded that cause for concern did exist. He told the
CIA that Mossadeq was willing to give "reasonable compensation" but
unwilling to "mortgage" the country's future.[55] He explained that
Mossadeq would agree to either a specified lump sum or arbitration
with stated limits. Even before the Eisenhower-Churchill letter,

[52] Dr. Abdol Bashar Farman Farmaian, Iran's Best Interests (August 1953), CIA
     Electronic Library, www.cia.gov/library/readingroom/search/site/Iran.
[53] NSC, Memorandum on Meeting (18 March 1954), www.cia.gov/readingroom/
     search/site/Iran.
[54] Hassebi, Speech, 17th Majles, 21 December 1952.
[55] Henderson, Memo to the CIA (11 December 1952), *FRUS* (2017), 426.

Henderson stressed that Mossadeq wants Britain to "state immediately amount of compensation they intend to ask of Court before he agrees to submit to the Court ... He suspects that Britain wants to put Iran into bondage for twenty-five years and if he accepted this bondage Iran would be not better off than before nationalization."[56] Acheson himself admitted he feared the British were thinking of an "astronomical figure."[57] When one American oil expert suggested a "lump sum" could possibly break the deadlock, the State Department stepped in to quash the idea.[58]

In fact, Mossadeq's suspicions were well founded. In drafting the letter, Churchill had written a personal note to Eisenhower waxing nostalgic about the good old days of World War II when they had worked together. He then raised the question of compensation, insisting the issue had to be submitted to the International Court.[59] The CIA surmised that even though Mossadeq was willing to pay compensation the British were unwilling to settle for simple loses of current assets.[60] The British later admitted they wanted compensation to be so onerous as to "deter other countries from nationalizing their oil industries."[61] Even in 1978, the British foreign minister applauded his distant predecessor for insisting that the International Court should determine the amount of compensation. "Otherwise," he wrote, "British (or American) interests in foreign countries would not be safeguarded against breach of contract."[62]

The CIA in early 1953 concluded that the negotiations over compensation were completely stalemated. Britain was adamant that loss of future profits must be taken into account; Iran was equally adamant that Britain should either state a specific sum or a figure based on

[56] Henderson, Letter to the State Department (9 March 1953), *FRUS* (1989), 703–6.
[57] Foreign Office, Minutes of the Persian Official Meeting, FO 371/Persia 1952/34–98647.
[58] NSC, Conversations in Washington, *FRUS* (2017), 599.
[59] Letters between London and Washington (21–7 August 1952), *FRUS* (1989), 459–69.
[60] CIA, Oil Talks (March 1953), CIA Electronic Library, www.cia.gov/library/readingroom/search/site/Iran.
[61] CIA, Bulletin on Question of Compensation (2 July 1954), CIA Electronic Library, www.cia.gov/library/readingroom/search/site/Iran.
[62] A. Heath, Note to the Middle East Department, FCO 8/2730.

the current book value of the oil installations.[63] A State Department policy paper warned that if the USA sided with Iran "such action might be regarded as flouting a recognized principle of international economic relations through countenancing appropriations without compensation."[64] In simple English, it would undermine international contracts.

An NIE drafted in March 1953 was quite blunt in admitting that the British insisted on wording which would permit the AIOC to include projected profits in their claims.[65] Another NIE argued that even though nationalization per se was no longer an issue, the British continued to insist that an international body should determine the amount of compensation in part because of public opinion at home and in part because they "feel that capitulation to Iran would threaten their own and the Western oil position generally in other parts of the Middle East."[66]

Compensation was the topic of long discussions between Mossadeq and Henderson in February 1953. The former suspected the AIOC was thinking of a sum totaling as much as £150 million. The latter replied that international judges were "reasonable men" and that compensation could be limited to 25 percent of annual sales. The former asked for how many years. The latter could not specify.[67] At one point, Iran offered 25 percent of sales for ten to fifteen years, but the United Kingdom insisted on its previous position.[68] The MI6 man heading the coup operation later admitted that the British were not really interested in the compensation issue. As he explained, "We would have wanted to oust Mossadegh regardless of whether he would have signed an agreement favourable to the British."[69]

63   CIA, "Briefing Note for Director (4 February 1953), Information Only (31 January 1953)," CIA Electronic Library, www.cia.gov/library/readin groom/search/site/Iran.
64   US Embassy, Memo for Ambassador Henderson (19 May 1953), *FRUS* (2017), 567.
65   CIA, NIE Estimate (11 March 1953), *FRUS* (2017), 494.
66   NIE-75, Probable Developments in Iran through 1953 (7 January 1953), CIA Electronic Library, www.cia.gov/library/readingroom/search/site/Iran.
67   Henderson, Meeting with Mosadeq (28 January 1953), *FRUS* (1989), 655.
68   *Ettela'at*, 12 May 1953.
69   Granada TV, "Interview with Derbyshire," *End of Empire*, Channel 4, UK, 1985. This is in the transcript of the interview.

Later narratives tend to repeat the claim that Mossadeq refused outright to pay any compensation. The British annual report for 1953 argued that Mossadeq had been unwilling to pay compensation for future profits because of his "childish" attitude.[70] A much later CIA history claimed categorically that the British began to think of overthrowing Mossadeq when it became "clear" he had absolutely "no intention of paying" compensation.[71] This same history insisted that the root difficulty was Mossadeq's refusal to compensate. Similarly, a senior American diplomat later reminisced that the coup became inevitable when Mossadeq refused to pay any compensation whatsoever.[72] This certainly would have been news to the actual negotiators. The press in the West went along with this false narrative. Only the American journal *The Reporter* – but only after the coup – admitted the sticking point had been compensation for future loses. It wrote: "Negotiations broke down because the British wanted compensation for future profits ... If idea got around that oil concessions could be broken without compensation, the monarchs and politicos of the Middle East would lose no time proving that they too were sovereign."[73]

Thus the Eisenhower-Churchill letter was dead on arrival. Mossadeq concluded that the former was fully siding with the latter. At the same time Saleh, the Iranian ambassador in Washington, was informed by a middle-level State Department official that senior personnel were "too busy" to see him and that the International Court should have full discretion on defining "fair compensation." This issue, he was told, was important because American companies had major investments in other oil producing countries.[74]

Mossadeq even then did not technically reject the Eisenhower-Churchill letter. Instead, he put the ball back into the US court. He told Henderson he would be happy to let the president himself define "fair compensation." Henderson replied he did not think the president

[70] Foreign Office, Summary of Events in Persia in 1953, FO 416/107.
[71] Koch, *"Zendebad Shah!" The CIA and the Fall of Iran Prime Minister Mohammed Mossadeq, August 1953.*
[72] John Stempel, *Inside the Iranian Revolution* (Bloomington: Indiana University Press, 1981), 62.
[73] Harlan Cleveland, "Oil, Blood, and Politics," *The Reporter*, 10 November 1953.
[74] Allahyar Saleh, *Gozaresh-e Siyas-ye Vashington* (Political Events in Washington) (Tehran: Sukhan Publications, 2010), 345.

could do that.[75] Eisenhower privately sided with the United Kingdom on the grounds that he did not want any agreement that would have grave effects on US investments elsewhere.[76] Secretary Dulles seconded him even though he admitted Mossadeq feared putting his country into "protracted economic bondage."[77]

Eisenhower, in his final message to Mossadeq – designed to undermine him – clearly sided with the British. "There is considerable sentiment in the United States," he stated, "to the effect that a settlement based on the payment of compensation on merely for losses of the physical assets of a firm which has been nationalized would not be what might be called a reasonable settlement and that an agreement to such a settlement might tend to weaken mutual trust between free nations engaged in friendly economic intercourse."[78] In other words, compensation should include possible future losses.

Communism

The NSC in Washington was sharply divided over Iran – especially over its periodic NIEs on Iran. On one side were State Department advisers and some analysts inside the CIA – academics such as Joseph Upton who later taught at Harvard, and William Langer, Assistant Director of the Office of National Estimates and author of *The Diplomacy of Imperialism* who later chaired the history department at Harvard. On the other side was Allen Dulles, the deputy director of the CIA and his main cohorts – Roosevelt, Helms, Wisner, Waller, and Wilber. They had manned the Iran desk at the CIA ever since January 1951. Allen Dulles, who had been in the CIA since its very inception in 1947, became deputy director in July 1952 – full six months before Eisenhower entered the White House and his brother Foster Dulles became Secretary of State. This inner division within the NSC and the CIA remained hidden until the declassification of government documents in 2017.

[75] Henderson, Telegram (4 May 1953), *FRUS* (2017), 546–7.
[76] NSC, Meeting (4 March 1953), *FRUS* (2017), 474–92; see also NSC, Meeting (11 March 1953), *FRUS* (1989), 713.
[77] NSC, Meeting (11 March 1953), *FRUS* (2017), 491.
[78] President Eisenhower, Message to Mosadeq (30 June 1953), *FRUS* (2017), 607–9.

On the whole, the analysts in the State Department during the Truman administration held a fairly down-to-earth evaluation of the situation in Iran. At the start of the crisis, a top-level meeting of the Foreign Office and the State Department, led by McGhee, agreed that the "present situation contained no Russian incitation and ought not to be seen primarily as part of the immediate short term 'cold war' problems."[79] An NIE, dated February 1952 and titled "Probable Developments in Iran in 1952," depicted Mossadeq as "highly popular," "astute," "intensely nationalistic," and a "social reformer" who favored parliamentary government, limitations on royal prerogatives, as well as freedom of speech, assembly and the press.[80] It concluded the Mossadeq administration was stable and unlikely to be replaced in the near future.

Many other NSC reports endorsed this conclusion. One declared: "It is unlikely that Mossadeq can be overthrown during this critical period except by violence or by the establishment of a semi-dictatorial regime under the aegis of the Shah. Such a course of action would involve risks which the Shah has thus far shown no willingness to take."[81] Another predicted that Mossadeq would survive through 1952–3, despite the British embargo, because his "popularity derived in large part from his success in 'liberating' Iran from Britain ... His popular prestige makes him still the dominant political force in Iran."[82] These estimates also stressed that the Tudeh was not an "imminent threat" – it was small, smaller than in 1946, had no arms and paramilitary organizations, and had failed to "penetrate" any of the key ministries. A later CIA history of the coup admitted the Tudeh did not pose an imminent threat:[83]

Neither Langer nor any of the Iran specialists in CIA's clandestine service – the Office of Special Operations (OSO), and the Office of Policy Coordination (OPC) – thought the Tudeh was strong enough by itself to

[79] Foreign Office, First Meeting held in State Department (9 April 1952), *FO 371/ Persia* 1951/34–91471.
[80] NIE-46, Probable Developments in Iran (4 February 1952), *FRUS* (2017), 175–82.
[81] NSC, Special Estimate: Current Developments in Iran, *FRUS* (2017), 91–2.
[82] NSC, Prospects for Survival of Mossadeq Regime in Iran (14 October 1952), *FRUS* (2017), 367–70.
[83] Koch, *"Zendebad Shah!": The CIA and the Fall of Iranian Prime Minister Mohammad Mossadeq, August 1953*, 11.

topple Mossadeq. As long as the central government remained able to deal with events, Langer and others saw the danger of a Tudeh coup as negligible. "Tudeh represents a serious threat in view of the opportunities awaiting it," OSO and OPC specialists agreed in January 1952, "but does not yet have the intention or the ability to gain control of the government at this time either by force or political means." CIA's operators thought that the Tudeh would come to power only through chaos and impotent central authority.

This full paragraph was redacted from the same document published in previous years.

Allen Dulles, however, had a very different assessment of the situation. On 9 March 1951 – mere days after Mossadeq's election – he conveyed to the CIA director the message from Eden, the shadow British foreign secretary, whom he had just met quietly in Paris, that the only way to deal with Mossadeq was to throw him out.[84] He also lobbied to have Roosevelt assigned the task of revamping the existing NIE on Iran.[85] After the July Uprising, he described the situation as "urgent" and dismissed all the previous NIEs as "poor" and "too optimistic." Failing to get a new NIE, he requested periodic "oral reports."[86] Just before the February crisis, he claimed that the situation was "highly dangerous," "more explosive than any time," and "collapse was imminent."[87]

Roosevelt amplified these alarms. He claimed the Mossadeq administration was weak and the Tudeh posed a dire and imminent danger. In April 1952, he claimed that the "political and economic situation was fast deteriorating," that Mossadeq was unwilling to reach an oil settlement, that his popularity was rapidly "waning," that "xenophobia" was now directed at the USA, that the Tudeh was gaining strength, and that the majority of people remained oblivious to the rising communist threat.[88] He requested a brand new NIE. The Dulles group also continued to feed alarmist reports to their newspaper friends. For example,

---

[84] CIA, Minutes of the Director's Meeting (9 May 1951), *FRUS* (2017), 87; CIA, Letter from Allen Dulles (14 August 1951), CIA Electronic Library, www.cia.gov/library/readingroom/search/site/Iran.

[85] CIA, Memo for the Record (9 November 1951), *FRUS* (2017), 150.

[86] CIA, Memo on Staff Meeting (19 September 1952), CIA Electronic Library, www.cia.gov/library/readingroom/search/site/Iran.

[87] CIA, Brief Notes (18 February 1953), *FRUS* (2017), 442.

[88] Roosevelt, Memo to the Director of CIA Operations (5 April 1952), *FRUS* (2017), 227.

the *Wall Street Journal* ran articles claiming Stalin had "instigated" the whole crisis because he was running out of oil.[89]

This policy debate at times ventured into political sociology. For the academic-minded, Mossadeq and the National Front represented the new middle class – an emerging force that was reformist as well as nationalistic. In short, the National Front was on the right side of history. For the Dulles group, however, Iran was not yet a "class conscious society" and its urban middle class remained small and insignificant. The National Front had failed to advocate social reforms, and its leaders, notably Mossadeq, came from the landed upper class. On the other hand, the shah, who like FDR came from the upper class, could well end up championing social reforms similar to the New Deal. The CIA pushed to incorporate into the 1952 NIE for Iran the following paragraph from its own long study entitled "An Evaluation of the Significance of the National Front in Iran":[90]

The position of the traditional ruling group does not appear to have been seriously undermined, even though its members have been conspicuously absent from the highest government posts during the past year ... Members of the "old guard" have been "rolling with the punch" during the past year. They have supported oil nationalization and the elimination of British influence as strongly as the National Front has itself. However, they have, particularly since last fall, placed progressively more emphasis on Mossadeq's failure to solve the critical financial and economic problem resulting from the oil issue. ... Their attitude toward the oil controversy is, however, more realistic and prospects for an oil solution would improve if they returned to power. They have at no time lost their controlling position in the Senate and Majlis and have the numerical strength not only to block legislation desired by the National Front, but also to overthrow the government when they consider such action to be desirable.

Upton retorted that the National Front advocated "electoral reform, more effective taxation, and social justice." He added that many "liberal aristocrats" in Iran supported the National Front and social reform; that the "old guard" was not only divided but also lacked the "courage and capacity" to reach an agreement with Britain; and that Qavam was

---

[89] British Embassy in Washington, Dispatch (4 April 1951), *FO 371*/Persia 1951/ 34–91471.

[90] Office of National Estimates, an Evaluation of the Significance of the National Front in Iran (1 July 1952), Declassified CIA-RDP79T00937A000200010066-8. Declassified on 29 August 2000. See also *FRUS* (2017), 261–5.

"more tenacious than Mossadeq in making political power as an end in itself."[91] He concluded: "In view of the astonishing rapidity and degree of change in urban life in Iran during the past five years, there seems little justification of the conclusion that the strength of the urban middle class will probably not increase greatly for many years. Any policy based upon that assumption would, in our opinion, be very hazardous."

The more down-to-earth analysis was presented to the outside world by Professor Cuyler Young, an academic consultant who had lived for decades in Iran. He later chaired the Middle East Department at Princeton. In an article entitled "The Social Support of Current Iranian Policy," he argued that Mossadeq had "endured" and retained wide "support" because he articulated the "nationalistic spirit" of the middle classes – both of the new middle class formed of intellectuals, physicians, lawyers, engineers, journalists, civil servants, teachers, and university students, as well as of the traditional middle class of businessmen, merchants and tradesmen in the bazaars.[92] This movement, he continued, challenged the traditional power structure but was "primarily concerned with securing independence from foreign especially British domination and influence." He concluded,

Everyone knows that the Shah has not approved of much, if indeed most of what Prime Minister Mosaddeq has done in the last year. But the fact that he has nevertheless continued to support him, or perhaps more accurately, to refrain from opposing or ousting him, is cogent evidence that His Majesty perceives that the Prime Minister has the majority of the Iranian people behind him.

Cuyler Young retained this perspective long after the coup.[93] Professor Manfred Halpern, also of Princeton and former consultant to the State Department, expanded on this theme of the modern middle class as the progressive force in his well-known book *The Politics of Social Change in the Middle East and North Africa*.[94]

---

[91] Upton, Staff Memo (18 July 1952), Declassified CIA-DP79T009370002000100 57-8. Declassified on 8/29/2000/. See also *FRUS* (2017), 271–3.

[92] T. Cuyler Young, "The Social Support of Current Iranian Policy," *Middle East Journal*, Vol. 6, No. 2 (Spring 1952), 125–43.

[93] T. Cuyler Young, "Iran in Continuing Crisis," *Foreign Affairs*, Vol. 40, No. 2 (January 1962), 275–92.

[94] Manfred Halpern, *The Politics of Social Change in the Middle East and North Africa* (Princeton: Princeton University Press, 1963).

The Dulles group, meanwhile, recruited the oil expert Max Thornburg to bolster their case. Thornburg was deemed a leading specialist on Iran since he had for years advised the Tehran government on its oil negotiations with the AIOC and the Foreign Office. At the same time, he had secretly advised the AIOC and the Foreign Office. He supported Dulles' conviction that only a military coup would solve the oil problem.[95] He, together with a CIA operative in Tehran, produced a long report entitled "The Rise of an Iranian Nationalist." The report dismissed the oil nationalization campaign as irresponsible and unmanageable "xenophobia."[96] It depicted Mossadeq as a "demagogue," "slanderer," "reckless," "ruthless," "tyrannical," "dictatorial," "self-centered intriguer," "political trickster," "opportunist," as "lacking a conscience," "full of fantasies," and perhaps suffering from "hereditary insanity." His colleagues were "power hungry," "selfish," and "extremists." What is more, his "masses" were "vane," "ignorant," "irresponsible," "fatalistic," "suffering from inferiority complex," "Asian rather than Western," and full of "Haji Babals [sic]."

The Thornburg report equated nationalization with "expropriation," warning that Mossadeq's xenophobia would soon search for new targets. It concluded that Iranians were "incomprehensible" because they had "different values, different appeals, different customs, and characteristics quite peculiar to themselves." Without any sense of self-awareness it repeated the old quote about "patriotism being the last refuge of a scoundrel." A State Department official could not resist scribbling on the margin: "Who is the scoundrel: AIOC or Mosadeq?" The CIA in mid-1952 admitted that "considerable differences" existed among Iran analysts. It hoped these differences could be resolved before the completion of the next full NIE on Iran.[97]

Despite the persistence of the Dulles team, the NIEs on the whole remained sanguine. The NIE completed in November 1952 reiterated previous assessments that Mossadeq would survive through the forthcoming year.[98] He had weathered economic difficulties, retained

[95] John Leavitt, Memo to Roosevelt (23 September 1953), *FRUS* (2017), 351.
[96] John Stutesman, The Rise of Iranian Nationalism (16 February 1952), *FRUS* (2017), 185–214.
[97] John Leavitt, An Evaluation of the National Front in Iran (1 July 1952), *FRUS* (2017), 261–5.
[98] NIE-75, Probable Developments in Iran Through 1953 (13 November 1952), *FRUS* (2017), 407–16.

the capability of controlling social unrest and the Tudeh, remained eager to have US support, and because of "popular prestige was still the dominant political force in Iran." Moreover, the Soviet Union was unlikely to initiate any moves. The consensus within the NSC was that Mossadeq was secure because "neither the groups opposing the National Front nor the Tudeh are likely to develop the strength to overthrow the National Front by constitutional means or by force in 1953." The alarmists tried – unsuccessfully – to smuggle this paragraph into the new NIE:[99]

Conditions in Iran are unfavorable to the maintenance of control by a non-communist regime for an extended period of time. In wresting the political initiate from the Shah, the landlords, and other traditional holders of power, the National Front politicians now in power have at least temporarily elim-inated every alternative to their own rule except the Communist Tudeh Party. However the ability of the National Front to maintain control of the situ-ation indefinitely is uncertain. The political upheaval which brought the nationalists to power has heightened popular desire for promised economic and social betterment and has increased social unrest. At the same time, nationalist failure to restore the oil industry to operations has led to near exhaustion of the government's financial reserves and to deficit financing to meet current expenses, and is likely to produce a progressive deterioration of the economy at large.

The new NIE, entitled "Probable Developments in Iran through 1953," did not include the requested paragraph.[100]

Surprisingly even official CIA reports, especially from Tehran, remained remarkably cool headed. An extensive report dated 13 August 1953 – literally two days before the scheduled coup – stressed that Mossadeq was secure in power and could overcome all opposition and economic difficulties.[101] The Tudeh, the report added, lacked the ability to make a direct bid for power. It was "numerically small," concentrated in Tehran, incapable of resisting "firm repres-sion," and had failed to make inroads into the security forces. It concluded:

---

[99] CIA, Proposed Rewording (14 November 1952), *FRUS* (2017), 417.

[100] NIE-75, Probable Developments in Iran through 1953 (9 January 1953), *FRUS* (2017), 432–42.

[101] Sherman Kent, Current Outlook (13 August 1953), CIA Electronic Library, www.cia.gov/library/readingroom/search/site/Iran. See also Embassy, Telegram (12 August 1953), *FRUS* (1989), 743.

We do not believe that Iran will come directly or indirectly under Communist domination in 1953 ... There are no indications that the Tudeh will be able to significantly increase its own capabilities for a coup ... Over a long period if present economic and political deterioration continues, Tudeh might achieve sufficient popular support to gain power by parliamentary means.

Such means to power would have needed decades, if not centuries, since the CIA calculated in 1953 that the Tudeh and all its front organization could at most muster 400,000 votes – 2.3 percent of the population.[102] The CIA could have added that the Tudeh had to work under certain limitations: its organization was semi-underground; its social clubs and front newspapers were often closed down by martial law; and its top leaders had been sentenced to death and had lived in exile since early 1947.

Other CIA reports on the Tudeh came to similar conclusions. A detailed analysis in January 1953 concluded the party presented "no clear or crucial threat."[103] It had no paramilitary organization. It was "unlikely to increase strength through 1953." It had mere 1,500 sympathizers in the armed forces – the military at the time had over 66,000 officers. The true number of Tudeh officers turned out to be less than 600.[104] No Tudeh officer held an important post in the army. Another report mentioned that the Iranian G-2 monitored them closely and in April 1953 sidelined many to harmless posts in the outlying provinces.[105]

The January 1953 report also estimated that of the 200 individuals who ran the country none were communists. "Fellow travellers" numbered at most ten. The party's main objective "appears to be to get control of the government by constitutional means." The party had some 1,000 core activists and 35,000 rank-and-file members. Another CIA report took issue with newspapers' claims that the Tudeh was

---

[102] Office of Intelligence Research, Communism in Free World: Iran (January 1953), CIA Electronic Library, www.cia.gov/library/readingroom/se arch/site/Iran.

[103] Office of Intelligence Research, Communism in Free World: Iran (January 1953), CIA Electronic Library, www.cia.gov/library/readingroom/se arch/site/Iran.

[104] General Timour Bakhtiyar (ed.), *Ketab-e Siyah darbareh-e Sazman-e Afsaran-e Tudeh* (Black Book on the Organization of Tudeh Officers) (Tehran: Matbouat Press, 1955).

[105] CIA, Situation in Iran (28 December 1953), CIA Electronic Library, www .cia.gov/library/readingroom/search/site/Iran.

responsible for much of the street violence. It put the blame on right-wing thugs.[106] Yet another report mentioned that the Tudeh on the eve of the coup had instructed its members to "protect the government against a coup."[107] One CIA operative, in a study specifically on the Tudeh, mentioned in passing that cadres were required to read something he garbled as *The Manifest* [sic] and *Communism's Infancy Diseases* [sic].[108] This operative clearly missed the significance of what he was citing: a party thinking of revolution was unlikely to have used as required reading Lenin's famous *"Left Wing Communism": An Infantile Disorder*. It appeared that CIA operatives had limited knowledge of what they were monitoring.

The down-to-earth assessments were reinforced by the French military attaché who was well versed in the ins-and-outs of Iranian politics and knew personally the young army officers who had studied at St. Cyr. In a visit to Kabul, he assured the British ambassador – and through him the State Department – that the Tudeh had "little chance of seizing power in the near future." He emphasized that Mossadeq was "still fairly firmly in the saddle" and retained the "support of the great majority."[109] He expected Iran to soon become a republic like Egypt. The Foreign Office in London – at that time lacking an embassy in Tehran – judged the French attaché's views to be "sound" and "valuable."

The Conventional View

The internal documents bring out the central significance of oil and relative insignificance of communism in the whole crisis. The prevalent view, however, continues to be that the communist fear was paramount with the oil issue playing little, if any, role in American decision-making – especially in the eventual coup. How does one explain the discrepancy? The following four pressures help: First, the US and the UK governments, armed with an extensive array of media outlets,

---

[106] CIA, December Riot in Tehran, CIA Electronic Library www.cia.gov/library/readingroom/search/site/Iran.

[107] CIA, Political Prospects in Iran (July 1953), CIA Electronic Library, www.cia.gov/library/readingroom/search/site/Iran.

[108] CIA, Minutes of the Board of the Central Committee of Student Organization, CIA Electronic Library, www.cia.gov/library/readingroom/search/site/Iran.

[109] British Ambassador in Kabul, Visit of Colonel Buvis (10 June 1953), *FO 371/Persia* 1953/104562.

waged a concerted campaign to sell the notion they had fully accepted nationalization, and, therefore, were more than happy to offer a "fair compromise." They hammered away on this theme so consistently and so thoroughly that they convinced not only their own diplomats and journalists but also historians much later – even ones sympathetic to Mossadeq. The *New York Times*, in leaking the CIA document on the coup, claimed in 2000 that Mossadeq had rejected compromise because he had become "a prisoner of his own nationalism."[110] The *Washington Post* argued in 2012 that the "tragedy" of the failed "democratic dream" in Iran lay in Mossadeq's rejection of a fair compromise.[111] The *New York Review of Books* in 2016 described Mossadeq as a man "who when he saw a hole he had an irrepressible inclination to dig deeper." "His high principle," it added, "trumped judicious compromise too often to make him a successful politician."[112] The *Times Literary Supplement* in 2012 was equally adamant: "In the greatest mistake of his career, Mossadegh squandered American goodwill by rejecting the offer of an equal split of oil profits by an international consortium that would have respected Iran sovereignty."[113]

Similarly, a recent book entitled *The Future of Islam*, while sympathetic to Iran, insists that Mossadeq's "adamant refusal to a accept an [oil] settlement proved fatal."[114] Christopher de Bellaigue, in a flattering biography entitled *Patriot of Persia: Muhammad Mossadegh and a Tragic Anglo-American Coup*, writes:[115]

In the spring of 1953 Mossadegh was offered an arrangement whereby the Iranians would retain charge of the oil industry and Anglo-Iranian (Oil Company) would be reduced to the status of a participant in an international

---

[110] Elaine Sciolino, "Mossadegh: Eccentric Nationalist Begets Strange History," *New York Times*, 16 April 2000. This issue contains a long front-page article by James Risen, "How a Plot Convulsed Iran in '53 (and in '79)." This article introduced the newly leaked Donald Wilber's CIA document on the coup.

[111] Tara Bahrampour, "Lost Leader of Iran's Dream of Democracy," *Washington Post*, 21 July 2012.

[112] Roger Cohen, "A Crass and Consequential Error," *New York Review of Books*, 16 August 2016.

[113] Wm. Roger Louis, "Fusspot Visionary," *Times Literary Supplement*, 29 June 2012.

[114] Shirin Hunter, *The Future of Islam and the West: Clash of Civilizations or Peaceful Existence* (London: Praeger, 1998), 137.

[115] Christopher de Bellaigue, *Patriot of Persia: Muhammad Mossadegh and a Tragic Anglo-American Coup* (New York: HarperCollins, 2012), 206.

consortium that would market Iranian oil exports. The essence of privatiza-
tion, not merely its form, would be preserved. This would be the last serious
deal Mossadegh was offered and his rejection of it was as grave a failure of
leadership as any in his premiership.

Roger Louis, the preeminent authority on the British Empire and
a leading Anglo-American historian of the coup, concurs. In a study
of the crisis, he faults Mossadeq for being highly unreasonable for
refusing to accept the reasonable Western offers which recognized
nationalization. In the same study, however, he admits that such offers
included arrangements in which "the new managing company" would
be a "façade" to save face for the Iranians. He also admits the new
agreements would include guarantees to prevent Iran from interfering
"in the company's day to day operations."[116] In other words,
Mossadeq was "unreasonable" for not accepting a "reasonable"
offer that promised an empty form of nationalization – nationalization
in theory but not in practice.

One could speculate that contemporaries and historians relying on
secondary sources were easily misled by US-UK public pronouncements since they did not have access to internal documents and closed-
door negotiations. But a skeptical observer reading public declarations
closely, especially Mossadeq's statements, could have reached the conclusion that no real offer was ever placed on the table. Professor Elwell-
Sutton, who had no access to confidential information but who had
worked in the AIOC and the Foreign Office, managed to hit the nail on
the head: "Put very succinctly, the British attitude was that, in return
for their recognizing the principle of nationalisation, the Persian government should forego its insistence on that principle."[117] In other
words, one side would accept the principle of nationalization if the
other side would be willing to forgo implementation. In plain English,
the United Kingdom-USA would publicly accept nationalization on
condition Iran privately agreed not to insist on its actual enforcement.
Not surprisingly, the British embassy requested the BBC to blacklist
Elwell-Sutton, even though he had earlier served as a press attaché and

---

[116] Wm. Roger Louis, "Musaddiq, Oil, and the Dilemmas of British Imperialism,"
in *Ends of British Imperialism: The Scramble for Empire, Suez and
Decolonization* (London: Tauris, 2006), 727–87.

[117] L. P. Elwell-Sutton, *Persian Oil: A Study in Power Politics* (London: Lawrence
& Wishart, 1955), 252.

headed the BBC Persian service. He was deemed to be "anti-British, anti-colonial, and anti-Shah."[118]

Second, the political discourse of the day was very much that of the Cold War – both in the USA and the United Kingdom. Of course, the Cold War did exist and was very real – especially in Korea and Eastern Europe. This, however, did not necessarily mean that every crisis in every part of the world was directly related to it – or that every rhetorical resort to it should be taken at face value. Invariably, NSC documents in the 1950s begin with warnings about the ever-present and ever-increasing dangers of international communism. Likewise, pronouncements in the contemporary Islamic world inevitably begin with "In the Name of God, Most Benevolent, Ever Merciful." Such pious introductions may be sincere, but the document's inner content may not necessarily tally with the opening mantra. Historians eager to place the Iran crisis firmly within the Cold War can easily do so by copiously citing these opening paragraphs. In eagerness to do so, they often overlook such jarring phrases as the need to "preserve sanctity of contracts," "prevent breaking of agreements," "avoid setting danger-ous precedents," and "check contagious expropriations." Such phrases may be short but they are pregnant with significance. They speak louder than elaborate public pronouncements.

Legalistic and bureaucratic considerations further amplified the dominant discourse. The famous NSC 68 – Truman's foreign policy guideline – focused solely on communism and the Soviet Union.[119] It conspicuously contained nothing on neutralism, non-alignment, and what would soon become the Third World. It stated forthrightly that the predominant objective of the US government was to "reduce the power and influence of the Kremlin inside the Soviet Union and other areas under its control." It also gave the CIA the writ to carry out covert actions against the Soviet Union and its allied communist parties. To carry out acts against non-communist entities and countries, the CIA, as well as other US agencies, had to bend facts, distort reality, and resort to creative language. They had to pigeonhole such operations as part-and-parcel of the war on communism and the Soviet Union – that is, to make the issue an integral part of the Cold War. Thus the policy of

---

[118] British Embassy, Telegram (5 August 1951), *FO 371/Persia 1951/34–91548.* See also British Embassy, Telegram (30 July 1951), *FO 248/1528.*

[119] Ernest May (ed.), *American Cold War Strategy: Interpreting NSC 68* (New York: St. Martin's Press, 1993).

interfering in Iran was depicted not as intervention in a neutral country but as an essential part of the Cold War. The overthrow of a non-aligned government was technically and even legally outside the bounds of NSC 68. But it could be placed within the bounds if that government could be depicted as possibly allying with the Soviet Union in the future – even distant future. Acheson was a rare participant who was willing to publicly admit that there was no serious communist threat in Iran – but only sixteen years later.[120]

Third, the British often boasted that they had cleverly conjured up the communist specter to scare the Americans into acting against Mossadeq. In private, the British were confident there was no such danger having closely monitored Iran, including its military, ever since 1941. When the oil crisis started, the Foreign Office assured the British government that financial difficulties produced by the economic embargo would not increase the danger of communism in Iran.[121] Mostafa Fateh, who, in his famous book *Fifty Years of Oil* stressed the role of the Tudeh both in the 1951 oil strike and in the July Uprising, privately reassured the Foreign Office that the party did not pose any "danger" since the "ruling class is well on guard and capable of stopping" any leftist coup.[122] Even after the July Uprising, the British embassy assured London that the Tudeh was absorbed in build-ing its labor organizations and it was "difficult to foresee under what circumstances it could attempt a coup." If it did so, the embassy assured London, the armed forces were quite capable of deal with the situation.[123] In early 1952, the British military attaché reported that "energetic measures" were being taken to remove Tudeh influence from the Tehran garrison.[124] Churchill's special aide later admitted his government never took seriously the supposed communist danger.[125] Acheson also later admitted that Eden was consistent in discounting the likelihood of a Tudeh take-over.[126]

---

120 Acheson, *Present at the Creation*, 506.
121 Foreign Office, Memo (14 November 1951), FO 371/Persia 1951/34–91495.
122 Anglo-Iranian Oil Company, Mr. Fateh's Diary, FO 371/91464.
123 Foreign Office, The Tudeh Party, FO 975/Persia 1953/69.
124 Military Attaché, Annual Report for the Persian Army for 1952, FO 371/Persia 1952/98638.
125 Stephen Dorril, *MI6: Inside the Covert World of Her Majesty's Secret Service* (New York: Free Press, 2000), 583.
126 Acheson, *Present at the Creation*, 685.

Despite these assessments, the British Treasury advised the Foreign Office to use the "communist bogey" whenever communicating with the Americans.[127] The Foreign Office, in turn, advised embassy officials in Tehran to "play on this theme" whenever dealing with their American counterparts – even though admitting that Mossadeq was "genuinely anti-Russian."[128] Falle boasted he had talked Stewart Alsop of the *New York Herald Tribune* into writing articles claiming the "Soviets could well take over Iran in twelve months."[129] "Monty" Woodhouse, the MI6 liaison with the CIA, admits in his memoirs that in his dealing with Washington he intentionally "emphasized the Communist threat."[130]

Such admissions come in handy for American historians eager to shift the onus of the coup onto the British. To accept this shift, however, one would have to believe that the top CIA and State Department officials were both naïve simpletons and willfully ignorant of their own internal assessments. Dulles, Roosevelt, and Helms were anything but naïve and ignorant. On the contrary, they were hard-nosed realists unlikely to be led astray by the "perfidious" British. If they responded to these alarm bells it was not because they found them convincing – but because they found them politically convenient.

They eagerly picked up – and freely used inside Iran – the recent communist takeover of Czechoslovakia. They claimed the Tudeh could do in Tehran what Czech communists had done in Prague. Royalists even today raise the specter of Czechoslovakia.[131] Similarly, Woodhouse, half a century later, claimed that Czechoslovakia played an important part in the eventual decision to carry out the coup.[132] But no two countries could have been more different. Czechoslovakia was a highly industrialized society with a large working class and a formidable communist party. The party and its allies represented half the electorate, controlled armed militias, and dominated key ministries – especially those of the interior, defense, and

---

[127] British Treasury, Memo (23 March 1952), *FO 371*/Persia 1952/34–98652.
[128] Foreign Office, Telegram to the Tehran Embassy (4 May 1951), *FO 371*/Persia 1951/34–91530.
[129] Falle, Telegram (12 December 1951), *FO 371*/Persia 1951/34–91493.
[130] C. M. Woodhouse, *Something Ventured* (London, Granada, 1982), 117.
[131] Ardasher Zahedi, *Katerat-e Ardasher Zahedi* (Memoirs of Ardasher Zahedi) (Maryland: Ibex Publishers, 2006), 196.
[132] Roger Louis, "How Mussadeq Was Ousted."

communications.[133] The Czech officer corps, unlike the Iranian one, was Soviet-trained. Iran, on the other hand, was predominantly an agricultural society – even a "feudal" one – where the intelligentsia, the working class, and the Tudeh were confined to a few urban centers. Although the Tudeh could organize strikes and even impressive demonstrations, the CIA decision-makers were hardnosed enough to know the difference between organizing such activities and pulling off a coup or a revolution. As Mossadeq retorted at his trial when the prosecutor asked him the rhetorical question if he had ever worried about a communist coup: "How on earth could they have done that when they did not have even a single plane or tank?"[134] He repeated this in prison, and later argued that "foreign powers" had used the fear of communism as a pretext to overthrown him and "regain control over the country's oil."[135]

Furthermore, Iran – unlike Czechoslovakia – contained large tribes armed by MI6 and the CIA. By early 1953, the CIA boasted it had armed as many as 10,000 Qashqayis.[136] It added that MI6 had done the same with many neighboring tribes.[137] The CIA was mystified why the Soviets showed no interest in the Kurds – the only tribes susceptible to their wooing.[138] In fact, the Soviets remained remarkably inactive in Iran throughout these years: when their oil agreement was rejected in 1947; when the nationalization campaign against Britain was in full swing; and even when Mossadeq in 1953 nationalized their Caspian fisheries. The State Department was somewhat disappointed the Soviets failed to react strongly against the take-over of their fisheries.[139] In planning for the coup, the CIA worked on the assumption that the Soviet reaction would continue to be "limited in

[133] Morton Kaplan, *The Communist Coup in Czechoslovakia* (Princeton: Woodrow Wilson School, 1960).

[134] Jalel Bozorgmehr (ed.), *Muhammad Mossadeq dar Mahakemeh-e Nezami* (Mohammad Mossadeq in the Military Court) (Tehran: Jahan Publication: 1984), Vol. I, 573–4.

[135] Iraj Afshar, *Toqrerat-e Mossadeq dar Zendan* (Mossadeq's Comments in Prison) (Sazman-e Ketab Publication, 1980), 136; Muhammad Mossadeq, *Khaterat va Ta'alumat* (Memories and Sorrows) (Tehran: Elm Publications, 2007), 205.

[136] CIA, Memo for Directorate of Plans (25 February 1953), *FRUS* (2017), 453.

[137] CIA, Tribes may be a Factor in Ousting Mosaddeq, *FRUS* (2017), 487.

[138] CIA, Internal Threat to Iran's Security (18 February 1953), *FRUS* (2017), 442.

[139] CIA, Memo for Directorate of Plans (25 February 1953), *FRUS* (2017), 455.

nature."[140] So much for the notion the 1953 coup was carried out to preempt an imminent communist coup.

In fact, the shah in early 1951 had written a secret letter to Molotov complaining that the USSR – unlike the United Kingdom and USA – was showing remarkable little interest in his country.[141] The shah, who, at least in public, liked to conjure up the image of the tsarist bear as well as the communism threat, was now poking awake the same beast. One British report admitted the "Russians have shown no sign of wishing to intervene in the crisis."[142] One US dispatch reported, the "USSR has been content to maintain silence."[143] Another was even more forthright: "Diplomatically the USSR has continued its policy, inaugurated in the latter half of 1950, of displaying friendship to the Iranian government and not interfering in the government problem connected with oil nationalization, internal issues, and relations with the British. There is no evidence that the Soviet ambassador in Iran has put any pressure on the Iranian government."[144] Of course, some suspected some sinister ulterior motive behind this apparent lack of interest.

The fourth and final reason why the conventional interpretation has gained widespread acceptance is that many American historians as well as politicians tend to shy away from economic, especially oil, issues in discussing US foreign policy. Other countries, including allies, may be motivated by such "base" interests, but US foreign policy was seen as inspired by ideas, ideals, and well-meant intentions. The driving force was deemed to have been the desire to save the world from the evils of international communism. According to Kermit Roosevelt, the British interest in Iran was to undo oil nationalization but the American concern was the "obvious communist threat."[145] One leading American expert on the coup brushes off the oil issue as smacking of "economic determinism" – as if the taking account of the economic implications of nationalization is tantamount to embracing such larger

---

[140] Donald Wilber, Factors in the Overthrow of Mossadeq (16 April 1953), *FRUS* (2017), 526.

[141] Artemy Kalinovsky, "The Soviet Union and Mosaddeq: A Research Note," *Iranian Studies*, Vol. 47, No. 3 (May 2014), 401–18.

[142] NSC, "British Paper of Communist Danger in Persia," *FRUS* (2017), 377.

[143] Embassy, Telegram (30 October 1952), *FRUS* (2017), 385.

[144] CIA, "The Soviet Attitude to Situation in Iran," *FRUS* (2017), 70.

[145] Kermit Roosevelt, *Countercoup: The Struggle for the Control of Iran* (New York: McGraw Hill, 1979), 3.

philosophical concepts as Historical Materialism, Dialectical Materialism, and the Inevitable March of Human History.[146]

Similarly, Malcolm Byrne, who at the National Security Archive has successfully lobbied to declassify government documents, insists that at the time of the coup the "communist threat was uppermost on the US list of concerns." He claims that in general American foreign policy is "not driven by animosity towards countries that bear the brunt"; that the main motive is the desire to do good for those counties; and that Eisenhower's coup in Iran, like Bush's invasion of Iraq, was "pre-emptive" and designed to "get them before they got us."[147] In other words, the road to hell can be paved with good intentions. How do we know these decisions were motivated by good intentions? Because, we are told, the decision-makers themselves assure us they were. As a well-known nineteenth-century philosopher cautioned: "As in private life one differentiates between what a man thinks and says of himself and what he really is and does, so in historical struggles one must distinguish still more the phrases and fancies of parties from their real organism and their interests, their conceptions of themselves, from their reality."[148] This remains as true now as in the nineteenth century.

---

[146] Mark Gasiorowski, "The Coup (Book Review)," *Middle East Journal*, Vol. 67, No. 2 (Spring 2013), 315–17.

[147] Malcolm Byrne, "New Documents about 1953 Coup Enliven Regime Change Debate," *Atlantic Council*, 13 July 2017. See also Azadeh Moaveni, "History Should be Messy and Complicated: An Interview with Malcolm Byrne," *Iranwire*, http://iranwire.com/en/projects/2164.

[148] Karl Marx, "The Eighteenth Brumaire of Louis Napoleon," in *On Revolution* (ed. Saul Padover) (New York: McGraw Hill, 1971), 267.

3 | *Parliamentary Politics*

There were six strategies designed to bring down my administration . . . The fourth was resorting to obstructions and immobilization in the majles against the government. Once this failed, they resorted to the military coup d'état.

Mossadeq at his trial

The Constitution

Iran was blessed – or cursed – with two constitutions. The first came from the fundamental laws of the 1906 Constitutional Revolution; the second from precedents set by Reza Shah from 1925 until 1941. Since Mohammad Reza Shah was reluctant to partake in a coup and preferred to have Mossadeq removed by parliament the oil crisis became inevitably interwoven with these two different interpretations of the constitution. The USA and the United Kingdom – with a reluctant shah dragged along – resorted to the coup only when they realized that Mossadeq had out maneuvered them on the parliamentary terrain.

The fundamental laws were borrowed from the constitutional monarchy of Belgium.[1] Parliament – officially known as Majles-e Shura-ye Melli (National Consultative Assembly) – was established as the country's central institution. The majles "represented the whole nation" with the addendum that "powers of the realm were all derived from the people" and "sovereignty is a trust, as a Divine gift, confided by the people to the person of the Shah." The majles was endowed with full authority over legislation, taxation, state budgets, foreign concessions and international agreements, and, most important of all, selection of

[1] Edward Browne, *The Persian Revolution of 1905–1909* (New York: Barnes and Noble, 1966), 353–400. For an analysis of the fundamental laws, see Fakhreddin Azimi, "The Constitutional Revolution: The Constitution," *Encyclopaedia Iranica* (Leiden: Brill, 2011).

cabinet ministers – implicitly including the prime minister. It could also elect its own speaker or president (*rayis*); set its own house rules, regulations, and committees; submit bills to relevant committees for debate on the floor; and bring urgent bills directly to the floor if a majority deemed them necessary. Deputies could scrutinize credentials (*e'tebar nameh*) of fellow members; speak on any topic before formal debates; hold closed meetings; enjoy immunity from arrest during sessions; and bring legislation to standstill through boycotts and parliamentary obstructionism – the assembly needed a quorum of two-thirds to start a meeting and of three-quarters to take a vote. Legislative sessions lasted two years; only the majles could dissolve itself. Elections for a new majles were to be announced before the closing of the existing one. The electoral law initially restricted the vote to property owners, but later expanded to include all adult males. The monarch was described as the chief executive, but ministers were deemed responsible not to him but to the majles. Since the primary aim of the constitutional revolution had been to curtail the power of the shah, he did not attain even the authority to veto legislation. A State Department brief for the US president written in 1949 categorically stated "because of the fear and suspicions of the then (Qajar) Shahs, the constitution was so drawn as to give almost complete monopoly of power to the Majlis."[2]

When the fundamental laws worked as intended, as in 1941–53, Iran can be said to have had a truly parliamentary form of government. The majles first nominated, through a majority vote, the prospective prime minister – this was known as the "vote of inclination" (*ezhar-e tamayul*). The shah next issued the nominee the automatic *farman* (royal decree) to form a cabinet and a program. The nominee then returned to the majles to seek the required majority vote for himself, his cabinet, and his program – this became known as the "vote of confidence" (*ray-e e'temad*). What is more, the majles – if the majority wished – could any time question (*estyzah*) individual ministers or call for a "vote of no confidence" (*salb-e e'temad*) on the whole government.

---

[2] State Department, Background Memorandum on Visit to the United States of His Imperial Majesty Mohammad Reza Shah Pahlavi Shahinshah of Iran (1 November 1949). Declassified File 891.001 on Pahlavi, Reza.

The constitution, furthermore, required the shah to take his coronation oath before the majles. The fundamental laws categorically emphasized that ministers were responsible not to the monarch but to the majles; that the shah was exempt from responsibility; and that "ministers could not divest themselves of responsibility by pleading verbal or written orders from the shah." In the words of one Western expert on the Iranian constitution: "Although with the Constitutional Revolution the Shah remained head of the State, he had to govern through his ministers who were responsible not to him but to the Majles. Majles controlled finances, conclusion of treaties, and granting of concession."[3]

Reza Shah, while ruling with a firm hand, never scrapped the written constitution. Instead, he reduced the majles into a pliant body packed with "yes men" and "placemen." Local notables – large landowners, tribal chiefs, religious leaders, and wealthy businessmen – were permitted to herd their peasants, tribesmen, and clients to voting polls where supervisory councils appointed by the interior minister counted the ballots and named the winners. Of course, the ultimate decision remained with Reza Shah, who, together with his interior minister, would evaluate candidates as "suitable," "unsuitable," "average," "sly," "arrogant," "statuesque," "empty headed," "ambitious," "idiotic," "obstinate," "crazy," and "lacking self-respect."[4] One candidate for the Jewish seat was eliminated on the grounds of being a *Yahud-ye Bad* (Bad Jew).

Thus the assembly – beginning with the 5th Majles and Reza Shah's coronation in 1925 and ending with the 13th Majles and his forced abdication in 1941 – became an exclusive landowners' "club" formed of many "rotten boroughs." In the words of one former premier: "The Shah, throughout his reign, was always insistent on having the deputies legitimize all his actions, decrees, and appointments to the cabinet."[5] With parliament reduced to a rubber stamp, the shah was able to exercise autocratic powers. He handpicked the prime ministers;

[3] Laurence Lockhart, "The Constitutional Laws of Persia," *Middle East Journal*, Vol. 13, No. 4 (Autumn 1959), 372–88.
[4] Mohammad Keshavarz (ed.), *Asnad az Enteqabat-e Majles-e Shura-ye Melli dar Dowreh-e Pahlavi-e Aval* (Documents on Parliamentary Elections during the Reign of Pahlavi I) (Tehran: Ministry of Culture, 1999), 37–44.
[5] Ahmad Matin-Daftari, "Memoires from Past Elections," *Khandaniha*, 5 April 1956.

selected his cabinet ministers; and dispatched them off to the majles to obtain the pro forma vote. He shuffled at will premiers and ministries, and drew up budgets and bills for parliamentary approval. Even more important, he established total and sole control over the armed forces. Having seized power through a coup in 1921, he first created the post of Sardar-e Sepah (Army Commander); and then, with his coronation in 1925, the royal title of Commander-in-Chief of the Armed Forces. He viewed himself first and foremost as the top military commander. He favored the military budget; expanded the armed forces from 40,000 men in 1925 to 127,000 in 1941; invariably appeared in public wearing military uniforms; raised his heir to be first and foremost an army officer; scrutinized promotions above the rank of major; shopped for modern weaponry – in 1940 he tried to buy sixty British bombers, telling London they would be useful for bombing Baku; and, most important of all, handpicked all the top military personnel – the war ministers, the chiefs of general staff, as well as those of the army, navy, police, and gendarmerie. Reza Shah, in the apt words of a Pentagon historian, created a "military monarchy."[6]

The abdication of Reza Shah in the aftermath of the Anglo-Soviet invasion sharply diminished but did not eliminate royal power. Mohammad Reza Shah, the twenty-one-year-old heir, promptly made a series of calculated concessions to preempt more radical demands coming from the public and from his father's own handpicked 13th Majles. The British strongly advised such concessions. Bullard, the wartime British ambassador, urged him to act as a constitutional monarch, travel widely in the provinces, and persuade his Egyptian-born queen to spend less time on clothes and more on learning Persian.[7] Even before the invasion, Bullard had reported: "Reza Shah has become so unpopular that he could not rely even on the army and any movement for his removal or even of his dynasty would be popular."[8] He even speculated that "most people would welcome revolution, however caused."[9] Similarly, the American ambassador described Reza Shah as "a brutal, avaricious, and inscrutable despot in his later years, his fall

[6] J. C. Hurewitz, *Middle East Politics: The Military Dimension* (New York: Praeger, 1969), 265–95.
[7] Bullard, Merits and Demerits of the Shah (13 July 1943), *FO 371*/Persia 1943/ 38–55072.
[8] Bullard, Telegram (7 May 1941), *FO 371*/Persia 1941/42–27149.
[9] Bullard, Telegram (12 May 1941), *FO 371*/Persia 1941/42–27149.

from power when the country was occupied in 1941 by the British and Russian forces and his death later in exile, were regretted by no one."[10] The State Department was just as blunt: "His growing avarice in the later years of his reign and the ruthlessness with which he suppressed all opposition aroused widespread fear and hatred."[11]

The new shah took his oath of office before the majles deputies and vowed to reign as a "constitutional monarch." Wearing civilian clothes, he played down his military training and instead emphasized his four-year education in "democratic" Switzerland – Le Rosey, the secondary school in Geneva he attended, catered predominantly for sons of wealthy Europeans and Americans. He signed a law abolishing the title of Sardar-e Sepah. He handed over the large number of villages his father had accumulated – often through forced sales – to the state to return to their original owners. He also handed over some of his father's urban property to a new charity foundation to fund hospitals and schools. What is more, he transferred $1,000,000 from London to New York as a "nest egg," and, $500,000 to Tehran to use for the forthcoming 14th Majles elections.[12]

Although the shah had no choice but to give up the title of Sardar-e Sepah, he fought tooth and nail to remain the real as well as the nominal Commander-in-Chief of the Armed Forces. In a study on the "Shah's Prerogatives in the Constitution," the British embassy concluded: "The Shah is Commander-in-Chief but what this involves is in dispute since interpretation of the laws, according to the Fundamental Laws, is the business of the Majles and it is for the Majles to say to what extent the Shah should command the armed forces."[13]

The shah lived with the knowledge there would be no monarchy without the military – at least no Pahlavi dynasty. In Bullard's words: "The Shah, doubtful of the popular enthusiasm for the dynasty, has jealously resented any limitations of his personal control of the

---

[10] US Ambassador, Telegram to Secretary of State (26 June 1945) in State Department, *FRUS* (1964) (Washington, DC: US Printing Office, 1964), 1945, Vol. VIII, 385.

[11] State Department, Background Memoranda on Visit to the United States of the Imperial Majesty Mohammad Reza Shah Pahlavi Shahinshah of Iran, November 1949 (1 November 1949), unpublished but declassified document.

[12] Bullard, Telegram (16 December 1943), *FO 371/Persia* 1943/38–35077; Bullard, Telegram (11 April 1944), *FO 371/Persia* 1944/189–40187.

[13] British Embassy, Shah's Prerogatives in the Constitution (6 May 1944), *FO 371/ Persia* 1944/34–40187.

army."[14] He determined to continue his father's personal interest in the armed forces – in maneuvers, inspections, uniforms, training, salaries, fringe benefits, and promotions above rank of major – especially among tank officers. He quickly named thirty new generals. His father, in twenty years, had named only eight.[15] In the next six years, he created another 105 generals and 89 colonels.[16] In a memo to the White House on the shah's forthcoming visit, the State Department noted the young monarch was "obsessed about tanks," "considers himself a qualified strategist and tactician," and "would be mortally offended if he were to be bluntly contradicted in matter of opinion on military matters." It added:[17]

While the Shah has during the course of the past few years endeavored to strengthen his hand in order to make the functioning of the government a bit less chaotic, and while he greatly admires his late father, a brutal, oriental despot, he is not consciously, as many Iranians have charged, endeavoring to set up a dictatorship. However, there is always a chance the shah, surrounded by assorted advisers, many of them dangerous, might be talked into taking some very foolish step. If the Shah launches into a discussion of the difficulties inherent in running Iran under a democratic system and the need for a stronger hand, generalized remarks to the effect that the path of democracy is never smooth one and the millennium cannot be obtained overnight might be appropriate.

To secure his military turf, the shah insisted on making all decisions pertinent to the armed forces, especially in buying weapons, dealing with the three US military missions – to the army, police, and gendarmerie, and, most important of all, in preserving the existing chain of military command. Orders continued to go out from the military office within the royal palace, through the chief of staff, directly to the field commanders, bypassing the war minister. To ensure smooth working, the shah insisted on naming the war minister and placing royalists throughout the ministry. The war minister, in effect, served as a mere quartermaster. What is more, the chiefs of the various military

---

[14] Bullard, Annual Report for Persia for 1942, *FO 371/Persia* 1943/231–35117.
[15] *Rahbar*, 12 December 1944.
[16] British Embassy, Personalities in Persia-Military Supplement (1947), *FO 371/ Persia* 1947/62035.
[17] State Department, Background Memoranda on Visit to the United States of the Imperial Majesty Mohammad Reza Shah Pahlavi Shahinshah of Iran November 1949 (1 November 1949).

branches communicated only vertically with the shah; they could not communicate horizontally with each other or with the war minister or even with the chief of staff.

Conventional wisdom claims the young shah's appetite for personal rule was wetted only after the 1953 coup. But in the early 1940s, Bullard reported that the shah preferred "weak" ministers, tried to "suppress anti-court newspapers," and intended "govern through subservient cabinets as his father did."[18] "Over the year," Bullard explained in 1942,

the Shah has gradually increased his personal power. Guided by self-seeking courtiers and secure from public criticism, the young Shah has taken a direct interest in current affairs. Not only did he assume the powers and authority of an executive head of the army but he cultivated relations with certain deputies, subsidized certain newspapers, and attempted to force the resignation of ministers.[19]

The shah later complained to Henderson that the British had tried to talk him into acting like a European constitutional monarch with "his head in the clouds," but he had been convinced that Iran, "being what it was," needed a monarch who would participate fully in the country's political and military life. Otherwise, Iran would descend into chaos. The shah confessed that "he had not lived up to the oath he had taken to fully enforce the constitution."[20]

Qavam was the only early premier who tried, unsuccessfully, to trespass into military terrain by nominating his own war minister. When bread riots broke out in Tehran on 9 December 1942, the police and army – under the shah's instructions – refused to act, resulting in mass attacks on the premier's own residence as well as on local stores, especially Jewish ones.[21] General Amir Ahmadi, the military governor of Tehran, declared the crisis had once again shown that the army must remain firmly under his majesty's command.[22]

---

[18] Bullard, Telegrams (29 July 1943) (26 August 1943) (19 December 1943), *FO* 371/Persia 1943/110–35109.

[19] Bullard, Annual Report for Persia in 1942, *FO* 371/Persia 1943/231–35117.

[20] Henderson, Conversation with the Shah (30 May 1953), *FRUS* (2017), 275–80.

[21] Hussein Kuhi-Kermani, *Az Shahrivar 1320 ta Faje'eh-e Azerbaijan va Zanjan* (From August 1941 to the Tragedy of Azerbaijan and Zanjan) (Tehran: Muzaheri Publication, 1946), Vol. II, 312–42.

[22] General Amir Ahmadi, Speech, *1st Senate*, 23 April 1950.

Although the shah retained command of the military, he lost control of parliament – especially with the convening of the 14th Majles. He could no longer handpick premiers and cabinet members. Instead, parliamentary *fraksiuns* (caucuses) – a term borrowed from the German Reichstag – reverted to earlier constitutional practices. They bargained among themselves until a candidate mustered a majority and the required vote of "preference-inclination." Cabinets, thus, became uneasy coalitions of ministers dependent on constantly bargaining factions in the majles. The 13th–14th Majles in four years produced ten premiers and fourteen cabinets. Although parliament remained mostly an exclusive club of 136 deputies, its royalist component was reduced to less than 25 percent. These royalist deputies were mostly landowners linked to the palace or placemen "elected" from constituencies controlled by the military – often tribal regions under martial law.

The British military attaché reported that on the eve of the opening of the 14th Majles the shah was so "obsessed with the fear that the Constitutional group would obstruct his aspirations to autocracy" that he quietly approached Mossadeq – who had just received the top vote in the Tehran elections – with a last-minute gambit. The shah offered to help elect Mossadeq prime minister if the latter declared martial law and annulled the recent elections as null and void on grounds of "corruption and undue interference." Mossadeq countered that the new elections had to be carried out without delay and under a reformed law to restrict the influence of the military and the landed notables.[23] He suggested a referendum to amend the electoral law.[24] The shah decided he preferred the existing danger. This little-known behind-the-scenes bargaining reveals that the shah, even in 1944, deemed Mossadeq to be important enough to become prime minister. It also reveals that Mossadeq was thinking of referendums and electoral reform long before the 1950s' oil crisis.

The shah did not give up his aspiration to regain his father's lost powers. He often confided to British and American officials that Iran was not ready for "democracy," and that he needed the prerogatives to dissolve the majles, veto legislation, hold new elections, appoint prime

---

[23] Military Attaché, Bi-Weekly Reports (7 January 1944), *FO 371*/Persia 1944/422–40205; British Minister, Dispatch to the FO (20 January 1944), *FO 371*/Persia 1944/40–40186.

[24] Bullard, Telegram (22 January 1944). *FO 371*/Persia 1944/34–40186.

ministers, and create a counterbalancing upper house. The fundamental laws had mentioned the need for a Senate, but such an assembly had never been convened. Reza Shah, having full powers, deemed it unnecessary. The American ambassador reported in 1945 that the shah was "endeavoring to elicit some words that might encourage him to resort to personal rule without the benefit of parliamentary restraint." The shah claimed his people needed at least another forty years before they could appreciate democracy. He especially regretted he did not have the constitutional authority to convene the upper house and dissolve the lower house.[25]

Similarly, Bullard reported that the shah sounded him out on the same theme, but he advised against it on the "grounds that the public would attribute it to his desire to pack the Majles with his own men."[26] He added: "I fear the Shah wants not better but more subservient deputies." The British – who could always rely on deputies from the southern provinces with business ties to the British Empire – concurred with the Americans that the "Majles, with all its faults, served as a safety valve and was regarded by the Iranian people as the safeguard of their liberties."[27] Shepherd, Bullard's successor, reported that old-time politicians "differed markedly" with the shah over the constitutional role of prime ministers. While the shah felt he should have the power to appoint them, the politicians on the whole favored the British model.[28] Some staunch monarchists even claimed the constitution gave the shah the prerogative to summon and dismiss ministers at will, and treat premiers as mere court "servants." If so, the constitutional revolution had been much noise signifying and achieving nothing.

The shah continued to periodically raise the issue of constitutional changes. American ambassadors on a number of occasions threw cold water over such talk. They felt that the majles provided a "safeguard" and enjoyed "public sympathies" whereas the shah's "record is not one to inspire confidence in personal rule."[29] The British embassy

---

[25] US Ambassador, Telegram to the State Department (20 June 1945), State Department, *FRUS* (1964), 1945, Vol. VIII, 383–5.

[26] Bullard, Telegram (20 January 1944), *FO 371/Persia 1944/34–40186*.

[27] State Department, Memorandum (8 January 1943), *FRUS* (1964), 1943, Vol. IV, 325–9.

[28] Shepherd, 8 April 1950, *FO 371/Persia 1950/82311*.

[29] State Department, Memorandum (7 December 1947), *FRUS* (1964), 1947, Vol. V, 990–2.

responded curtly in September 1948 when sounded out once again about constitutional changes:

Instead the Shah might make a serious endeavor to improved conditions in Azerbaijan, where it is reported that fifty percent of the Persian troops are ready to desert and where there is dissatisfaction among the peasants because the Army is being bribed by landlords. The Shah's action would be particularly effective here in view of his close connexion with the Army.[30]

The State Department concurred on hearing "rumors the Shah intended to precipitate constitutional changes." On 1 February 1949, it instructed the ambassador to advise the shah "not to rock the boat too quickly" and to make it clear that "constitutional changes were neither desirable nor necessary."[31]

The situation changed drastically three days later – on 4 February – when a would-be assassin shot and injured the shah on the campus of Tehran University. Although the assailant was a suicidal loner, the shah took full advantage of the crisis. Informing the two ambassadors there was no time to waste, he declared martial law; closed down newspapers critical of the royal family; outlawed the Tudeh Party; again forced Qavam into exile; confined Mossadeq to his village; arrested vocal critics such as Kashani, Baqai, and Makki; and, most important of all, convened a Constituent Assembly to enhance his constitutional prerogatives.

This packed assembly voted unanimously to create a senate and to give the shah the prerogative to dissolve the majles – provided he simultaneously announced the date for new elections and convened the subsequent majles within three months. The shah also obtained the prerogative of naming thirty of the sixty senators. The other thirty were to be elected through a two-stage process. The senate – with a six-year term – was to consist exclusively of former ministers, governors, generals, ambassadors, judges, senior civil servants, majles presidents, deputies who had served in at least three parliaments, senior clerics, large landowners, and wealthy businessmen. Mossadeq, as well as many future National Front leaders, dismissed these changes as

---

[30] British Embassy in Washington, Shah's Constitutional Ideas (30 September 1948) *FO 371/Persia 1948/68714*.

[31] Secretary of State, Memorandum to the Ambassador (1 February 1949), *FRUS* (1964), Vol. VI, 476.

unacceptable and unconstitutional. Makki, for example, declared that members of the Constituent Assembly should be "hanged."[32]

The 1st Senate convened in mid-February 1950. It elected as its first president Taqizadeh, the famous veteran of the constitutional revolution. One senator waxed eloquent on how his colleagues were not *ayan* and *ashraf* (notables and aristocrats) as in the British House of Lords, but "ordinary citizens" reliant on hard-earned salaries.[33] In fact, the senate was very much an exclusive club of elderly and titled notables who had worked closely with Reza Shah – Dr. Ahmad Matin-Daftari (son of Mohammad-Ali al-Mamalek), Mehdi Farrukh (Mu'tasem al-Saltaneh), Morteza Qoli Bayat (Sham al-Saltaneh), Baqer Kazemi (Mu'azeb al-Dowleh), Ibrahim Qavam (Qavam al-Mulk), Asadollah Yamin Esfandiyari (Yamin al-Mamalek), Ibrahim Hakimi (Hakim al-Mulk), Abul Qassem Najm (Najm al-Mulk), Ghulam Ali Khajehnouri (Nizam al-Saltaneh), Mehdi Fatemi ('Emad al-Saltaneh), Amir-Hussein Ilkhani Bakhtiyari, and Nasser Qashqayi. It also included a number of retired generals: Zahedi, Amir Ahmadi, Amanollah Jahanbani, Mohammad Nakhjevan, and Ali Akbar Zarghami. Senator Malekzadeh, the historian and notable exception, wished his chamber did not contain such a long list of "al-dowlehs, al-mulks, al-saltanehs, al-mamaleks."[34]

The shah scored other successes. Reza Shah's vast estates (totaling 180,000 hectares with 232,878 peasants), which had been entrusted to the state in 1941 to be handed over to their previous owners, were returned to the royal family. The title *Kaber* (Great) was bestowed on Reza Shah; his body was brought home and buried with much pomp and ceremony in a Napoleonic-style mausoleum in Tehran – senior clerics and opposition politicians boycotted the event. The British ambassador remarked that the whole show "offended Persian sense of propriety."[35] Not surprisingly, many complained the shah had turned the assassination attempt into a royalist coup d'état.

Thus, by the time the oil crisis erupted royalists and their opponents interpreted the constitution in two very different ways. The former saw the monarch as the kingpin of the constitution. The latter saw the

---

[32] Zaehner, Conversation with Ala (12 June 1952), *FO 248/Persia 1952/1531*.
[33] Sayyed Javad Imami, Speech, *1st Senate*, 1 March 1951.
[34] Malekzadeh, Speech, *1st Senate*, 25 November 1951.
[35] Sir John Le Rougetel, Dispatch to the Foreign Office (28 June 1949), *FO 371/Persia 1949/75504*.

majles as the country's central institution and the people as the ultimate source of sovereignty. The former based their claims on precedents set by Reza Shah. The latter, as strict constitutionalists, looked back to the fundamental laws. The former supplemented their claims by citing the recent constituent assembly. The latter dismissed the same assembly as totally illegitimate on grounds it had been rigged, packed, and failed to generate any public enthusiasm. The top candidate in the Tehran election had mustered mere forty-eight votes.[36]

In a study on the "Role of the Shah in Persian Politics," Pyman, the British counsellor, explained that the constitution was somewhat ambiguous on the monarch's proper role.[37] On one hand, the constitution entrusted full responsibility to the ministers, not to the shah. On the other hand, at least according to some, the shah had the prerogative to appoint ministers and act as supreme commander of the armed forces. This ambiguity, he reported, restricted the shah and provided politicians with the opportunity to "scapegoat" him and blame him for failing to set a firm course of action – especially during the oil crisis. Henderson, after a private conversation with the shah, reported the latter again complained that some continued to pressure him to act like a European monarch but he was convinced he needed to play an important role in the country's life – in both its political and its military life.[38]

17th Majles Elections

As the 16th Majles drew to a close in late 1951 Mossadeq tried – unsuccessfully – to reform the electoral law. He proposed replacing the supervisory electoral committees appointed by governors, and, if under martial law, by military governors, with independent bodies formed of judges, professors, senior civil servants, and school principals. He also proposed extending the majles term from two to four years, increasing Tehran's representation from twelve to twenty-five deputies, and restricting the vote to those who could write the names of their candidates on the ballot papers. He argued that "illiterate peasants and tribesmen" invariably became malleable "sheep" and "tools

---

[36] Editorial, "Fifteen Senators from Tehran," *Dad*, 30 October 1946.

[37] Pyman, Role of the Shah in Persian Politics (21 April 1952), FO 248/Persia 1952/1531.

[38] Henderson, Memorandum on Conversation (30 May 1953), *FRUS* (2017), 275.

of large landlords."[39] He looked forward to the day when all "peasants and tribesmen would be literate," and, thus, "free from the shackles of landlords."[40] He had so little regard for his own class that he had caused a major scandal in 1944 by denouncing the whole majles as a "den of thieves."[41] Establishment figures retorted that the electoral law should not "differentiate between literates and illiterates" and that "peasants and workers" were just as capable as anyone else of voting responsibly.[42] The landed class was not averse to resorting to populist rhetoric.

The American and British embassies both took keen interest in the 17th Majles elections. The voting started on 23 December 1951; it was scheduled to end on 1 March 1952. Pyman, Zaehner, and Falle – the three counsellors – kept close tabs, frequently consulting not only Zahedi and Sayyed Ziya but also an array of prominent politicians. This included Dr. Hadi Taheri, veteran wealthy deputy from Yazd – the British respected him for his profound knowledge of parliamentary procedures, but found him embarrassing because he often presented himself as their "mouthpiece" and attributed his own views to them;[43] Sayyed Hashem Malek-Madani, a longtime deputy from Malayer who boasted of having sixteen deputies in his pocket – Falle described him as "a slippery rogue";[44] Ahmad Human, the assistant court minister; Javad Busheri, a wealthy senator and former minister of economy; Senator Ibrahim Khajeh-Nouri, a radio celebrity, popular biographer, and Zahedi associate – the British embassy considered him a rare Iranian politician willing to publicly express pro-British sentiments;[45] Senator Ali Dashti, a well-known writer who, at the very start of the oil crisis, had privately urged the British to invade and occupy Abadan – the British embassy described him as a "hot-headed firebrand with neither scruples nor principles";[46] Abdul-Hussein Nikpour, a glass

---

[39] Mossadeq, Speech, *14th Majles*, 28 May 1945.
[40] Mohammad Mossadeq, "The Electoral Question," *Ayandeh*, Vol. III, No. 3 (September 1944), 55–60.
[41] Mossadeq, Speech, *14th Majles*, 4 March 1944.
[42] Abul Qassem Najm, Speech, *1st Senate*, 16 November 1951.
[43] British Embassy, Leading Personalities of Persia (1952), *FO 416/105*.
[44] Falle, Telegram (10 July 1952), *FO 248/Persia 1952/1539*.
[45] British Embassy, Leading Personalities in Persia (1952), *FO 416/105*.
[46] Pyman, Telegram (5 September 1951), *FO 248/Persia 1951/1514*; Foreign Office, Notes on Leading Personalities in Persia (1927), *FO 371/Persia 1927/ 12300*.

manufacturer who had presided over the Tehran chamber of commerce for some twenty years – the British felt he was willing to work quietly with the embassy as well as with Qavam;[47] Izaz Nikpay, a former governor and landlord-industrialist from Isfahan – he had also served in Qavam's cabinet in 1946–7; and, most important of all, Imami, the Imam Jum'eh of *Landan*.[48] As the election kicked off, Zaehner reported that the shah transferred $600,000 from New York to bolster his campaign war chest.[49]

The British embassy compiled a detailed electoral list taking keen interest in even distant provinces. It also took a keen interest in sowing dissension within the National Front. A senior official in London noted:

> Mr. Middleton's view, as explained to the Department, is that though there must always be a large element of speculation in our estimates, the National Front consists of separate elements – a fanatical right and a progressive and not wholly intractable left wing – which are held together largely by self-interest and that under intensified pressure combined with a sharp jolt from the outside the National Front might break up ... In Mr. Middleton's view, a deal with Makki would not be altogether impossible.[50]

The American embassy left no trace of compiling a similar electoral list, but commissioned studies on the intricate working of majles elections and procedures. The CIA inadvertently mentioned later – in a heavily redacted memo – that it had achieved "remarkable success" in the elections and added this was at the expense of the Tudeh.[51] But, of course, to achieve such success it would have had to support specific candidates. These candidates were unlikely to have been pro-Mossadeq figures. Fateh, the prominent historian of the oil crisis, writes that the Mossadeq government itself was determined no Tudeh candidate should be successful in any part of the country.[52]

The Wilber report mentions in passing that the original intention had been to remove Mossadeq through the parliamentary process. At a top-level meeting in Washington in mid-1953, Henderson repeated his

[47] Foreign Embassy, Leading Personalities in Persia (1952), *FO 416/105*.
[48] Pyman, List of Candidates (20 September 1951), *FO 248/Persia 1951/1514*; Zaehner, Conversations with Izaz Nikpay, *FO 248/Persia 1952/1541*.
[49] Pyman, Conversations with Izaz Nikpay, *FO 248/Persia 1952/1541*.
[50] A. Ross, Anglo-US Policy (29 February 1952), *FO 371/Persia 1952/34–98608*.
[51] CIA, Memo on Elections (20 February 1951), *FRUS (2017)*, 214–16.
[52] Mustafa Fateh, *Panjah Sal-e Naft* (Fifty Years of Oil) (Tehran, 1965), 596.

long-held conviction that Mossadeq had to go, that a coup could not succeed without the shah, that the USA would have to "pressure" the shah to participate, and, to top it all, that the shah would "insist" on first using "legal procedures" to replace the prime minister. The shah had made it clear that before he would issue a royal *farman* to a new premier the majles would have to give first a vote of censure or of no confidence, and then a vote of inclination or preference to the new candidate.[53]

The CIA plan for the elections stated: "In addition to the general authorization enabling the Tehran station to spend up to $1,000,000 in covert activities in support of Zahedi, the station was specifically authorized to spend one million rials a day in purchasing the cooperation of members of the Iranian Majles."[54] This would have totaled more than $11,000 per day. The report added:

It must be admitted that in the years and months of working with subsidized press and its venal (or patriotic) journalists in Tehran, the station was still not sure whether it was achieving results comparable to the sums so spend. In July and early August every segment of the press with which we or the United Kingdom had working relations went all out against Mossadeq.[55]

Wilber speculated the CIA would need at least forty-one votes to undercut Mossadeq in the majles – MI6 speculated on an additional twenty. Wilber repeated several times the feasibility of removing Mossadeq through this "quasi-legal method."[56]

The CIA study on elections described how in some constituencies "local landlords controlled the results," and in others, especially tribal ones, the army elected its own candidates.[57] For example, Imami of Tehran was elected from Mahabad – a Sunni Kurdish region with which he had absolutely no connections. Similarly, Mehdi Mir Ashrafi – the editor of the rightist *Atesh* (Fire) – was elected from

[53] John Waller, Memorandum on Conversation: Preliminary Operation Plan in Implementation of Project TPAJAX (6 June 1953), *FRUS* (2017), 583–7.
[54] Donald Wilber, *Overthrow of Premier Mossadeq of Iran, November 1952–August 1953* (Washington, DC: CIA Historical Division, 1954).
[55] Wilber, *Overthrow of Premier Mossadeq*, 90–1.
[56] Wilber, *Overthrow of Premier Mossadeq*, Appendix A.
[57] CIA, Memo on Elections (20 February 1951), *FRUS* (2017), 215.

Meshgin Shahr where the peasantry, according to the CIA, had never heard of him. The CIA explained:[58]

In the elections to the 17th Majles the Shah wanted Mir Ashrafi to be deputy from Meshgin Shahi [sic]. Mir Ashrafi is a former Army officer who was expelled from the Army for being *too* corrupt. During the war he acquired for himself the reputation of being one of the worst crooks in the country. However, Meshgin Shahi [sic] is a region inhabited by simple peasants who certainly had never heard anything of or about Mir Ashrafi. Since the Army controlled the area, the Intelligence Bureau of the General Staff communicated the royal desire to the Commanding officer at Meshgin Shahi [sic]. A few men were instructed to fill thousands of ballots with the name of Mir Ashrafi and the peasants were ordered to cast the ballots in the ballot boxes. It is probable that the majority of "voters" never learned whose name was on the ballots they cast. The whole thing was done so smoothly that even Mossadeq did not know what was afoot until the results were published.

Richard Cottam, a CIA analyst in Washington, later wrote that because Mossadeq was reluctant to intervene in rural regions under martial law these constituencies not surprisingly "elected" staunch monarchists such as the two Zolfaqari brothers, Mohammad and Nasser.[59] The two headed the Turkic-speaking tribe of the same name near Zanjan in Azerbaijan. The tribe had fought for the monarch in the Constitutional Revolution. The British embassy described the two brothers as the shah's "cronies." After the coup, Mohammad Zolfaqari was rewarded with the governorship of Isfahan.[60]

The elections became highly contentious not only because the shah, the British, and the Americans were deeply involved, but also because government supporters in many constituencies fielded rival slates – one led by the Iran Party, the other by Ayatollah Kashani. The Iran Party, Mossadeq's most reliable support, sponsored mostly professionals who had worked with or within the government ministries and was inspired by a mild brand of French socialism. It received support from the Pan-Iranist Party, a new ultra-nationalist group formed of high school students. They wore black shirts, dreamt of regaining the "lost territories of ancient Iran," and specialized in physical attacks on the Tudeh

[58] CIA, A Study of Electoral Methods in Iran (13 November 1953), *FRUS* (2017), 833–7.
[59] Richard Cottam, *Nationalism in Iran* (Pittsburgh: University of Pittsburgh Press, 1967), 256–7.
[60] British Embassy, Leading Personalities in Iran (1957), FO 371/127072.

and members of the religious minorities, especially Jews and Bahais. The CIA described them as obsessed with the fear of Iran being contaminated with alien ideas, especially Marxism.[61] The Pan-Iranists later discarded some of their ultra-right sentiments.

The Kashani slate was drawn up by his Mujahedin-e Islam (Fighters for Islam). In some constituencies, it was also supported by Baqai's Toilers Party and Shams al-Din Qonatabadi's Majma'-e Musulman-e Mujahedin (Society of Muslim Fighters). Qonatabadi, Kashani's relative, had been eased out of Qom because of his political activism. After the coup, he discarded his turban, entered the bazaar world, and co-edited *Atesh* with Mir Ashrafi. These groups were small, fluid, and unstructured. Baqai's support was concentrated in his hometown Kerman. Kashani wielded more clout – especially in Tabriz where his associates won five seats. As the election campaign heated up, Kashani began to distance himself from Mossadeq mainly because the interior minister had refused to help his many sons get elected. Adding insult to injury, Kashani failed to top the list of the elected candidates in Tehran. Makki, who at the time was still close to Kashani, topped the Tehran list. Makki later commented that if the interior minister had catered to Kashani the public would have concluded the "ayatollah had taken over Iran and packed the majles with his sons."[62]

The American embassy had coyly courted Kashani since August 1951. It had arranged an impressive array of dignitaries to visit him quietly at his home – Harriman, Christopher Warne of Point IV, Henderson and his embassy colleagues, Professor George Lenczowski of the University of California and of the CIA, correspondents from the *Herald Tribune*, *Daily Express*, and the *New York Times*, and an "unnamed American" (most probably from the CIA). They had buttered him up, praising him as a towering figure in the "whole Muslim world." Lenczowski, after one private session, told the press that Iran and the USA could work together since both abhorred "materialism."[63] One embassy report described Kashani as "important" albeit "fanatical," "ambitious," "bombastic," "opportunistic," "psychopathic," harboring "delusions of grandeur," encouraging

---

[61] CIA, *Pan-Iranist Movement* (10 May 1951), www.cia.gov/readingroom/search/site/Iran.

[62] Mohammad Movahhed, *Khavab-e Ashufeteh-e Naft* (Oil Nightmare) (Tehran: Karnameh Publication, 1999), Vol. I, 400.

[63] *Ettela'at*, 28 May 1953.

assassinations, and attracting "ignorant classes and fanatical elements in the bazaar." It repeated earlier assessments: "He can be bribed. He has at least on one occasion made overtures to the American embassy here for financial support in return, presumably, he would support US policies."[64]

Henderson reported he had a meeting with Kashani in late 1952 during which the ayatollah had asked in a friendly manner for help to strengthen his "enterprise" in the Muslim world. He added that a former cabinet member and friend of Kashani told him that the ayatollah probably needed financial help from the USA to send delegates to an international conference.[65] A CIA visitor reported that although Kashani was definitely a "megalomaniac" it would still be useful to continue relations with him and "penetrate his followers."[66] Middleton reported that Kashani in preparations for the elections had put out feelers to the shah and the Americans.[67] Earlier he heard rumors that Kashani – as well as Makki and Baqai – had put out similar feelers to Zahedi.[68] He added that Zahedi held regular secret meetings with Kashani, Baqai, and others.[69]

Middleton further reported that Makki had visited the American ambassador and had not disguised his serious differences with Mossadeq, especially over the appointment of "nonentities to the cabinet."[70] The US embassy noted that Makki was busy "grooming himself for the premiership."[71] In a meeting with representatives of "Old Commonwealth Governments," Middleton reported that Makki would be acceptable as a prime minister since "we could do business with him."[72] It was rumored that Makki had been offended by being excluded from the Iranian delegation to The Hague on the grounds that he knew no French and was not an expert on international law. Makki later admitted, without mentioning his own name, that Zahedi held regular secret meetings with former members of the National Front.[73]

---

[64] Arthur Richards, Recent Increase in Political Prestige of Ayatollah Kashani (20 August 1951), *FRUS* (2017), 126–31.

[65] Henderson, Telegram (9 November 1952), *FRUS* (2017), 398.

[66] CIA, Dispatch from Station (10 January 1952), *FRUS* (2017), 171.

[67] Middleton, Telegram, FO 371/91465.

[68] Middleton, Telegram (7 August 1952), FO 371/Persia 1952/98602.

[69] Middleton, Telegram (12 October 1952), FO 371/Persia 1952/98603.

[70] Middleton, Telegram (7 August 1952), FO 248/Persia/1531.

[71] US Embassy, Telegram (23 April 1953), FO 371/Persia 1953/104567.

[72] Middleton, Telegram (2 December 1952), FO 371/Persia 1952/98606.

[73] Makki, *The Coup of 19 August*, 234.

Reports by the CIA often mention the need to approach and fund other political entities. Their identities remain redacted, but most probably included Baqai's Toilers Party touted by the CIA as a Titoist movement.[74] The CIA mentioned that Baqai had been eager for some time to get in touch with them, and suggested that "controlling him" would be useful since he was a "valuable asset" and "important in the National Front."[75] Clearly, the intention was more to sow dissension within the National Front than to replace Mossadeq with the likes of Kashani, Makki, and Baqai. The shah, for his part, fueled dissension by dropping hints to Makki, Saleh, Baqai, and Fatemi that Iran was in dire need of younger leaders like themselves. Fatemi promptly reported this to Mossadeq. Makki, taken in by the ruse, confided to a friend that he hoped to become prime minister soon.[76] Meanwhile, the British embassy often received confidential reports that the shah was funding Baqai and was advising royalist newspaper editors not to attack Kashani and Baqai.[77]

In some constituencies, Kashani received active support from Fedayan-e Islam – the zealots notorious for their string of political assassinations. Although the Fedayan had broken with Mossadeq, they retained ties with Kashani even – or rather, especially – after being evicted from Qom by Grand Ayatollah Boroujerdi for their political activism and disruption of seminary classes. Surprisingly, the Fedayan established ties with Sayyed Ziya, the pro-British politician. In analyzing the Fedayan, Zaehner explained such ties as politically expedient. After all, he argued, the Fedayan opposed Mossadeq because of his refusal to implement shari'a and amnesty their leaders; Britain, however, had very different reasons for opposing Mossadeq. Fedayan was obsessed about sex, drink, American promiscuity, and Western decadence; Britain was not overly concerned over such matters. "The fact that Sayyed Ziya is pro-British," Zaehner concluded, "does not seem to bother the Fedayan unduly."[78] The CIA shared Zaehner's sentiments. In drawing up the coup plans, the CIA proposed that the Fedayan "should be encouraged to threaten direct action against pro-Mossadeq deputies."[79] It was at one such meeting that Henderson

---

[74] CIA, Project Outline Prepared in the CIA (26 July 1951), *FRUS* (2017), 121–3.
[75] CIA, Monthly Report (September 1953), *FRUS* (2017), 358.
[76] Falle, Telegram (12 June 1952), *FO* 248/Persia 1952/1531.
[77] Middleton, Memo, *FO* 248/1541.
[78] Zaehner, The Feda'yan-i-Islam (1 March 1952), *FO* 248/1540.
[79] Wilber, *Overthrow of Premier Mossadeq*, Appendix A (Initial Operation Plan).

interjected that Mossadeq should not be assassinated.[80] The USA, like the United Kingdom, was pragmatic and "open-minded" enough to seek allies anywhere for the higher goal of replacing Mossadeq. No one at these meetings seems to have questioned the wisdom or ethics of working with religious fanatics – not to mention local Nazis.

The elections in Tehran were on the whole fair simply because, as the CIA admitted, it was "almost impossible to control the vote in such a large city."[81] The government took the precaution of placing voting booths near mosques so monitors could sound the alarm from minarets at the approach of unauthorized military personnel. Presenting a joint slate, the government not surprisingly won all twelve seats. Makki and Kashani headed the slate. They were followed by: Kazem Hassibi, a petroleum engineer and cabinet adviser with long career in the AIOC; Abdul Hussein Haerizadeh, a veteran majles deputy famous for his denunciations of Reza Shah; Ali Shayegan, a law professor and longtime legal adviser to Mossadeq; Baqai of Kerman; Mohammad Nariman, former mayor of Tehran and career civil servant from the finance ministry; Ahmad Zirakzadeh, professor of engineering from the Iran Party; Hussein Fatemi, Mossadeq's future foreign minister; Yousef Mosher (Mosher 'Azam), another outspoken critic of Reza Shah; Hussein Ali Rashed, a professor of theology; and Ali Zaheri, editor of Baqai's paper *Shahed* (Witness). Five of the twelve – Hassibi, Shayegan, Baqai, Zirakzadeh, and Fatemi – had degrees from French universities.

The elections, however, became so contentious and so violent in some provincial constituencies that they had to be suspended.[82] Over thirty-five lives were lost in street clashes, especially in Baluchistan and Luristan. Nineteen candidates backed by ten newspapers competed in Boroujerd. Kashani issued a fatwa against one candidate. Twenty candidates with eight papers entered the race in Tabriz; one pro-Kashani paper denounced the government candidates as "pro-British." In Najafabad, according to Ayatollah Montazeri's later memoirs, Kashani supported an unknown candidate against a popular irrigation engineer sponsored by the Iran Party. Montazeri seems to have favored

---

[80] CIA, Memorandum of Conversation (6 June 1953), *FRUS* (2017), 586.
[81] CIA, A Study of Electoral Methods in Iran (13 November 1953), *FRUS* (2017), 834.
[82] Ali Tatari (ed.), *Negah beh Majles-e Shuray-e Melli* (Look at the National Assembly) (Tehran: Ministry of Culture, 2015).

the latter.[83] The campaign grew so tense in Khuzestan that martial law was declared and voting suspended in eight oil-producing constituencies. Farrukh, the royalist senator, even accused the government of sponsoring a *lamazhab* (atheist) in Behahabad. He also blamed the government for bloody clashes between the Tudeh and Pan-Iranists in Babul, and, most serious of all, for peasant unrest throughout Azerbaijan. "This peasant incitement," he warned, "will soon spread throughout the country like wild fire and eventually consume even Mossadeq's own village of Ahmadabad."[84]

By early March the British embassy reported that "dissension" between Kashani and Mossadeq was public knowledge, and that the former was now openly complaining that the latter was not supporting his candidates, especially his sons.[85] The embassy also reported that of the twenty-two national newspapers, fifteen were critical of the government, five were pro-government, and two, especially *Ettela'at*, were neutral.[86] These papers continued to be published throughout the 17th Majles. This belies the often-repeated accusation abroad and among the opposition that Mossadeq had silenced the Fourth Estate and established a personal political "dictatorship."

Once 79 of the 136 seats had been filled – enough to constitute the required quorum – Mossadeq suspended the remaining elections. These numbers became crucial in the forthcoming political struggles. At least four deputies never took their seats because they were travelling abroad or because they served in the executive branch. The constitution set the quorum at total number of elected deputies minus those whose absence had been duly allowed by the assembly; this meant that at least thirty-eight deputies had to be present. Majles rules further stipulated that the assembly could open debates when two-thirds of elected deputies were present, and could take a vote when three-quarters were in attendance. A simple majority of those present could pass a motion. Mossadeq's resort to stopping the elections once a quorum had been reached did have a historical precedent. The 2nd Majles (1909–11) – probably one of the most

[83] Hussein-Ali Montazeri, *Matn-e Kamel-e Khaterat* (Text of Full Memoires) (Sweden: Baran Press, 2000), 79.

[84] Farrukh, *1st Senate*, 21 April 1952.

[85] Middleton, Dispatch (10 March 1952), *FO 248/Persia 1952/1531.*

[86] G. Barker, Dispatch (1 March 1952), *FO 248/Persia 1952/1531.*

productive – had functioned well even though only 65 of its 120 seats had been filled.[87]

Of the seventy-nine elected to the 17th Majles, forty-nine were landlords. A detailed CIA study identified thirty as staunch Mossadeq supporters, four as waivers, and forty-five as potential opponents. It categorized the opponents as ten royalists, seventeen free floaters, eight Kashani followers, and ten defectors from the National Front – associates of Baqai, Makki, and Haerizadeh.[88] Meanwhile, the British reported that Sayyed Ziya and Imami boasted that they "controlled" twenty-one and fifteen votes respectively.[89] One version of the same CIA study described the majles as "*not* a factor" to be considered in the course of a forceful coup. Another version of the very same report described the majles as "another factor to be considered in the course of a forceful coup." The report continued: "However, in spite of this potential opposition Mossadeq has won overwhelming votes of confidence in the past. These votes have been on his handling of the oil issue." The CIA estimated that forty-two votes could remove Mossadeq; MI6 estimated that "20 deputies now not controlled must be purchased" to achieve the desired end of removing Mossadeq.[90] A US embassy study concluded that the government had twenty-eight secure votes and this was ten short of the thirty-eight needed to remain stable and pass legislation.[91] Wilber notes that the CIA station was instructed by the State Department in early June to spend an additional one million rials a week to "purchase the cooperation of the majlis" simply because the shah continued to insist that Mossadeq had to be removed by a "vote of inclination."[92]

[87] Mangol Bayat, *Iran's Experiment with Parliamentary Governance: The Second Majles 1909–1911* (Syracuse: Syracuse University Press, 2020).

[88] Wilber, Factors Involved in the Overthrow of Mossadeq (16 April 1953), *FRUS* (2017), 523–39.

[89] Zaehner, Conversations with Sayyed Ziya (15 May 1952), FO 248/Persia 1952/ 1531; Falle, Conversations with Imam Jum'eh (21 June 1952), FO 248/Persia 1952/1531.

[90] Wilber, *Overthrow of Premier Mossadeq*, Appendix A.

[91] Roy Melbourne (First Secretary of US Embassy), Report on the Majles (26 June 1953), FO 371/Persia 1953/104568.

[92] Wilber, *Overthrow of Premier Mossadeq*, 17–19.

The 17th Majles

The majles officially convened on 17 April 1952, but official business did not begin until 29 June. The deputies spent the first two months challenging each other's credentials. Mir Ashrafi, the cashiered army officer, was the most vociferous denouncing opponents endlessly with innuendos. He even smeared the reputation of Nariman's long-deceased father.[93] The pro-government deputies were equally vociferous challenging the credentials of Mir Ashrafi, Imami and Taheri – the latter for his long associations with the British. Haerizadeh, while still supportive of the government, accused a Baluch deputy of murdering his rival candidate. He also denounced Sheikh Abdul Rahman Faramarzi, the editor of *Kayhan*, for collaborating with the AIOC and Reza Shah, for having family origins in Bahrain and the Arab world, and for having no links whatsoever with his supposed constituency – the villages of Veramin outside Tehran owned by the shah.[94] Faramarzi counterattacked accusing Haerizadeh of having cooperated with Qavam and the Soviets in World War II, of being "illiterate" in Persian and Arabic, and of sowing dissension between Sunnis and Shi'is.[95] Both sides aired complaints of gross electoral irregularities including armed intimidation, packed supervisory committees, stuffed and switched ballot boxes, multiple and underage voting, and herding of whole tribes to designated voting polls. At times the sessions became so heated that the assembly had to go into recess. These preliminary squabbles ended once seventy-nine credentials were accepted. The real number turned out to be seventy-seven. Kashani deemed it beneath his clerical dignity to appear in the majles; and Fatemi was constitutionally barred since he had accepted the post of foreign minister.

The majles began formal sessions on 29 June by electing its president. This produced the government's first setback. On the first count, Imami received thirty-three votes; the pro-government vote was split with sixteen for Shayegan and seventeen for Dr. Abdullah Moazemi – a French-educated lawyer from the Iran Party representing Golpayegan where his family owned ancestral land. Since Imami had failed to receive the required majority, a second count was taken a few days later when Shayegan withdrew. Imami mustered thirty-nine votes

---

[93] Mir Ashrafi, Speech, *17th Majles*, 22 May 1952.
[94] Haerizadeh, Speech, *17th Majles*, 5 June 1952.
[95] Faramarzi, Speech, *17th Majles*, 10 June 1952.

to Moazemi's thirty-five. The shah's strategy against Mossadeq seemed to be working.

A second setback came on 5 July. According to convention, the prime minister would hand in his resignation at the convening of a new parliament and then seek a fresh "vote of inclination" to head the next government. Mossadeq did so, receiving fifty-two votes out of sixty-four in the majles, but only fourteen out of forty-five in the senate. Arsanjani, Qavam's adviser, suspected the shah had something to do with this outcome in the senate.[96] The shah had tried to privately persuade Imami – probably prodded by Henderson and Middleton – to convene a joint majles-senate session to vote for change of premier on the grounds that the oil crisis was over and the country deserved a new administration.[97] Henderson and Middleton themselves had doubled their behind-the-scenes lobbying on behalf of Qavam. The National Front countered by flooding the majles with letters, petitions, and telegrams from all parts of the country pledging full support for Mossadeq.[98]

Aware of these intrigues, Mossadeq initiated the crisis that turned into the July Uprising. On 16 July, in announcing the formation of his new cabinet and government program, he kept the portfolio of the war ministry for himself and requested special six-month powers to deal with the economic embargo imposed by Britain. When the shah resisted, Mossadeq promptly resigned. On the very next day, forty out of forty-two deputies present gave their "vote of inclination" to Qavam in a secret closed session – even majles orderlies were barred. Twenty-seven deputies refused to attend.[99] The British embassy later reported that Baqai had sent a secret letter to Qavam pledging "full support."[100] Baqai's bodyguard, who had sworn personal allegiance to him, years after his boss's death revealed that the latter had worked secretly with Imami and Qavam against Mossadeq.[101] The shah signed the requisite *farman* for Qavam to form a cabinet.

---

[96]   Hassan Arsanjani, *Yaddashtha-ye Siyasi-e Man: Siyum-e Tir* (My Political Memoirs: 21 July) (Tehran: Atesh Press, 1956), 11–12.
[97]   Middleton, Developments in the Persian Internal Situation (9 July 1952), *FO 416/Persia 1952/105*.
[98]   Collection of Petitions Presented to the Majles, *17th Majles*, 8 July 1952.
[99]   Makki, *The Events of 21 July*, 80.
[100] R. J., Confidential (21 August 1952), *FO 248/Persia 1952/1531*.
[101] Morteza Kashani, *Khaterat* (Memoirs) (Tehran: Islamic Revolution Publications, 2011), 66–9.

This sparked off the July Uprising, which, in turn, led to Qavam's ouster and Mossadeq's triumphant return. His triumph was reinforced by the coincidental verdict issued from The Hague. The court voted eight to four in favor of Iran; it ruled it had no jurisdiction over a dispute between a sovereign state and a private company. Critics in the West denounced the Hague judgment as violating "natural law," the "sanctity of private property, and the viability of internationally signed pledges."[102] Mossadeq had not only won the fight hands down but had also foiled the attempt to remove him through the parliamentary process. Acheson put it bluntly: "As a result of events last week, it appears to us that Mossadeq is clearly in a stronger position vis-à-vis the Shah, the Majles and the public now than at any time since the nationalization of Iran oil in April 1951."[103] Middleton concluded that hope of replacing Mossadeq through constitutional means had ended once for all.[104]

Returning triumphant to the majles, Mossadeq received an overwhelming "vote of inclination" – sixty-one out of sixty-four votes in the majles, thirty-three out of forty-one in the senate. He gained not only the war ministry but also the six-months special powers and a cabinet fully of his own choosing – the previous ones had contained royalists as well as half-hearted supporters. In late January 1953, the majles extended the special powers to a full twelve months. It also gave him another vote of confidence with fifty-nine out of sixty-one deputies supporting him.

In the new cabinet, the foreign ministry went to Fatemi; interior to Dr. Ghulam Hussein Sadeqi – a sociology professor at Tehran University; finance to Baqer Kazemi, a senior diplomat and former cabinet minister; justice to Abdul Ali Lofti – a strict constitutional jurists educated in a Najaf seminary; education to Dr. Mehdi Azar, a professor of medicine; post and telegraph to Sheifollah Moazemi, the brother of the Iran Party leader; economy to Dr. Ali Akbar Akhavi, a recently returned businessman from New York; agriculture to Khalel Taleqani, an irrigation engineer; health to Dr. Sabar Farmanfarmayan, a physician from the well-known aristocratic family; and labor to

---

[102] Jolanat Sierakowska-Dyndo, "Polish Judge Defended the Iran Stance," *Studia Litteraria Universitatis Iagellonicae Cracowiensis 2019*. Special Issue, 231–43.
[103] Acheson, Letter to the US Embassy in London (26 July 1952), *FRUS* (1989), 415.
[104] Middleton, Summary of Events for Persia in 1952, FO 416/106.

Dr. Ibrahim Alemi – a French-educated jurist who had recently drawn up a progressive labor law – the British embassy deemed him "completely subservient to Dr. Musaddiq."[105] Most – with the notable exception of Lofti – were French educated and longtime members of the Iran Party.

The CIA and the right-wing press soon targeted Azar and Lofti–as well as Shayegan, Mossadeq 's legal adviser – as Tudeh fellow travelers: Azar, because he had a brother in exile in the Soviet Union; Lofti and Shayegan, because as strict jurists, they insisted civilians should not be tried in military courts. Lofti was unlikely to have been a "fellow traveler" since he had close ties to Grand Ayatollah Boroujerdi. The CIA probably did not believe its own claims; both Azar and Shayegan later obtained visas to live in exile in the USA. Farrukh, an independent-minded conservative royalist, vouched for both Azar and Lofti on the senate floor.[106] Soon after the coup, Lofti was physically attacked, seriously injured, and subsequently died in hospital. Sayyed Ziya, who had no political reason to like Lofti, described him as "The most just Minister of Justice Iran has ever had."[107] Lofti had purged corrupt judges and officials out of the judiciary. It was rumored that Baqai had taken out a contract on him with one of the gang leaders.

The special powers given to Mossadeq enabled him to decree extensive reforms. He introduced a 2 percent tax on wealth; 20 percent increase in the share of the annual crop going to the peasants – 10 percent was to go directly to them and 10 percent to village councils for local projects; and the total eradication of labor dues owed by peasants to their landlords. He did not resort to the standard form of land reform and place a ceiling on ownership for the simple reason no cadastral survey had been carried out and it would have taken years to complete such a survey. He also used the powers to abolish special tribunals that had been set up outside the justice development department – such tribunals had been set up after the 1949 assassination attempt. He decreed a press law entrusting the supervision of newspapers, especially censorship, to a council of academics, lawyers, intellectuals, and education ministry representatives. Moreover, he introduced social insurance

---

[105] British Embassy, Leading Personalities in Persia (1952), *FO 416/105*.
[106] Farrukh, *1st Senate*, 2 August 1953.
[107] Peter Avery, *Modern Iran* (London: Benn Limited, 1965), 433.

for factory workers – pensions, unemployment benefits, medical coverage, free literacy classes, and maternity leave. Furthermore, he drew up the long-anticipated reform of the electoral system. A bill for city elections – portend for national elections – limited the vote for literates, introduced female suffrage, and set up secret ballots and supervisory councils independent of provincial governors and the central government.[108] A similar law was drafted for future parliamentary elections. The legislation for these special powers stipulated that all decrees issued by the government had to be eventually submitted to the majles. Needless to say, the CIA analysts who had earlier found fault with Mossadeq for failing to advocate social reforms were not impressed by such wide-ranging legislation. They merely ignored them.

Mossadeq also struck a series of heavy blows on the shah. He replaced Ala, the court minister, with Dr. Abul Qassem Amini, an independent-minded aristocrat. He restricted the shah's access to foreign ambassadors. He renamed the ministry of war to that of defense; trimmed the top-heavy officer corps and proposed cutting the military budget; transferred jurisdiction of tribes from the army to the interior ministry; and instructed the chiefs of staff to communicate directly with the defense ministry bypassing the shah. He appointed General Mohammad Taqi Riyahi – a Saint-Cyr educated member of the Iran Party – as his chief of general staff. The British embassy commented that the only influence now left to the shah was any "loyalty" the officers had to the crown.[109] Mossadeq also exiled Princess Ashraf and the Queen Mother; transferred Reza Shah's estates, including twelve villages near Veramin, back to the state to be returned to their original owners; closed down foundations led by members of the royal family; and shifted allocations from the palace budget to the ministry of health.

Mossadeq also forced Imami to resign as majles president. Kashani replaced him with forty-two votes. The American naval attaché reported that Kashani was elected after a late-night secret meeting of his son, Mostafa Kashani, with Baqai, Makki, Mir Ashrafi, Ardasher Zahedi, the general's son, and some unidentified deputies. The attaché implied that some of the forty-two votes had been bought. He

[108] Bill for City Councils, *1st Senate*, 11 June 1952.
[109] Melbourne, Control of High-Level Army Appointments (21 May 1953), FO 371/Persia 1953/104601.

explained that although the election was secret, the ballots were surreptitiously marked so recipients could be identified if they reneged.[110] Kashani, however, continued to stay away from majles debates. The assembly was instead presided over by his elected deputy Ahmad Razavi – a French-educated engineer and longtime member of both the Iran Party and the National Front.

The majles, meanwhile, declared 30th Tir a National Uprising (*Qeyam-e Melli*) and proclaimed the dead as national martyrs (*shahed*). Even royalists, such as Nasser Zolfaqari, took turns to hail the uprising as a National Revolution (*Enqelab*) and praise Mossadeq as the "true voice of the masses fighting imperialism (*estemari*)."[111] The lower house, moreover, exercised its constitutional authority to reduce the upper house's term from six to two years – thereby in effect closing it down. No deputy rose to oppose the motion. Former National Front deputies now in the opposition – such as Kashani, Baqai, Makki, Haerizadeh, and Qonatabadi – could hardly object since they themselves had vehemently opposed the creation of the senate in the first place. Middleton commented it was "relatively easy" to depict the senate as "a reactionary, blood-sucking body totally subservient to foreign interests."[112] One senator had openly threatened to vote against any bill proposed by the existing government.[113]

The majles, furthermore, immediately after the February Crisis, had elected a Committee of Eight to study the fundamental laws and resolve the constitutional differences between the government and the monarch. This conjured up images of 1789 when the National Assembly in Paris had formed a Committee of Eight to look into the constitutional crisis in France.[114] Six of the eight deputies elected to the majles committee had been longtime critics of the Pahlavis for violating the 1906 constitution.[115] Not surprisingly, the committee now came up with a report siding with the government – even though one member,

---

[110] Eric Pollard, Memorandum Prepared by Naval Attaché (11 June 1953), *FRUS* (2017), 587–90.

[111] Nasser Zolfaqari, Speech, *17th Majles*, 29 July 1952.

[112] Middleton, Telegram, FO 248/1539.

[113] Kamal Hedayat, *1st Senate*, 14 March 1952.

[114] Lord Acton, *Lectures on the French Revolution* (New York: Noonday Press, 1959), 87.

[115] The Committee of Eight was formed of Hussein Makki, Javad Ganjei, Abdul-Hussein Haerizadeh, Bahman Majzadeh, Abdul Moazemi, Mozaffar Baqai, Reza Rafi, and Karim Sanjabi.

Haerizadeh, now in the opposition, tried to take back his original vote. The report also recommended the creation of a committee of law professors, senior clerics, and high court judges to update the 1906 fundamental laws.[116] The strategy of using parliament to remove Mossadeq had failed dismally.

Parliamentary Obstruction

Having failed to bring down the government through the legislative process, the opposition deputies – fully encouraged by the USA and the United Kingdom – resorted to parliamentary obstructionism. They aimed both to prevent the government from replacing the assembly with a new one, and to "question" (*estyzah*) individual ministers and threaten a vote of no confidence in the government (*ezhar-e tamayul* or *salbe-e e'temad*). In an updated analysis of the majles, Roosevelt noted it would be easy to grind the assembly to a halt since few had questioned the problem of having only eighty deputies. He again noted the Iranian constitution stipulated the majles needed two-thirds of its members present to begin debates; three-quarters to take any vote; and a majority plus one to pass a law or accept a motion.[117] Thus a small but determined bloc could immobilize the whole assembly. The CIA put the issue bluntly:

The Majlis had a powerful weapon – the quorum veto. The constitution stated that the Majlis could only be considered convened when two-thirds of its 136 deputies had reached Tehran, and half of those in the present in the capital constituted a quorum. Thus, if 91 deputies were in Tehran, the absence of 46 of them could keep the assembly from functioning.[118]

The majles soon divided into two warring blocs. On one side were some thirty pro-government deputies. They initially called themselves the *Fraksiun-e Vatan* (Homeland Caucus), but, when joined by some *Enferadi* (Independents), renamed themselves *Fraksiun-e Nahzat-e Melli* (National Movement Caucus). On the other side were some forty deputies clustered around rival personalities with their own *fraksiuns*. They used labels such as *Azadi* (Freedom), Iran, *Ettefaq* (Alliance), *Vahadat* (Unity), *Ettehad* (Unity), *Keshvar* (State),

---

[116] *Ettela'at*, 24 May 1953.
[117] Roosevelt, Memorandum (15 July 1953), *FRUS* (2017), 623.
[118] CIA, *Battle for Iran* (Washington, DC: CIA Near East Division, n.d.), 8.

Mottafeq (Confederate), and *Najat-e Nahzat* (Save the Movement). Azadi, the most vociferous, was led by Haerizadeh, the longtime critic of the Pahlavis who now joined hands with staunch royalists such as Mir Ashrafi, Faramarzi, and the Zolfaqari brothers. Zaehner, who through his All Soul's connections was certainly familiar with Lewis Namier's famous *Structure of Politics at the Accession of George III*, probably relished the idea of funneling "secret service" money to such "placemen" and "King's friends." Namier famously depicted the Georgian parliament as an "ant-heap with human ants hurrying in long files along their various paths."[119]

The opposition caucuses could readily deprive the majles of a quorum. By April 1953, the loss of further deputies due to deaths, resignations, and travel abroad had reduced the total number present in the capital to sixty-nine – which meant that forty-six were required to be in Tehran to begin debates and fifty-two to take a vote.[120] This provided the opposition with the easy opportunity of bringing business to a total standstill. Whenever the government tabled an important motion – especially the report from the Committee of Eight – the opposition would promptly walk out of the chamber, even leave the capital. Azadi often found the urgent need to go on a pilgrimage to Qom. Obstructionism continued intermittently for over forty days, starting in April and continuing into August. The government was left frustrated with 180 bills ready to bring to the floor but no functioning majles to debate and vote on them.

In obstructing the government, the opposition on the whole avoided the subject of oil and acted as if the whole issue had been resolved. It even reaffirmed support for the government on this issue. The opposition instead attacked the government on a host of other issues – sometimes from the far right, sometimes from the far left, sometimes from the supposed moderate center. The intention was to immobilize the government, not to provide a coherent critique or consistent criticism.

The opposition deputies targeted the six-months and twelve-months special powers. They equated them with the Nazi Enabling Act accusing Mossadeq of being a new Hitler and Goebbels. The government

---

[119] D. W. Hayton, *Conservative Revolutionary: The Lives of Lewis Namier* (Manchester: Manchester University Press, 2019), 170–2.
[120] *Ettela'at*, 9 May 1953.

retorted that previous parliaments in Iran, as well as the National Assembly in France, had enacted similar powers. It also reminded them that all decrees enacted under the special powers needed the eventual endorsement of the majles. It is unlikely that Henderson in his many private chats with Baqai, Kashani, and other vociferous member of the opposition, would have explained that Executive Orders gave American presidents similar powers. Haerizadeh, the most vocal opponent of the special powers, completely lost interest in the topic after the coup. He accepted first a sinecure abroad and then a safe seat in the subsequent parliament. In attacking the government, Haerizadeh suddenly discovered that Mossadeq must have been a "British agent" all his life. "Otherwise," he argued, "how could he have become governor of Fars in 1921 when the British controlled all of southern Iran?"[121] He also argued the majles – not the cabinet and the prime minister – should have the sole authority in appointing the chiefs of staff, police, and gendarmerie.[122] Mir Ashrafi seconded Haerizadeh in accusing Mossadeq of being a British "agent." "The best evidence of this," he argued, "was that the British judge at The Hague had voted in favor of Mossadeq."[123] It is not surprising foreign diplomats often joked that they felt like Alice in Wonderland.

The opposition deputies also took turns to denounce the government for resorting to martial law. They reminded the public that Mossadeq himself had previously depicted such measures as "unconstitutional." Sumka, Arya, and the Toilers Party would often instigate public disturbances, especially against the Tudeh, and when the government resorted to martial law they would raise hue and cry that the prime minister was a "dictator." Faramarzi, the royalist deputy, was especially vocal in denouncing the government for using martial law to "illegally" detain the Sumka leader.[124] He also criticized the annual budget for shortchanging schools in the southern provinces where they were needed – "unlike Kurdestan where people are uninterested in education."[125] Mir Ashrafi, the cashiered army officer, complained that the government was spending too much on prisons and not enough

---

[121] Haerizadeh, Speech, *17th Majles*, 20 March 1953.
[122] Haerizadeh, Speech, *17th Majles*, 14 May 1953.
[123] Atesh, *Qeyam dar Rah-e Saltanat* (Revolt for the Monarchy) (Tehran, Majles Publication, 1954), 5.
[124] Faramarzi, Speech, *17th Majles*, 19 September 1952.
[125] Faramarzi, Speech, *17th Majles*, 18 December 1952.

on hospitals and schools.[126] Baqai and his right hand man, Zaheri, criticized the new Social Stability Law – mainly directed at Tudeh – for violating workers' rights, especially their right to strike.[127] Nasser Zolfaqari claimed he still supported Mossadeq but not his ministers – especially that of education and justice – who, he claimed, wanted to turn Iran into another Czechoslovakia.[128] Some complained about censorship – although their publications outnumbered those supporting the government. Others complained that their majles speeches were not being aired on national radio, even though there was no such precedent.

Mir Ashrafi also claimed that in the past he had backed the government but was now withdrawing support because he had discovered the prime minister to be not only incompetent, but also, far more serious, financially "corrupt."[129] Qonatabadi complained the government permitted music during Ramadan and failed to draft serious legislation to ban alcohol. He praised Kashani for being the real leader of the nationalization campaign and the Fedayan-e Islam for "executing" traitors.[130] He also accused Riyahi, the chief of staff, of being a "National Socialist," Amini, the new court minister, of being a conservative aristocrat, and General Daftari, the head of custom guards, of dealing with contraband – especially sugar, tea, and rice.[131] He proclaimed that he, as a religious man, "worshipped no individual but only God."[132]

Ahmad Safayi, a pro-Kashani cleric who retained his seat after the coup, began his speeches with "In the Name of God, the Compassionate" – previous clerical deputies had not observed this formula. He also praised Kashani as the "true leader of oil nationalization"; demanded that religious lands be returned to clerical foundations; and reminded his audience that private property was sacred in Islam – this came when the government introduced bills to nationalize the bus and telephone companies. He also called for the purge of

---

[126] Mir Ashrafi, Speech, *17th Majles*, 8 March 1953.
[127] Baqai, Speech, *17th Majles*, 2 November 1952.
[128] Nasser Zolfqari, Speech, *17th Majles*, 9 December 1952.
[129] Mir Ashrafi, Speech, *17th Majles*, 29 May 1952.
[130] Qonatabadi, Speech, *17th Majles*, 5 June 1952; 13 November 1952.
[131] Qonatabadi, Speech, *17th Majles*, 11 February 1953.
[132] Qonatabadi, Speech, *17th Majles*, 10 March 1953.

women teachers from boys' schools and the removal of all French influence from the educational system.[133]

Baqai, Makki, Qonatabadi, and Haerizadeh also took turns to denounce Mossadeq for consulting petroleum experts from previous administrations and for offering to pay "compensation" to the Anglo-Iranian Oil Company.[134] "The British," Haerizadeh exclaimed, "should pay us compensate for all these years of exploitation. There is no reason we should give them any compensation. The fact that Mossadeq has agreed to give compensation proves beyond doubt that he is a British agent."[135] They further claimed that the nationalizing of private companies would set dangerous precedents and that the printing of paper money would produce runaway inflation and thus "enflame class conflicts."[136]

Baqai, seconded by Qonatabadi, constantly denounced Mossadeq – now referring to him by his defunct title of *al-saltaneh*. They accused him of protecting Qavam, a fellow aristocrat, by not imprisoning him, not confiscating his property, and not declaring him a "sower of corruption on earth."[137] They claimed the same *dastgah* (establishment) and *taba-qeh-e momtazeh* (privileged class) that had traditionally ruled Iran continued to do so under Mossadeq.[138] Mossadeq responded that the judiciary – not the legislature and the executive – had the authority to judge Qavam. Qontatabadi retorted Qavam should be promptly executed since the whole country had already found him guilty.[139] Insiders – especially in the Foreign Office – found Baqai's grandstanding somewhat rich since he had secretly supported Qavam's bid for power.

Meanwhile, Karimi Akhgar, a royalist deputy from Busher, exclaimed that the land reform bill violated property rights enshrined in the holy shari'a.[140] Baqai, however, exclaimed that it did not go far enough to meet peasant expectations.[141] He avoided explaining how he

---

[133] Ahmad Safayi, Speech, *17th Majles*, 14 August 1952; 13 November 1952.
[134] Baqai, Speech, *17th Majles*, 21 December 1952; Qonatabadi, Speech, *17th Majles*, 23 December 1952; See also Ali Shayegan, Speech, *17th Majles*, 19 September 1952.
[135] Haerizadeh, *17th Majles*, 21 May 1953.
[136] Haerizadeh, *Ettela'at*, 20 May 1953.
[137] Baqai, Speech, *17th Majles*, 23 November 1952.
[138] Haerizadeh, Speech, *17th Majles*, 27 November 1952.
[139] Qonatabadi, Speech, *17th Majles*, 2 November 1952.
[140] Karimi Akhgar, Speech, *17th Majles*, 3 August 1952.
[141] Baqai, Speech, *17th Majles*, 14 August 1952.

would improve it. At the same time, Makki, as chair of the banking committee, protested that the government was illegally printing bank notes without parliamentary permission.

These majles attacks increased after the February Crisis – especially when the Committee of Eight fully sided with the prime minister against the shah. It reported that the "monarch is exempt from responsibility," "ministers are responsible to the majles in all matters," and "all decrees must be countersigned by the responsible ministers." Mir Ashrafi not surprisingly siding with the shah, and claimed that during the war the Soviet Union had conspired with the British to force the shah out of the country. The monarchy, he claimed, had been saved in the nick of time by Zahedi and Kashani. He hailed the latter as "the real father of the constitution."[142] Baqai, Haerizadeh, and Makki – long-time critics of the Pahlavis – found excuses to absent themselves whenever the Committee of Eight tried to present its final report to the majles.

The crisis intensified on 21 April when General Mahmud Afshartous, the chief of police, was kidnapped. His badly tortured body was found six days later dumped in the wilderness outside Tehran. The kidnapping was clearly designed to destabilize the government, and send the clear message that the authorities could not protect even their top officials. Norman Darbyshire – an MI6 operator – later claimed one kidnapper had lost his temper and shot the general.[143] This, however, does not explain the badly tortured body. Investigators soon linked the murder to a network of officers associated with Baqai and Zahedi. General Nasrollah Bayondor, one of the suspects, confirmed this link.[144] The investigators also reported that "a foreigner" had been involved in the kidnapping.[145] This foreigner was probably Darbyshire. Lofti, the justice minister, requested the majles withdraw parliamentary immunity from Baqai so he could be prosecuted. Baqai – as well as Zahedi – promptly sought sanctuary inside the majles building. After the coup, Henderson remarked in passing that the new

---

[142] Mir Ashrafi, Speech, *17th Majles*, 10 March 1953.
[143] Anonymous, "Interview with Norman Darbyshire," Unpublished Transcript for ITV Film *End of Empire*. The interview was not filmed.
[144] Anonymous, "The Confession of General Bayondor," *Umid-e Iran* (Iran's Hope), 19 August 1979.
[145] *Ettela'at*, 26 June 1953.

government could at any time terminate Baqai's political career simply by releasing damaging information about the Afshartous murder.[146]

Kashani, as majles president, promptly gave sanctuary to Baqai and Zahedi, and issued periodic denouncements of the government. He criticized "Mossadeq al-Saltaneh's dictatorship" for nationalizing private companies, resorting to martial law, printing bank notes, extending special powers to twelve months, and proposing radical changes in the electoral law. "He could not understand," he proclaimed, "what men had done wrong that women should be given the vote."[147] He also took Mossadeq to task for offering to compensate the British oil company with 25 percent of annual sales for ten to fifteen years. "There is no reason," he told a Japanese journalist, "for any compensation since Britain has exploited us for over fifty years."[148] It was strange for someone in regular contact with Henderson to be denouncing Mossadeq for willingness to pay compensation. It was equally strange for Henderson to be courting Kashani while insisting that Mossadeq should let an international body determine the amount of compensation.

The crisis further intensified in June when those arrested in the February crisis – especially Sha'aban Brainless – were brought to trial. Opposition papers repeated Western insinuations that communists had infiltrated the justice ministry and put Iran on the same trajectory as Czechoslovakia. They denounced the High Court for ruling that anyone accused of political offenses, including Tudeh members, should be tried in civilian, not military, courts. Clashes erupted almost daily in the streets, especially outside the majles building. Hand grenades were even thrown into the majles gardens. And, most sensational of all, a mysterious fire destroyed the old Armenian quarter near the 200-year-old Saint Thaddeus Church close to the central Tehran bazaar. Some suspected "arson" and speculated about "political motives."[149]

By late spring of 1953, the majles had ceased to function. Deputies took turns in denouncing each other as "wolves," "crooks," "foreign agents," "hypocrites," "sinners," and "apologists for dictatorship." Makki tried to physically dislodge Razavi from the speaker's chair. Mir

---

[146] Henderson, Letter to NSC (20 October 1953), *FRUS* (2017), 799.
[147] M. Dahnowi, *Majmu'ah-e az Maktubat, Sukhanraniha va Paymanha-ye Ayatollah Kashani* (Collection of Ayatollah Kashani's Teachings, Speeches, and Messages) (Tehran: Ashna Publications, 1982), Vols. I–III.
[148] *Ettela'at*, 16 May 1953.   [149] *Ettela'at*, 16 June 1953.

Ashrafi – pistol drawn – attempted to evict an opponent and threatened to beat up Nariman. He also assaulted a Tabriz deputy calling him a dangerous *akhund* – a derogatory term for cleric. Armed guards had to intervene. Fifteen deputies, including Haerizadeh, Zohari, Faramarzi, and Mir Ashraf, joined Zahedi and Baqai in their majles sanctuary. The CIA reported that those taking sanctuary had received financial help from "unknown sources."[150] At one point the Toilers Party packed the visitors' gallery with supporters shouting "Long Live Baqai, Death to Mossadeq."[151] One deputy told the press that these shenanigans were designed to bring down the government. He specu-lated that Mossadeq would have no choice but to resort to a referendum.[152] Long periods passed without formal majles sessions. Whenever the government tried to bring an important issue – especially the report of the Committee of Eight – to the floor the opposition would head for the exit doors; or retreat to committee meetings; or introduce endless amendments; or just leave town.

The majles was unable to hold any formal sessions for much of April and May. Meanwhile, the National Front, as well as the Tudeh, organ-ized rallies outside parliament in support of the Committee of Eight. They avoided "inflammatory slogans" and instead passed resolutions in support of the committee.[153] Their main slogan was Mossadeq's old refrain: "The Shah must reign not rule." Baqai, who had signed the original report, now insinuated the government wanted to limit the monarch's authority because the shah and royal family wanted to implement "real" land reform.[154] Haerizadeh, who had also endorsed the original report, now wanted to take back his vote. A British report explained the opposition had been reduced to boycotting the majles because the Committee of Eight had concluded the "Government, not the Shah, was responsible for civil and military administration." "The approval of the report," it concluded, "would give Dr. Musaddiq complete victory over the Court."[155]

---

[150] Roosevelt, Memorandum (17 July 1953), *FRUS* (2017), 627.
[151] *Ettela'at*, 12 May 1953.   [152] *Ettela'at*, 18 May 1953.
[153] US Embassy, Report on the Majles (6 July 1953), in *FO 371*/Persia 1953/
       104568.
[154] US Embassy, Report on the Majles (29 May 1953), in *FO 371*/Persia 1953/
       104568.
[155] Foreign Office, Summary of Events in Persia, 1953, *FO 416/107*.

When it became clear that parliamentary work had ground to a complete halt, Mossadeq asked the deputies to resign. This, as a matter of course, would dissolve the 17th Majles and pave the way to elections for the 18th Majles. On 15 July, fifty-two deputies – twenty-nine from the Nahzat-e Milli caucus plus twenty-three others – resigned, depriving the assembly of any possible quorum, and, in effect, dissolving the majles. The numbers soon increased to fifty-six.[156] The opposition – counseled by the US embassy – pointed out that according to majles bylaws such resignations were not valid until ratified by the assembly itself.[157] In other words, self-proclaimed resignations were not valid in themselves. The government countered by calling for a national referendum on dissolving the majles.

To celebrate the anniversary of the July Uprising, the National Front and the Tudeh held separate rallies in Parliament Square. The National Front met in the morning. Spokesmen from the cabinet, the parliamentary caucus, the Society of Merchants, Guilds and Tradesmen, as well as the Iran Party, Pan-Iranist Party and Third Force took turns to address the crowd. *Ettela'at* described the size of the crowd as "unprecedented."[158] The Tudeh met separately that same afternoon to hear representatives from its front organizations – especially from the Peace Partisans and the Society against Imperialism. *Ettela'at* did not estimate its size but implied it rivaled the first. Both rallies called for a referendum to dissolve the majles as well as justice for Afshartous. The Tudeh rally also called for an end to martial law, lifting of the ban on the Tudeh, and a united front against "colonial enemies." The CIA, in a confidential report, estimated the Tudeh crowd to be near 50,000.[159] The *New York Times* correspondent – who later complained of being used unwittingly by the CIA – reported that the "Red Crowd" was the "biggest popular demonstration in Iran's history." He claimed it surpassed even its organizer's expectations, numbered at least 100,000 and easily dwarfed the morning one – which he reported to have been fewer than 5,000 people.[160] Clearly this

---

156 *Ettela'at*, 19 July 1953.
157 Roosevelt, Majles Politics (12 July 1953), *National Security Archives*, Document 5, Declassified on 21 June 2011.
158 *Ettela'at*, 22 July 1953.
159 CIA, Background Information on Iran, CIA Electronic Library, www.cia.gov /libraryroom/search/site/Iran.
160 Kennett Love, "100,000 Reds Rally in Iranian Capital," *New York Times*, 22 July 1953.

reportage was designed to reinforce the official line that Iran was about to fall behind the Iron Curtain.

Mossadeq address the nation with a radio broadcast on 27 July. He called for a national referendum to end the existing majles and hold immediate elections for a new one. He explained that for months he had tried hard to work with the existing majles, but disruptive "intriguers" in league with "foreign powers" had obstructed all parliamentary work. He concluded the people could determine the fate of the majles since in a "true democracy and constitutional government there was no authority above the people." He argued "since parliaments, governments, and laws are all derived from the people, the people have the right to make the ultimate decisions and even change their minds." Mossadeq, a strict constitutionalist most of his life, was now resorting to populism – but traces of this element could also be found in his long career.

Mossadeq accused the opposition of undermining the government by instigating tribal uprisings, such as the Bakhtiyari revolt, by assassinating political figures, such as Afshartous, by rioting, such at the 28 February crisis, and now by obstructing parliamentary legislation – thus necessitating a referendum.[161] Qonatabadi retorted that Mossadeq sought the referendum to distract attention from his scheme of rewarding Britain with generous "compensation."[162] He claimed the real issue was not the constitution but the scheme of sneaking in undeserved compensation. Others repeated the charge that Mossadeq was a new Goebbels – if not Hitler. They clearly did not shy away from hyperbole.

The referendum was held in Tehran on 3 August; in the provinces on 10 August. Tehran had 112 polling stations with distant separate ballot boxes for yes and no voters. By all accounts, the voting was heavy and continued into late in the day. Women appeared at some stations demanding ballots, but, according to *Ettela'at*, their votes were not counted.[163] *Ettela'at* – without comment or sense of irony – reported near 2,250,00 voted in Tehran.[164] Not surprisingly, the yes vote won overwhelmingly. Fewer than 1,500 voted no.[165] In the provinces, the

---

[161] Mossadeq, Radio Address, *Ettela'at*, 27 July 1953.
[162] *Ettela'at*, 1 August 1953.   [163] *Ettela'at*, 4 August 1953.
[164] *Ettela'at*, 30 July 1953.
[165] Foreign Office, Persia: Quarterly Political Report – July to September 1953, *FO 416/106*.

total vote was supposed to have been as much as 1,530,00 – with supposedly fewer than 700 voting no.[166] Clashes broke out in a number of places, especially in Mashed, Maragheh, and Malayer.

Immediately after the referendum the interior ministry issued preparations for the forthcoming 18th Majles. It also promised to issue immediately a new electoral law. The US embassy cabled Washington that Mossadeq had "eliminated" the parliamentary threat by successfully outwitting the majles opposition.[167] The CIA begrudgingly conceded that despite increasing parliamentary opposition, Mossadeq had continued to receive votes of confidence mainly because of his apt handling of the oil crisis.[168] Once again Mossadeq had outmaneuvered all the opposition – the shah as well as the USA and the United Kingdom. But by doing so, he had inadvertently foreclosed the "quasi-legal" strategy for regime change. Instead, he had provided the temptation for a conventional military coup d'état to bring about the required change of regime.

---

[166] *Ettela'at*, 11 August 1953.
[167] Mattison, Telegram from the Embassy (17 July 1953), *FRUS* (2017), 630.
[168] Waller, Memorandum to Roosevelt, *FRUS* (2017), 531.

4 | *The Road to the Coup*

We had admitted, as a nation, the right of a country to nationalize foreign-held properties provided they are paid for promptly and adequately. The British finally accepted the right of the Iranians to nationalize but it was rather too late. By then Mossadegh and his followers were beyond deal making. In the end, the British set out to overthrow him. In October 1952 Mossadegh discovered the plot. He ordered the British Embassy shut down and its diplomats expelled. A few weeks later the British asked the Americans to help them with a coup. The request came just after Dwight Eisenhower had been elected but before he took office. The outgoing Truman Administration opposed the idea of a coup. But Eisenhower did not.

Averell Harriman, Special Assistant to President Truman

Government Removal

Averell Harriman – troubleshooter for Presidents both Roosevelt and Truman – was a consummate diplomat. He mastered the art of giving misleading pronouncements without resorting to actual lies. He set the template for the standard picture of the coup. In addition to the claim the USA-United Kingdom had fully accepted nationalization, he left the distinct impression the Truman administration had been willing to coexist with Mossadeq but Eisenhower had made the fateful decision to overthrown him. The road to the coup, however, was more circuitous. The decision to resort to a coup came only after the Truman administration had tried and failed many times to use political means to "replace" Mossadeq. The word "replace" was often substituted for "remove." Our contemporary term would be "regime change." In other words, the coup came as a result of policies initiated under Truman well before the advent of the Eisenhower administration.

The CIA's adamant opposition to Mossadeq clearly predated his election in late April. In a long memorandum drafted a month earlier – many paragraphs remain redacted – the CIA begrudgingly admitted that Mossadeq was "too widely admired to be subject of successful attack."[1] Instead it recommended: waging an "intense propaganda campaign (by both overt and covert means) to support the Shah and Ala"; "establishing relations" with parliamentary groups; using "clandestine publications" to insinuate that Mossadeq's "conspicuous followers," such as Makki and Haerizadeh, had covert ties to the Soviet Union; splitting Baqai from the National Front; and buying off Ayatollah Kashani who "could be influenced with US money." These recommendations came even before Mossadeq was elected prime minister.

This same memo proposed intensifying "black propaganda" against the Tudeh by forging issues of its paper *Mardam* [sic] with "instructing" for an armed uprising, with list of those to be executed, and with boasts of having assassinated Razmara, the earlier prime minister. In a separate memo, the CIA mentioned that the ambassador had approved a "direct dollar subsidy" – sums remain classified – to Ala to "strengthen his hand and confound his enemies." Since the transaction was for "Eyes Only" Ala was not required to provide receipts or detailed accounting.[2] Other memos – all from the very early days of the Mossadeq administration – mention subsidies going to an unnamed anti-Tudeh organization, most probably the "Titoist" Toilers Party. They also recommended "manipulating of religious prejudices and fanaticism," and "capitalizing on personal enmity and competition among enemy leadership."[3]

Thus talk of removing Mossadeq began early in Washington as well as in London. In their dealings with the Americans, the British repeatedly stressed that negotiations with Mossadeq were a waste of time because he was "stubborn," and his nationalism was "inauthentic," "unsustainable," "unbridled," and "irresponsible."[4] As Herbert Morrison, the Labour Foreign Secretary, told the American

---

[1] CIA, Paper Prepared for Directorate of Plans (14 March 1951), *FRUS* (2017), 19–23.
[2] Wisner, Memorandum to Assistant Director of the CIA (23 April 1951), *FRUS* (2017), 69–70.
[3] CIA, Project Outline, *FRUS* (2017), 121–3.
[4] Foreign Office, Telegram to British Embassy in Washington, DC (12 October 1951), *FO 371/Persia* 1951/34–91601; Shepherd, A Comparison between Persian and Asian Nationalisms (26 September 1951), *FO 371/Persia* 1951/34–91484.

ambassador in June 1951 if the shah had any "courage" he would with the help of the army dismiss Mossadeq and dissolve parliament.[5] The British also reminded Washington that prime ministers in Iran did not remain in office long. Even before Mossadeq had formed his first cabinet, the Foreign Office suggested that the "shah should be encouraged to appoint a new government willing to negotiate reasonably."[6] It repeated the earlier suggestion that the shah should declare martial law, dissolve the majles, and appoint a new prime minister.[7]

Only three weeks into the crisis, Shepherd, the British ambassador, predicted that Mossadeq would last "only one more week" and urged the shah to "replace him" as soon as possible.[8] The Butler postmortem admits that in early June 1951, Shepherd began advocating the "unseating" of Mossadeq.[9] Shepherd told the *Wall Street Journal*, "We have learnt from years of experience out here that you must be firm with these people – especially since they are 'volatile and unstable.'"[10] The *Journal* commented that the "British would be happy to have the prime minister fall." Butler admits that the Foreign Secretary, as early as 27 June 1951, recommended "a joint Anglo-American approach to the Shah to dismiss Dr. Musaddiq. This might involve a coup d'état."

To hasten Mossadeq's "inevitable" demise, the British reacted quickly. They instructed their nationals – totaling some 2,500 oil technicians – to evacuate Iran; warned that salaries from the Iranian government would not be convertible into sterling; and prevented some 1,400 Europeans, including 400 Germans, from replacing the British technicians.[11] These measures were explicitly designed to persuade the majles to "hasten Mussadiq's removal."[12] They also reinforced their

---

[5] CIA, Current Intelligence Bulletin (28 June 1951), CIA Electronic Library, www .cia.gov/readingroom/search/site/Iran:

[6] Foreign Office, Record of Special Meeting (20 March 1951), FO 371/Persia 1951/ Persia 1951/34–91524.

[7] British Ambassador in London, Letter to the State Department (26 June 1951), *FRUS* (1989), 69–71.

[8] Shepherd, Letter to the Foreign Office (19 May 1951), FO 371/Persia 1951/34–91535.

[9] Butler, *British Policy in the Relinquishing of Abadan in 1951*.

[10] Anonymous, GB Irked at US attempts to Speed Iran Settlement (9 June 1951) in Shepherd, Dispatch (5 June 1951), FO 248/Persia 1951/1527.

[11] G. Keating, Notes of Meeting with Herr A. Stahmer (29 October 1951), FO 371/ Persia 1951/34–91617.

[12] Norman Seddon, Letter to E. G. Northcroft (29 July 1951), BP/126359.

troops in Iraq, moved warships into the Persian Gulf, staged air displays over Abadan, and drew up plans for an invasion of Khuzestan. Shepherd predicted that "Musaddiq will not remain in power much longer" and "we should be well advised to wait for his fall before starting serious negotiations."[13]

The British, moreover, imposed an economic embargo on Iran. Avoiding the term "embargo" because of its legal implications, they froze Iran's assets in the Bank of England – thereby limiting sale of such crucial goods as rubber, spare parts, and machinery. They also imposed a naval blockade to prevent the export of Iranian oil. Such measures would later be redefined as "unilateral sanctions." To give bite to the embargo, they "cornered" the tanker market, and threatened to impound tankers leaving Abadan on the grounds the oil had been "pirated." Butler boasted that the "strangulation of Persian oil exports was a major British success."[14]

What is more, the British persuaded the Americans to participate in the embargo. The Truman administration instructed American tankers as well as oil companies – both major and minor oil companies – to stay clear of Iran. It limited emergency loans to Iran to $10 million. This went to three military missions – for the army, police, and gendarmerie – and to Point IV specializing in agricultural projects. These missions came in handy during the coup. Henderson was also instructed to "read" to Mossadeq the "Battle Act" – named after a congressman. The act threatened in no uncertain terms to cut off all US aid to any country contemplating the sale of "strategic goods" to the Soviet Union and its satellites.[15]

Harriman himself, after his July 1951 mission to Tehran, came to the conclusion that a deal with Mossadeq was "impossible." But he explained it was still necessary to go through the motions of negotiating so long as the shah was reluctant to remove him. He stressed the importance of protecting "basic British interests."[16] The British, meanwhile, reported that Harriman agreed "it was impossible to deal" with

---

[13] Shepherd, Notes (30 May 1951), *FO 371/Persia 1951/34–91541*.
[14] Butler, *British Policy in the Relinquishing of Abadan in 1951*.
[15] British Embassy in Washington, Telegram to the Foreign Office (22 December 1951), *FO 371/Persia 1951/34–91616*.
[16] British Ambassador in Washington, Letter to the Foreign Office (12 September 1951), *FO 371/Persia 1951/34–1529*; Harriman, Memo to the President (19 July 1951), *FRUS* (1989), 97–8.

Mossadeq but the "situation lay in a change of government."[17] They persuaded Washington in October 1951 – immediately after Mossadeq's visit to the White House – not to increase loans to Iran, "leaving him to face his internal difficulties and avoiding any move which might allow him to claim he was negotiating for an oil settlement." Their main message was "Patience is from God and haste is from the devil."[18] They reiterated their conviction that Mossadeq would "undoubtedly be ousted if the shah and the opposition acted with determination."[19] They also noted the American press was "evolving in a healthy way" and American oil companies were well aware of the "threat Middle East nationalism posed to world-wide concessionary interests." They mentioned, in passing, that "we need to stress to Americans the dangers of communism."

Henry Grady, the departing American ambassador in 1952, privately opposed nationalization and paid lip service to the communist danger, but publicly criticized the British. In an article in the *Saturday Evening Post* entitled "What Went Wrong in Iran," he described British policy as "fatuous," "unrealistic," "impractical," "dangerous," and product of a "colonial state of mind fashionable in Queen Victoria's time."[20] He elaborated:

The British were counting right along on economic and financial pressures to get rid of Mossadegh and expected us to join them in this. The concept that financial pressures would bring the Iranian into line and solve the oil problem was from the beginning the key to the British blunders ... Their attitude was just wait until the beggars need money badly enough – that will bring them to their knees. I have heard that vapid statement so often that it began to sound like a phonography record. ... They remain wedded to force and power politics, to the notion that if they cause enough economic chaos to get rid of Mossadegh, all would be well.

In private, meanwhile, he insisted the AIOC should remain in charge, but should agree to the 50/50 sharing of profits – the formula American oil companies tried to apply throughout the world.

---

[17] British Embassy in Washington, Telegrams to Foreign Office (12–13 September 1951), FO 371/Persia 1951/91472.

[18] Foreign Office, Comment (8 December 1951), FO 371/Persia 1951/34–91616.

[19] Foreign Office, Minutes (26 November 1951), FO 371/Persia 1951/34–91615.

[20] Henry Grady, "What Went Wrong in Iran?" *Saturday Evening Post*, BP/10624.

The AIOC invited Bullard, the wartime British ambassador, to respond to Grady. Bullard obliged. He wrote that Grady ignored the benefits the AIOC had brought to Persia, and the latter should be grateful to Britain for saving the country from Russian clutches.[21] He insisted the real issue for Mossadeq was not royalties, nor nationalism, but, horror of horrors, "neutralism." He warned that "all negotiations were a waste of time" and that "Iran needs not money but face realities and get down to work instead of sitting around complaining that the British have done this or that." He went into a long digression into the nineteenth century and how Britain had "civilized" Persia. His clear message was that the Americans were misguided in thinking that Mossadeq could be persuaded into accepting a fair compromise. Bullard would have fitted well into Lytton Strachey's *Eminent Victorians*.

Such public airings of differences could be misleading. Many, including Mossadeq, jumped to the conclusion the two Western powers differed on fundamentals. In fact, both were equally opposed to real nationalization. Once the Americans realized that Mossadeq would not settle for empty nationalization, they moved even closer to the British position. In early December 1951, Henderson had a two-hour discussion with the shah on the subject of "replacing the prime minister."[22] The ambassador insisted he did not intend to interfere in internal matters but that Mossadeq "was heading the country to destruction." The shah replied that only a military coup could bring about the require change, but he could not think of a suitable person to lead such a coup and the subsequent dictatorial regime. Henderson added such a person would have to be "a man of decision, courage, organizational ability, loyalty to the Shah and also genuine interest in welfare of Iran and its people." This conversation took place a mere eight months after the start of Mossadeq's administration and nineteen months before the eventual coup.

Thus the initial American ambivalence about a coup was prompted more by the shah's reluctance and less by principles or grand strategy. In the very first blueprint for a coup, drafted in the aftermath of the July Uprising, the main CIA analyst on Iran warned in a long memorandum that the military would not act without the shah and that the shah was

---

[21] Sir Reader Bullard, "Oil Crisis in Iran," *FO* 371BP/10624.
[22] Henderson, Telegram (26 December 1951), *FRUS* (1989), 298–300.

"extremely" reluctant precisely because it would "lay him open to the charges of being a Western puppet and thus increase rather than reduce opposition to him."[23]

The CIA analyst laid out four "basic assumptions" for a successful coup: the shah must play a key role; the shah would do so only "if more or less constitutional means were adopted"; the action would need significant support from elements within the National Front; and the course of action would have to have "whole-hearted support in the army." He recommended the dispatching of a senior emissary to talk directly to the shah; the launching of an intense publicity campaign to undermine Mossadeq and present the shah as a social reformer in favor of oil nationalization; and the developing of a network of "influential military officers" eager to "carry out a coup in the Shah's name, even if they do not have his authority for such action." He concluded that the USA and United Kingdom must make "every effort to de-emphasize the oil issue" and scrupulously avoid giving any "indication that they had anything to do with the coup or considered the coup as a development favoring their interests."

Donald Wilber who drafted many of the CIA proposals and participated in the eventual overthrow, stressed that coup plans would be worthless without the shah's active participation.[24] The shah himself, however, held firm to his original conviction that Mossadeq had to be eased out through the parliamentary process – so others, rather than he, would be held responsible. He continued to tell Henderson even in late May 1953 that he would support Zahedi for the premiership only if the latter came to office through parliamentary means and not a coup – besides he was not convinced the general had the military support to pull off a coup. Henderson responded that intricate politics inside the majles made the parliamentary road difficult. In reporting his conversation with the shah, Henderson concluded with his refrain that there was "no chance of any oil settlement so long as Dr. Mosadeq was Prime Minister."[25]

---

[23] John Leavitt, Memorandum from Chief of the Iran Branch to the Director of Plans in the CIA (22 September 1952), *FRUS* (2017), 351–5.

[24] Donald Wilber, Memorandum (23 September 1952), *FRUS* (2017), 355–6.

[25] Henderson, Memorandum on Conversation (30 May 1953), *FRUS* (2017), 575–80.

Coup Plans

The CIA – chiefly Wilber – drew up more detailed plans after the February Crisis. Forty-eight hours after the crisis, Allen Dulles rushed to Eisenhower a memorandum claiming the country was on a downward spiral into the abyss of revolution. He speculated the shah could now be persuaded to act, and warned that Western "influence" was in danger of further decreasing "even without a Communist Tudeh victory."[26] In listing "assets available" for a coup, he gave prominence to the agency's station in Tehran. In the late 1940s, the station had launched a project named TPBEDAMN with the avowed goal to target the Tudeh Party. Its original chief, Roger Goiran, was transferred out when he questioned the wisdom of carrying out a coup. Despite TPBEDAMN and the claim of recruiting a high-ranking member of the party, the CIA remained remarkably ignorant of the inner workings of the Tudeh. It claimed the identity of the leaders was secret. In fact, their names and biographies had been well circulated in party newspapers. It also claimed its real mastermind was an old Bolshevik living in the Soviet Union named Sultanzadeh (Ovaness Mikaelian).[27] In fact, Sultanzadeh had been shot during the Stalinist purges.

Wilber listed other assets available for a coup: the embassy with its large staff; the three US military missions with eighty-six officers; and the CIA presence among the Qashqayis. The 1989 version of this document redacted two short sentences: "He [Mossadeq] might resent Henderson's activities": "The elimination of Mossadeq by assassination or otherwise might precipitate decisive events."[28] The plan remained silent on other "assets" such as General Gilanshah, former air force chief; Colonel Abbas Farzandegan, a staff officer with special communications training in the USA;[29] and the American community in Iran, which, according to *The Times of India*, was the largest in the Middle East. It totaled over 1,000, and included Point IV specialists,

---

[26] Allen Dulles to President Eisenhower, Memorandum on the Iranian Situation (1 March 1953), *FRUS* (2107), 469–72.

[27] State Department, Leaders and Members of the Tudeh Party (21 August 1950), OSS/State Department, *Intelligence and Research Report: The Middle East, 1950–61: Supplement Part XII*.

[28] Allen Dulles to President Eisenhower, Memorandum on the Iranian Situation (1 March 1953), *FRUS* (1989), 689–91.

[29] CIA, Monthly Report for September 1953, *FRUS* (2017), 778.

some of whom were deemed to be "spies."[30] Dulles requested a more detailed plan.

The CIA promptly presented one. It recommended the continued funding of the "network of numerous press, political, and clerical contacts" capable of disseminating large-scale "black" and "grey" propaganda.[31] It mentioned use of "poison pen, personal denunciations, and rumor mongering" to undermine any political leader, and to organize pro-shah "riots, mobs, and demonstrations, etc." It warned that such activities should not appear to be against Mossadeq. It also mentioned – without names – that it had "paid agents inside the security services."

This report appears to have been too modest to cite its most recent success – the bloody 15 July 1951 riots that had coincided with Harriman's arrival in Tehran. Months earlier, the Tudeh front organizations had announced they would hold a rally that day to commemorate the 1946 general strike in the oil industry. The rally had been assaulted by the Toilers Party, Sumka, Arya, and Sha'aban Brainless. The assault had been aided and abetted by General Zahedi, then interior minister, and General Hassan Baqai, the police chief. General Baqai, unrelated to his namesake politician, was a close Zahedi associate since they had both been interned during World War II for their links to the Third Reich.[32] The 15 July clash – the worst until then in Tehran – left 16 dead and 280 injured. One senator claimed over 100 had died.[33] Mossadeq replaced Zahedi and accused General Baqai of dereliction of duty. The shah used his influence to protect the latter at his court-martial.

The Foreign Office reported that "hooligans" from the Toilers Party were mainly responsible for the bloodshed. The CIA later boasted that their local friends, especially the Toilers Party and Sumka, were capable of sparking such riots even though their membership was "limited."[34] It touted the riot as a great success. It had created the impression the country was in the midst of a major crisis and the government was

---

[30] G. K. Reddy, "Iranian Round-Up," *Times of India*, 1–3 June 1953.

[31] CIA, Capabilities of CIA Clandestine Services in Iran (3 March 1953), *FRUS* (2017), 472–4.

[32] Roy Melbourne, Anti-Tudeh Campaign (5 November 1953), *FRUS* (2017), 824.

[33] Kemal Hedayat, Speech, *1st Senate*, 31 July 1951.

[34] Wilber, *Overthrow of Premier Mossadeq of Iran, November 1952–August 1953*, Appendix B, 20.

incapable of keeping order. It had highlighted the supposed communist "danger." It had put the Tudeh in bad light by making them appear rude towards "national guests."[35] More important, it had shown the CIA was capable of challenging the Tudeh on its own turf – in the streets. The CIA claimed the riot had "raised morale" and had shown effective opposition to the Tudeh.[36]

Two CIA operatives had helped the riot. Roosevelt named them the "Boscoe Brothers" – nicknamed after the milk-chocolate drink. Their cover names were Cilley and Nerren; their true names were Farrokh Keyvani and Ali Jalali. Both had ties with Baqai's Toilers Party and Sumka, and claimed connections with the *zurkhanehs* in southern Tehran. According to Roosevelt, they spoke German, had business connections in Hamburg, and years earlier received espionage training from an unnamed foreign agency.[37] During the war, the British had detained Jalali for disseminating pro-Nazi propaganda.[38] When they began working for the CIA, the two agreed to take the required poly-graph test on condition they would not be asked about their previous espionage training. No polygraph was needed to uncover the mystery.

The 15 July "success" was followed by the 5 December *Ghaeleh* (Uproar). On that day, the Tudeh student organization led a procession from Tehran University to parliament to protest curriculum changes. The procession was assaulted by the Toilers Party, Aya, Sumka, and Sha'aban Brainless. Sha'aban worked so closely with the police that he was now dubbed *temsar* (general). In the clashes, Saedi Theatre and newspaper offices associated with the Tudeh were ransacked. In all, over fifty were injured before order was reestablished. Opposition deputies used the incident to claim the government should resign since it was incapable of preserving law and order. Mossadeq appeared personally on the majles floor and reminded the deputies that they if they were dissatisfied with his administration they had the right to call for a no-confidence vote. They declined to do so. Outside, one Fedayan

[35] CIA, Current Strength of the Tudeh Party (13 September 1951), *FRUS* (2017), 132–4.

[36] CIA, Intelligence Memorandum (13 September 1951), CIA Electronic Library, www.cia.gov/library/readingroom/search/site/Iran.

[37] Roosevelt, *Countercoup*, 79, 91–4, 98, 165.

[38] Hamid Ahmadi, *Asrar-e Kudeta (Coup Secrets)* (Tehran: Ney Publications, 2001), 35.

leader denounced him as a "hysterical old man," "bloodthirsty," and "mad with syphilis (*divaneh-e sifilytyk*)."[39]

The CIA also established ties with Neru-ye Sevum (Third Force) – a new but small Marxist offshoot from the Toilers Party. Khalel Maleki, a veteran socialist who had broken from the Toilers Party and created his own organization immediately after the July Uprising when it became obvious Baqai was working against Mossadeq. A prominent member of the Third Force mentions, without realizing its implication, that a journalist named Ali Jalali – one of the Boscoe Brothers – financed the new organization claiming the money came from businessmen fearful of the Tudeh.[40] The new "Titoists," like their parent organization, seem to have been linked wittingly or unwittingly to the CIA.

The Third Force did its very best to sow friction between the Tudeh and the National Front. It adamantly opposed – against Mossadeq's wishes – any joint Tudeh-National Front rallies. Its organ, *Neru-ye Sevum*, praised Marshall Tito and reprinted articles from Western journals denouncing the Soviet Union – articles on the Stalinist Purges as well as Andre Gide's famous travels in Russia. It translated articles from *Newsweek* and *Time* stressing the worldwide communist danger. It even claimed that the Soviet ambassador was meeting secretly with the shah, that the Tudeh was scheming to support the shah, AIOC, and General Eisenhower, and that the Mossadeq administration was under siege from a joint attack from the communists, the royalists, and such *monafeqin* (hypocrites) as Baqai, Kashani and Haerizadeh.[41] On the morning of the coup, it raised the alarm that the main threat to Iran now came not from the shah and army but from the Tudeh.[42] This fitted nicely into CIA plans to sow dissension among government supporters. In a confidential report on the National Front, Pyman, the British counsellor, wrote that for some time "our friends have been trying to win over Khalel Maleki."[43]

---

[39] Rahnema, *Religious Forces*, 586.

[40] Masoud Hejazi, *Dovedad-ha va Davari-e Khaterat* (Memory's Runs and Judgments) (Tehran: Golshin Publications, 1999), 54.

[41] *Neru-ye Sevum*, 6 March–19 August 1953. See especially Editorial, *Neru-ye Sevum*, 8 August 1953; and article, "People of Iran be Aware," *Neru-ye Sevum*, 19 August 1953.

[42] Hejazi, *Memory's Runs*, 681; *Neru-ye Sevom*, 19 August 1953.

[43] Pyman, Confidential (20 September 1951), FO 248/1514.

The CIA coup blueprints also emphasized the importance of "grey propaganda" – probably because this was part of Wilber's own specialty. The CIA in Washington would write articles, and then have them translated and planted in compliant papers in Iran. One such article declared:[44]

As long as foreigners have been coming to Iran – since the days of Shah Abbas – they have written many flattering things about Iranians in their books published in Italy, Germany, France and England. They compliment us highly and listed us as the most polite people in the world and among the most hospitable. They told their readers in Europe and America that we are polite to visitors and very tolerant of men of different race and religion ... But what has happened in Iran since the dictator Mossadegh made an alliance with the Soviet Tudeh Party? In place of our traditional friendliness, politeness, and hospitality, Iranians are becoming rude and unfriendly. Some of our people have been insulting foreigners on our streets. In place of our traditional tolerance, Iranians are acting increasingly hateful towards people who are different. Ever since the alliance between the dictator Mossadegh and the Tudeh Party, Iranians have been less polite, less hospitable, and less tolerant. Iranians have been rude, rough, and unfriendly. Many of our people are acting more like Bolsheviks than like Iranians. Dictator Mossadegh, you are corrupting the character of the Iranian people.

In mid-April 1953, the CIA presented a more detailed coup plan. Its main author was again Wilber.[45] The fourteen-page plan spelled out steps to take to undermine the government. Over one hundred lines of the document remain classified. It built on the following "assumptions": that "Mossadegh must go"; that Zahedi was the only figure with chance of pulling off a successful coup; that Zahedi needed the shah's "energetic support" since the monarch had a following among younger officers; that Soviet reaction would be "limited in nature"; that Zahedi was anxious to "settle the oil issue"; that the future oil offer should *appear* (italics in the original) more generous than previous ones and should drop insistence on compensation for future losses; and, finally, that Zahedi would include in his cabinet not only US-approved candidates but also exclude Kashani supporters. The plan mentioned in passing that any attempts to bring down the government

---

[44] CIA, *National Security Archives*, Document 20, Declassified 21 June 2011.
[45] CIA, Memorandum from Chief of Iran Branch (John Waller) to Chief of the Near East and African Division (Roosevelt): Factors Involved in the Overthrow of Mossadeq, *FRUS* (2017), 523–37.

through political means, especially in the majles, were unlikely to succeed. The CIA held on to its earlier premise that Zahedi lacked his own real "source of power." After the coup he boasted, "I came in on a tank and if necessary I will go out on a tank."[46] Wilber, however, points out that the "intent was to present Zahedi with a concrete plan in which each one knew exactly what specific action was required of him" mainly because "Persians tended to be long-winded and illogical."[47] He adds: "Zahedi appeared lacking in drive, energy, and concrete plans. The station concluded that he must be closely guided and that the necessary plans must be made for him."[48]

The blueprint also weighed the strengths and weaknesses of the entities involved – Zahedi, the shah, the army, the tribes, the religious leaders, and the various political parties. The CIA was clearly divided over Zahedi. It noted his support was limited to the Association of Retired Army Officers even though he claimed the backing of Kashani, Qavam protégées, royal courtiers, leading merchants, and the "majority of the people [sic]" (emphasis in the original). It stressed Zahedi would not even contemplate a coup without US backing and without the shah's "whole hearted support." It explained that commissioned officers would not follow Zahedi without the shah's endorsement. Wilber soon discovered Zahedi "possessed almost no military assets."[49] On the eve of the coup, the CIA station warned that Zahedi was not only "vague in his thinking," but also lacked "guts," "stature," and "forceful leadership qualities." It stressed "every effort should be made to stimulate his ambition and maintain his morale."[50] Wilber, however, depicted him as "pro-American" and a "man of courage," but "venal" and lacking followers among field commanders.[51] Despite these misgivings, the CIA concluded Zahedi would be the best person to lead since he was the "main contender for power and appears to have the widest local support." It cited one unnamed source as describing him as "competent, energetic, aggressive, and patriotic."[52] A later CIA history noted:

[46] CIA, Replacement of Prime Minister Indicated (23 January 1955), www.cia.gov /readingroom/search/site/Iran.
[47] Wilber, *Overthrow of Premier Mossadeq*, 19.
[48] Wilber, *Overthrow of Premier Mossadeq*, 27.
[49] Wilber, *Overthrow of Premier Mossadeq*, Appendix D, 3.
[50] CIA, Memorandum (23 July 1953), *FRUS* (2017), 635.
[51] Wilber, *Overthrow of Premier Mossadeq*, Appendix E, 6.
[52] John Waller, Memorandum from the Chief of the Iran Branch (16 April 1952), *FRUS* (2017), 527.

"Although a staunch anti-Communist, the CIA thought him like all Iranians on the political scene to be not noted for honesty, certainty, reliability, and strength of convictions."[53] One CIA history reveals that the Tehran office was advised to find a "substitute" since Zahedi had a "negative background" and that his career had "nearly as many minuses as pluses."[54] Clearly, the pickings were slim.

The Wilber blueprint also dismissed as negligible the street clout of Baqai, Sumka, Arya, and even Kashani. Small shopkeepers, the memo noted, support not Kashani but Mossadeq, and continue to "admire him for his strong stand against the British and as a symbol of resurgent nationalism." "This element, however, is of no practical value unless effectively organized and led." The blueprint concluded by emphasizing that to avoid the Qavam fiasco the coup would have to prevent the appearance in the streets of Tudeh and pro-Mossadeq "mobs." It stressed "all available assets engaged in the operation" of overthrowing Mossadeq should concentrate on the dual task of building up the pro-shah "mobs" and weakening the ability of the Tudeh and Mossadeq to call out theirs. It clearly identified the key to success would be to prevent Mossadeq from mobilizing his mass support into the streets.

The CIA was instructed to work closely with the British Secret Intelligence Service (SIS) – better known as MI6. The latter had ready-made plans named BOOT. The CIA and MI6 convened a joint meeting in Cyprus in April. The British brought to the table their clandestine MI6 assets since they had lost all their diplomatic presence. Their many consulates – in Ahwaz, Bushire, Khorramshahr, Kermanshah, Shiraz, Isfahan, Mashed, Rasht, and Tabriz – had been closed down in January 1952. And their Tehran embassy had met the same fate that October when diplomatic relations had been broken. The MI6 network, nevertheless, survived mainly because Norman Darbyshire, their young Persian-speaking operative, managed to continue going in and out of the country. Their network included Colonel Hassan Akhavi, who, as longtime G-2 chief, personally knew many field commanders. Hussein Fardoust, the shah's childhood friend and future intelligence chief, later described Akhavi as the "real Iranian brain behind the

---

[53] Koch, *"Zendebad Shah!" The Central Intelligence Agency and the Fall of Iranian Prime Minister Mohammed Mossadeq August 1953*, 18.
[54] CIA, *Battle for Iran* (Washington, DC: Middle East Department, n.d.), 26–9.

coup."[55] Ever since 1941, he had worked closely with MI6 and General Arfa to keep leftist officers out of sensitive positions.

The MI6 network included Suleiman Behboudi, chief of court protocol; Ahmad Human, deputy chief of court protocol; Perron, the shah's friend from Switzerland – Perron had ties also with the CIA; Shahpour Reporter, a Zoroastrian from Delhi working as correspondent for the London *Times* – he was knighted immediately after the coup; General Nasserollah Mobadder, the recently appointed chief of police; and, most important, the three Rashidian brothers (Sheifollah, Gadrollah, and Assadollah), who, with businesses in London, regularly transmitted funds to majles deputies, journalists, bazaar businessmen, and pro-British politicians such Sayyed Ziya. The latter, in turn, kept in touch with Kashani, who, despite his public Anglophobia, was more than willing to deal privately with such prominent Anglophiles. The Rashidians also cultivated ties with such gang leaders as Tayyeb, Sha'aban, and Hassan Arab. The CIA described them as "low grade mobsters."[56] The British, in addition, had outside Iran a number of experienced Persian-speaking advisers – some had served at various times as embassy counsellors. They included Lambton, Zaehner, Pyman, Falle, Middleton, and Colonel Geoffrey Wheeler. The poet Basil Bunting, who had served as vice consul in Isfahan during the war, remained in Tehran during the oil crisis as special correspondent for the London *Times*.[57] He had probably helped arrange Dylan Thomas' visit to Abadan in the last days of AIOC presence there.

According to Wilber, the most valuable asset MI6 brought to Cyprus was their detailed biographies of top military officers. Surprisingly, the USA, despite the three military missions, had no such biographies. The most important lesson Wilber drew from the whole experience was the need to compile for other countries similar lists of Who's Who. In his words, the agency needed to collect personal information, "however trivial," on "who the officer is, what makes him tick, who his friends are, etc ... It is vital to have as detailed biographical information as possible on all military personnel whose presence might bear upon the problem, including possible enemies as well as friends."[58] He admitted

---

[55] Hussein Fardoust, *Khaterat* (Memoirs) (Tehran: Ettela'at Publications, 1982).

[56] CIA, Monthly Report for October, *FRUS* (2017), 780.

[57] Keith Alldritt, *The Poet as Spy: The Life and Wild Times of Basil Bunting* (London: Aurum Press, 1998).

[58] Wilber, *Overthrow of Premier Mossadeq*, Appendix E, 1–10.

that while the CIA declined to share the identity of the Boscoes with MI6, the British were more than willing to follow the lead of the Americans since the latter were "better equipped in the way of funds, personnel, and facilities." He also admitted the Rashidians outdid the Boscoes in their working relations with *zurkhaneh* gang leaders.[59]

Wilber presented an expanded version of his blueprint in early June. He later incorporated this into his CIA report entitled *Overthrow of Premier Mossadeq of Iran, November 1952–August 1953*. This work, intended for internal use only, may not have progressed through agency publishing channels. The copy leaked to the *New York Times* in 2000 was probably the author's own first draft; it contains many typos and misspellings.[60] Now famous as the Wilber Report, it totals over 175 pages and remains the closest to a primary source on the coup. Of course, Wilber respected obvious limitations. He censored himself when necessary, observing the taboo on diplomats and cloak-and-dagger missions, and avoiding putting on paper specific information about bribe recipients and political assassinations.[61]

The CIA and MI6, as well as the State Department and the Foreign Office, approved the final plan in late June 1953. According the Wilber, Eisenhower put his signature on the plan in mid-July; no such signature has been found.[62] Eisenhower may have preferred to keep presidential hands clean. The final plan combined MI6's BOOT with CIA's original TPBEDAMN to create a larger operation codenamed AJAX – an inauspicious title since Homer's hero of the same name had met an unfortunate and untimely end. To provide the operation with the requisite anti-Tudeh Party veneer it was retitled TPAJAX.

The actual directive for the operation interestingly contained little on the Tudeh and communism. Entitled "Campaign to Install Pro-Western Government in Iran," it instructed the CIA to use "legal, or quasi-legal, methods to replace the Mossadeq government with a pro-Western one under the Shah's leadership, with Zahedi as Prime Minister."[63] It further instructed the CIA to: "launch an intensive

---

[59] Wilber, *Overthrow of Premier Mossadeq*, Appendix B, 20.
[60] Wilber, *Overthrow of Premier Mossadeq*, Appendix C, 10.
[61] Tim Weiner, "CIA Plotted Killing of 58 in Guatemala," *New York Times*, 18 May 1997.
[62] Editorial Note, *FRUS* (2017), 602.
[63] CIA, Memorandum Prepared in the Directorate of Plans (11 July 1953), *FRUS* (2017), 910–2.

propaganda campaign to disenchant the Iranian population with the myth of Mossadeq's patriotism"; "conduct a 'war of nerves' against Mossadeq designed to reveal to the general populace that increased economic aid would not be forthcoming"; and "develop covertly and independently a military apparatus within the Iranian Army which could be counted on to back up any legal actions taken by the Shah to remove Mossadeq."

The plan contained four parts. The first directed the CIA to "weaken" the government through "grey" and "black" propaganda. "Grey" propaganda meant planting articles and cartoons in some twenty publications. These publications probably included *Kayhan* (The World), *Shahed* (Witness), *Atesh* (Fire), *Farman* (Decree), *Mellat-e Iran* (National of Iran), *Seda-ye Mardom* (People's Voice), *Dad* (Justice), *Mellat-e Ma* (Our Nation), *Mard-e Asiya* (Man of Asia), *Asiya-e Javanan* (Youth's Asia), *Aram* (Named after a Zoroastrian God), *Tolu* (Sunrise), *Shalaq* (Whip), *Mehr-e Mellat* (Nation's Sun), *Nabard-e Mellat* (National Struggle), *Neday-e Sepehr* (Sepehr's Voice), and *Setareh-e Islam* (Star of Islam). *Kayhan*, the country's second largest daily, was subsidized by the shah and owned by the Faramarzi family – two of whose members sat in the majles.

The planted articles accused the government of corruption, misman-agement, leniency towards communists, and rejection of "reasonable" offers on the oil dispute. One article insinuated that Mossadeq had Jewish ancestry; another that Fatemi, the foreign minister, was an apostate who had converted first to Bahaism and then Christianity. This could have earned him two separate death sentences from reli-gious fanatics. Not surprisingly, the Fedayan shot and wounded him seriously, requiring him to go Germany for medical treatment. The CIA plan did not name names but explicitly stated that the "Fedayan-e Islam should be encouraged to threaten direct action against govern-ment deputies."[64]

"Black propaganda" meant circulating pamphlets and provoking actions under the name of the Tudeh Party. These included placing bombs outside homes of clerical leaders; handing out broadsheets promising to "execute" them "after the revolution"; ridiculing their beliefs in a major pamphlet entitled *Negahbanan-e Sehre-Jadu*

---

[64] CIA, Preliminary Operation Plan for TPAJAX (6 June 1953), *FRUS* (2017), 586–7.

(Guardians of Sorcery); and "leaking" documents that "revealed secret agreements" between the Tudeh and the government. Wilber, whose specialty was forgery and "psychological warfare," tends to give undue prominence to this component of the coup. A royalist book relates that *Atesh* translated from the American paper *This Week* reminiscences by a supposed Russian defector named Vassilov who claimed the Tudeh not only "controlled" the National Front but also had secret ties to the British. The supposed defector also claimed that the Soviet ambassador during the July Uprising had threatened the shah and distributed free food to the street protestors.[65] Years later, Ayatollah Montazeri remembered that the newspaper editor most active mailing poison letters to the clergy turned out to have dubious foreign links – but not to the Tudeh and the Soviets.[66]

The coup plan's second component proposed that the US government itself should wage a simultaneous "intense war of nerves." It should openly withhold economic assistance; damper prospects of further oil negotiations; and keep out of Iran senior diplomats such as its ambassador, Point IV director, and Secretary of State. It should amplify pronouncement about the "deteriorating economic situation" and the "increasing danger of communism." The media, led by the *New York Times*, *Time*, and *Newsweek*, fully obliged. The *New York Times*, in an editorial entitled "Mossadegh Plays with Fire," declared: "We now know he is a power-hungry, personally ambitious, ruthless demagogue who is trampling over the liberties of his own people ... He is encouraging the Tudeh and is following policies which will make the Communists more and more dangerous."[67]

The third component proposed the secret dispatch of an influential emissary to privately persuade – if necessary pressure – the shah to participate in the coup. The following were seriously considered for the mission: Princess Ashraf, the shah's twin – Wilber considered her "forceful and scheming"; George Allen, the wartime ambassador in Tehran; Kermit Roosevelt himself; McGhee, Truman's special oil negotiator – this choice belies the notion that Democrats opposed the coup; and Brigadier General Norman Schwarzkopf, the former head of the

---

[65] *Atesh* Paper, *Qeyam dar Rah-e Saltanat* (Uprising for the Monarchy) (Tehran: Atesh Publications, 1954), 30–2.
[66] Hussein-Ali Montazeri, *Matn-e Kamel-e Khaterat* (Text of Complete Memoirs) (Sweden: Baran Press, 2000), 83.
[67] Editorial, "Mossadegh Plays with Fire," *New York Times*, 15 August 1953.

US gendarmerie mission in Iran. Schwarzkopf was preferred, but accepted only after being promoted to rank of full general. The shah eventually met Schwarzkopf and Roosevelt, as well as General Pollard, the head of the current US Military Mission. Princess Ashraf, who had been forced into exile in Paris after the July Uprising, was induced to fly back to Tehran. She later claimed the shah had refused to see her.

The pressure was designed to persuade the reluctant shah to sign either one *farman* or two *farmans* replacing Mossadeq with Zahedi – thus providing the coup with a dubious but "quasi-constitutional" cover.[68] The shah was to be told in no uncertain terms that if he did not cooperate "US-UK backing would cease and his dynasty would fall." The main aim of the emissaries would be to convey to the shah the seriousness of the "implications" if he failed to cooperate. To reassure the shah the future premier would not pose a threat, Zahedi agreed to sign an undated letter of resignation.[69]

The fourth, and most important, component of the blueprint required the CIA to draw up for Zahedi a detailed "plan of action." He, as prime minister, was to name a new chief of staff, who, in turn, was to instruct tank commanders to come out of barracks and take over the key points in the capital – the prime minister's home, the radio station, the telephone-telegraph office, and the headquarters of the chiefs of staff. For the plan to succeed, the streets had to be empty of Tudeh and National Front crowds. Miles Copeland of the CIA was dispatched to Tehran to carry out a "feasibility study." Copeland claims in his memoirs he had recently pulled off a successful coup in Syria by personally starting a gunfight in central Damascus and thus inducing tanks into the heart of the city.[70] The Syrian coup had taken place under the Truman administration. Wilber mentions in this report that his study would include an annex listing the names of all officers, journalists, majles deputies, and clergymen involved in the overthrow of Mossadeq.[71] No such annex, however, appears in the leaked document. It was either not completed or remains hidden.

After the coup, Wilber drafted for the NSC a brief on the CIA's success in using "legal and quasi-legal methods to effect the fall of

---

[68] Wilber, *Overthrow of Premier Mossadeq*.
[69] Foreign Office, US Report on Iran (7 April 1953), FO 371/Persia 1953/104564.
[70] Miles Copeland, *The Game Player: Confessions of the CIA's Original Political Operative* (London: Aurum Press, 1989), 190.
[71] Wilber, *Overthrow of Premier Mossadeq*, Appendix B, 29.

Mossadeq."[72] He summarized how the USA had "launched an intense propaganda campaign" to disenchant the Iranian people with the myth of Mossadeq's patriotism and to expose the government's collaboration with the communists; how it had waged an "intense war of nerves" by "revealing to the populace that economic aid would not be forthcoming"; and, most important of all, how it had "developed a covert military operation within the Iranian army."[73]

The Wilber plan was fine-tuned first in Beirut in early June with the help of operatives from Tehran; and further fine-tuned in New York, London, and Washington by representatives from both the CIA and MI6. Henderson flew in to attend the Washington meeting.[74] He "categorically stated" that the shah's "active" and "energetic" participation was vital for success, but to obtain this it would be necessary to exert extreme pressure in the form of making it clear to him that the USA was seriously contemplating his replacement with one of his brothers, perhaps Prince Ghulam Reza. Wilber noted cryptically: "From the very beginning it had been recognized that the Shah must be forced to play a specific role, however, reluctant he might be ... The measures were also intended to produce such pressure on the Shah that it would be easier for him to sign the papers required of him than it would be to refuse." Meanwhile, the shah's other brother, Ali-Reza, who had some following among younger officers, was in Tehran threatening to "act on his own if the shah did not do so."[75]

At the Washington meeting Henderson speculated that the influential Amini brothers could also be enlisted since they had privately indicated dissatisfaction with the government. General Mahmud Amini was chief of the gendarmerie; Abdul-Qassem Amini had recently replaced Ala as minister of court; and Ali Amini, the future minister of finance, had considerable influence with fellow old-time politicians. At the end of the meeting, Henderson suddenly interjected his remark that the CIA should not contemplate assassinating Mossadeq. This may have been prompted by a small paragraph in the plan urging the

---

[72] CIA, Campaign to Install Pro-Western Government in Iran (8 March 1954), *FRUS* (2017), 910–12.

[73] CIA, Campaign to Install Pro-Western Government in Iran (8 March 1954), *FRUS* (2017), 912.

[74] Waller, Memorandum of Conversation (6 June 1953), *FRUS* (2017), 583–7.

[75] CIA, Zahedi Campaign to Replace Prime Minister Mossadeq (17 April 1953), *FRUS* (2017), 542.

Fedayan to assassinate pro-Mossadeq politicians. It may have also been prompted by a recent CIA booklet on political assassinations.[76] In fact, the taboo word was now cropping up every so often. For example, the military attaché in Tehran – the main link with the army officers – informed Washington that Ardasher Zahedi, the general's son employed by Point IV, had stressed the importance of the CIA paying "special attention" to General Riyahi, Mossadeq's chief of staff. He advised assassinating him if he could not be recruited or persuaded to change "his attitude."[77] The Washington meeting ended with the firm decision that Henderson should absent himself from Tehran in the weeks before the coup – both to distance the State Department from the coup, and to fuel the "war of nerves" against Mossadeq.

The shah saw two special emissaries – Roosevelt and Schwarzkopf – but did not sign on until 10 August. He insisted he was not an "adventurer" and "risk taker" willing to gamble away his throne. According to Wilber, he agreed only when Colonel Akhavi – his former G-2 chief – provided him with the actual names of some forty line-commanders willing to act. The shah, who had dismissed Zahedi's boasts, took Akhavi's assurances more seriously. General Fardoust, shah's childhood friend who later became his chief security adviser, described Akhavi as the "real brain" on the Iranian side of the coup.[78] Historians eager to downplay the CIA role in the coup could focus on Akhavi. Unfortunately for them, Akhavi had a nervous breakdown after the failure of the first coup attempt. He was persuaded by Mossadeq's chief of staff, who happened to be an old friend, not to blow out his own brains. On the day of the successful coup, Akhavi was sedated in hospital.

Wilber does not provide the names on Akhavi's list, but they probably included some deputy brigade commanders in the five bases in the Tehran region – especially Lieutenant Colonels Ali Mohammad Rouhani, Zand Karimi, Farhang Khosrowpanah, Mohammad Yousefi, and Iskandar Azmudeh. They also probably included some majors and captains in those barracks.[79] A later CIA history mentions

---

[76] CIA, *A Study of Assassination* (West Virginia: Shadow Warrior Publications, n.d.).

[77] Military Attaché, Memorandum (11 June 1953), *FRUS* (2017), 587.

[78] Fardoust, *Memoirs*.

[79] A contemporary source provides many of the names: Anonymous, "From 15th to 19th August," *Salnameh-e Donya*, Vol. X (1954), 117–27.

that the US military attachés had confirmed the suspicion that most line officers would obey the shah rather than anyone else.[80] Few of these forty officers received much credit in the years after the coup.

The CIA also established contact with Colonel Timour Bakhtiyar, the military commander in Kermanshah; Colonel Vali Qarani, the military commander in Rasht; Colonel Ghulam Hussein Oveissi, the acting commander of the Imperial Guards at Baq-e Shah (Royal Gardens); General Modabber, the chief of police in Tehran; Colonel Akbar Dadestan, the shah's cousin who immediately after the coup was promoted and appointed military governor of Tehran; Colonel Darakhshan, member of the Qajar family; and General Mohammad Daftari, the commander of the Custom Guards – Daftari was Mossadeq's grandnephew. CIA dispatches indicate Zahedi had met secretly with both Modabber and Daftari.[81]

The coup plan was surprisingly simple. The shah would sign a *farman* or *farmans* dismissing Mossadeq and naming Zahedi as prime minister. The sources sometimes use the singular, sometimes the plural. Colonel Nematollah Nasseri, the Imperial Guard com-mander, would deliver the *farman* dismissing Mossadeq at his home late in the night of 15 August. He would arrive with a convoy of troops – trucks and armored vehicles – in case Mossadeq resisted. At the same time, three other convoys would set out: one to arrest cabinet ministers sharing a Shemiran summerhouse in northern Tehran; one, led by General Nader Batmanqalech, the designated chief of staff, to secure the military staff headquarters in central Tehran; and one headed by Colonel Azmudeh to occupy the central post and telegraph offices. The plan included a list of those to be promptly arrested: Mossadeq, his ministers, and close advisers; National Front leaders; sixty Tudeh activists; and key military officers, including surprisingly General Modabber, the police chief, and Colonel Ashrafi, a brigade commander in Tehran. The CIA explained that Modabber and Ashrafi were included in the list because their allegiances were "uncertain" despite their contacts with Zahedi.[82]

[80] Koch, *"Zendebad Shah!"* 29.
[81] CIA, Memorandum (22 July 1953), *FRUS* (2017), 631–2; CIA, Telegram (17 August 1953), *FRUS* (2017), 671–2.
[82] CIA, Memo from Acting Chief of Near East Division (22 July 1953), *FRUS* (2017), 631.

According to the plan, Batmanqalech, as chief of staff, would promptly order tank officers to drive their vehicles out of the five barracks and take over strategic points in the capital. Success hinged on this movement into central Tehran. Soon after the July Uprising, General Riyahi, Mossadeq's trusted chief of staff, had set up what the CIA feared was an almost coup-proof system. He had broken up the large Tehran garrison into five separate brigades – two heavily armored and three lightly armored mountain brigades. The armored contained heavy M4 (Sherman) tanks. He placed the five brigades in five separate barracks – at Saltanatabad, Qasr, Eshratabad, Mahabad, and Jamshidieh. Of these, Saltanatabad, in northern Tehran on the Shemiran Road, was the most crucial; it contained an armored brigade with twenty-four tanks, including twelve Shermans. Riyahi also removed all tanks from the Imperial Guards in the Royal Gardens.

Even more crucial, Riyahi entrusted command of the brigades to full colonels he trusted – Colonels Rostam Nowzari, Nasser Shahrokh, Hussein Ali Ashrafi, Ali Parsa, and Ezatollah Momtaz. All tank officers, including seconds in command, had to have signed written permission from their brigade commanders before they could obtain fuel and ammunition, and move vehicles out of barracks. Of these five colonels, Ashrafi was in touch with MI6, but for reasons best known to himself he sat out the coup. This earned him, on one hand, a prison sentence after the coup, and, on the other hand, the aura of being a true patriot. Nowrazi, the Saltanatabad commander, was arrested after the failed coup on August 16 on suspicion of having contacts with Nasseri. Wilber, unaware of Ashrafi's and Nowrazi's connections, described Riyahi's set up as a major obstacle to the coup. To short circuit it, the coup plan required a higher authority, the chief of staff, to bypass the brigade colonels and send orders directly to seconds in command – some of whom were lieutenant colonels and majors in Akhavi's list.

Failed Coup

The original plan went haywire. Mystified, Wilber blamed "typical Iranian inefficiency." Unknown to the CIA – despite the fact it was probably monitoring the prime minister's home from Point IV offices next door – Mossadeq had been tipped off through his wife's private phone. Captain Mehdi Homayuni, an Imperial Guard selected by Nasseri to accompany him on his midnight mission, happened to belong to the secret Organization of Tudeh Military Officers. He had immediately informed his superiors, who, in turn, had informed Nuraldin Kianouri of the Tudeh central committee. Kianouri, in turn, had promptly informed Mossadeq through his wife's private phone. His wife and Mossadeq's were close relatives and often spoke on their own phone lines. Once assured that Kianouri's information was precise and reliable, Mossadeq had instructed Riyahi to rush tanks to both his own residence and to the staff headquarters in central Tehran.

Consequently, when Nasseri and Batmanqalech reached their assigned destinations they found themselves confronted by tanks. Riyahi had placed two tanks outside the premier's home and another two outside staff headquarters. Nasseri was immediately arrested; Mossadeq dismissed the *farman* as a forgery arguing that the royal signature was grossly misplaced. He also argued the shah would not have signed such a decree since he lacked the constitutional authority to dismiss a duly elected prime minister. Batmanqalech, according to Wilber, "lost heart" when he saw the tanks and abandoned his mission. Homayuni was arrested together with Nasseri and immediately after the coup was promoted to the rank of a major. But two years later, unmasked as a Tudeh member, he was sentenced first to death and then to life imprisonment. He lived to tell his tale after the 1979 revolution.[83] A CIA history describes this midnight venture as "a conventional military takeover, reinforced by the Shah's signed orders."[84]

With Nasseri and Batmanqalech arrested, Farzandegan, who was in charge of communications, promptly informed Cyprus that the coup had failed for unknown reasons. He, together with Gilanshah, the two Zahedis, and the three Rashidians, took shelter in "safe houses" provided by the American embassy. The authorities, meanwhile, rounded up Perron, Human, Behboudi, Amini, and Colonel Nowzari, commander of Saltanatabad barracks.

Meanwhile, the shah together with his wife, a pilot, and one attendant flew first to Bagdad, then to Rome. In a press interview in Bagdad the shah claimed that he had issued a "letter" appointing Zahedi as

---

[83] Hamid Ahmadi, "Interview with Mehdi Homayuni," *Iranian Oral History Project* (Berlin: 1990). See also Nuraldin Kianouri, *Khaterat* (Memoirs) (Tehran, 1992), 246–66; Serge Barseqian, "Tudeh Party Gave Information about the Coup to Mossadeq," *Sharvand-e Emruz*, 13 August 2011.

[84] CIA, *Battle for Iran*, 57.

prime minister and that Mossadeq had acted unconstitutionally by arresting Nasseri. Taking US advice, he avoided the word "coup." The CIA suggested that if the word was used it should be applied to Mossadeq's actions. Privately the shah claimed that Roosevelt himself had advised sudden departure if unexpected difficulties arouse. The CIA, however, telegraphed Baghdad:

Had the Shah remained in place and not run away – and backed up Zahedi with his presence and his affirmation of sincerity – the change of government would have been effective in the first instant. The failure is in very part attributed to the fact that the Shah departed suddenly leaving behind only pieces of paper which are not very meaningful or powerful.[85]

Immediately after 15 August, some embassy officials in Tehran "gave up hope" and "strongly recommended discontinuing operations."[86] Their recommendation was conveyed to Washington; one cabinet member, in Eisenhower's words, suggested temporarily "snuggling up" to Mossadeq.[87] But Roosevelt, supported by the Zahedis, Rashidians, and Gilanshah, strongly disagreed. They argued that since only the "quasi-constitutional" part of the plan had failed and the main military component remained fully intact the enterprise should continue – with some improvisations. Informants within the Iranian G-2 assured them that their military networks remained "completely clean" and the government was still unaware of its existence.[88] "The station," Wilber writes, "was now faced with the task of rescuing the operation from total failure." The Tehran station broke communications with the outside world from 15 August until 19 August in case Washington ordered it to evacuate Iran.

The morning after the failed coup, the government – backed by Iran Party, Pan-Iranist Party, Third Force, trade unions, and Society of Merchants, Guilds, and Tradesmen – held a mass rally outside parliament. Ministers and National Front dignitaries took turns addressing the jubilant crowd. The partly disabled Fatemi denounced Reza Shah for the 1933 concession and accused Mohammad Reza Shah of absconding with crown jewels. He labeled him a "traitor" and "Felon of Bagdad" – play on "Thief of Bagdad." The large crowd cried "The

---

[85] CIA, Telegram to Baghdad (18 August 1953), *FRUS* (2017), 697.
[86] CIA, Telegram (18 August 1953), *FRUS* (2017), 683.
[87] President Eisenhower, Speech "Peace with Justice," White House, *Declassified Documents 1978/313*/White House.
[88] CIA Station, Telegram to Washington (19 August 1953), *FRUS* (2017), 699.

Shah must Reign, not Rule," "Death to the Shah," and "We Don't Want a Shah."[89] Fatemi's paper, *Bakhtar-e Emruz*, cheered on the destruction of royal statues, labeling them "idols," and denounced the Pahlavis, describing them as "dictators," "crooks," and "British lackeys."[90] These denunciations earned Fatemi a death sentence later despite Grand Ayatollah Boroujerdi's plea for clemency.[91] Karimpour Shirazi, editor of the gadfly magazine *Shuresh* (Insurrection), outdid Fatemi, mercilessly satirizing the royal family. After the coup, he was burnt alive in prison.

Although some called for a republic, the rally called for the establishment of a regency council. It also called for the trial of the coup leaders. It was later claimed that the Tudeh had outdone others in demanding the abolition of the monarchy. In actual fact, the *Third Force* had come out in the morning of 19 August with the headline demanding a republic and arguing that the "People of Iran would no longer accept the monarchy."[92]

Victory from the Jaws of Defeat

Henderson, who had been absent for over eleven weeks, rushed on a special military plane from Beirut to Tehran as soon as he heard of the failed coup. He arrived on 17 August to find the city in midst of mass jubilation. National Front, as well as Tudeh, crowds were still in the streets pulling down royal statues and changing street names – Shah Avenue had been changed to Mellat (Nation), Pahlavi to 15 August, and Reza Shah to Mossadeq. They were also attacking shops with pictures of the shah, and shouting "Long Live Mossadeq," "Down with the Shah," "Down with British Imperialism," and, even more disconcerting, "Down with American Imperialism." Some ministers urged Mossadeq to calm the crowds, but he felt they needed to vent their anger and let off steam.

Henderson was received at the airport by Mossadeq's son. He promptly arranged to have an emergency meeting the very next afternoon with the prime minister. On the way from the airport to the embassy, he passed large crowds and the remains of a royal statue – only the feet remained. At the embassy, he held a four-hour meeting with Roosevelt and General

---

[89]   Mohammad-Ali Safari, *Qalam va Seyasat* (Pen and Politics) (Tehran: Namak Publication, 1991), 25.

[90]   Correspondent, "Idol Smashing," *Bakhtar-e Emruz*, 18 August 1953.

[91]   Serge Barseqian, "Memoirs of Shah Husseini," *Tarekh-e Iran*, 17 May 2013.

[92]   *Neru-ye Sevum*, 19 August 1953.

McClure, the head of the US Military Mission. Both Wilber and Roosevelt describe the meeting as a "war council." They promptly communicated with the Zahedis, the Rashidians, and Gilanshah, who, according to Roosevelt, were "nearby." They were smuggled in and out of the embassy compound in closed jeeps. The "war council" determined to implement the military component of the coup on 19 August. Roosevelt writes: "It was after this that plans for 19th of August were put into operation. Only a few key Iranians – such as the chief of police, Ayatollah Behbehani, and those paying off demonstrators, knew details of the plan."[93] In a later confidential report, Roosevelt praised the military attachés for their work, but complained that McClure was "of no assistance."[94] The attachés probably communicated messages to tank officers in the army bases. McClure seemed to have had his own ideas for pulling off a successful coup.

The "war council" sent Farzendegan to Kermanshah to urge General Bakhtiyar to march onto Tehran; Ardasher Zahedi to Isfahan to win over the garrison commander – this seems to have failed; and Ayatollah Behbehani to Qom to persuade Grand Ayatollah Boroujerdi to issue a *fatwa* against communism – this too failed. The group also decided to circulate the royal *farman*(s) through local newspapers, especially *Kayhan, Shahed, Dad, Aram, Setareh-e Islam, Mard-e Asia*, and *Mellat-e Iran*. Wilber commented that the "sums" spent over years on the local "venal" papers had finally paid off.[95] The *farman* was also widely distributed through the Associated Press and the *New York Times*. The AP reporter was a CIA operative. The *New York Times* reporter, Kenneth Love, later complained that he had been used "unwittingly," that he did not even know of the CIA's existence then, and that he had kept knowledge of the goings-on to himself for years because of "misguided patriotism."[96] In a later paper presented to Professor Cuyler Young at Princeton University, Love concluded:[97]

---

[93] Anonymous, British Memorandum: Persia-Review of Recent Crisis (2 September 1953), *FRUS* (1989), 784.

[94] Roosevelt, Memorandum to the CIA (20 August 1953), *FRUS* (2017), 701.

[95] Wilber, *Overthrow of Premier Mossadeq*, 91.

[96] Special Reporter, "Ex-Times Reporter Accused of Role in the '53 Coup in Iran," *New York Times*, 26 September 1980.

[97] Kenneth Love, "The American Role in the Pahlavi Restoration on 19 August 1953," (Princeton University: Unpublished Paper, 1960), 1.

What part did the United States play in the overthrow of Premier Mohammed Mossadegh and the restoration of the Shah in Iran in the summer of 1953? It is probable that the American role was decisive, that the Iranian who participated in the royalist coup could not have succeeded without American help. It is doubtful that the coup would have been attempted without American cooperation.

At the close of the "war council," Henderson asked Roosevelt what he should answer if Mossadeq next day asked him whether the USA supported the shah.[98] Roosevelt replied: "I think you should tell him that while Americans do not want to, and will not, get involved in the domestic politics of sovereign country, they are bound to be sympathetic to the man they regards as the legitimate sovereign." Henderson concurred: "I will make it quite plain that we have no intention of interfering in the internal affairs of a friendly county." "To this," Roosevelt added, "I made no comment. Diplomats are expected, if not required, to say such things."

The scheduled Henderson-Mossadeq meeting was held the following afternoon – on 18 August. Much controversy surrounds the meeting. In a blow-by-blow account of the coup written specifically for Churchill, Roosevelt reported:[99]

Mr. Henderson called on the Prime Minister during the afternoon and, according to reliable report, warned him that his continued persistence in remaining in office was not in the best interests of Persia. It was learned that Dr. Musaddiq strongly resented this warning, and told Mr. Henderson that he had no right to interfere in the internal affairs of the country. Their meeting ended abruptly. According to well placed sources, it was soon after this that the plans for the events of the 19th August were put into operation.

Significantly, this paragraph was redacted when the document was first released in 1989. The full document was not released until 2001. Roosevelt, in his book *Countercoup*, claims that Mossadeq had been "visibly shaken" when the ambassador threatened to withdraw all Americans unless the authorities stopped all insults, threats, harassments, and physical violence against US citizens.[100] He claims

---

[98] Roosevelt, *Countercoup*, 183–4.

[99] Anonymous, British Memorandum, 780–8. The full version of this document has not been published but was declassified on 6 April 2001 (Declassified E0 12958).

[100] Roosevelt, *Countercoup*, 185.

Mossadeq had promptly instructed the police chief to clear the streets of demonstrators. "We agreed," Roosevelt commented, "that this had been a helpful move." Mossadeq, however, later wrote his decision to request people to keep off the streets had been made prior to the Henderson meeting.[101] *Ettela'at* later reported that at noon the interior minister had convened the chiefs of staff, police, gendarmerie as well as the military governor of Tehran to assess the situation. The paper made no mention of a ban on demonstrations. According to *Ettela'at* it was not until 4 pm that the military governor declared a total ban on all public meetings.[102] Makki, in his memoirs, claims ambiguously that the government banned all demonstrations, including pro-Mossadeq ones, in the *asr* (afternoon-evening).[103]

Henderson, in his follow-up report to Washington, provided a fuller, yet still sanitized, version of the meeting.[104] He reported that the one-hour meeting began on a polite note. Mossadeq, wearing a dark suit instead of his "usual pajamas," had been his "courteous self" but expressed a "certain amount of smoldering resentment." He blamed the British for the coup attempt, although he must have known from his own intelligence reports, that a "mysterious" American had been involved in secret meetings with Zahedi. At one point he made "little semi-jocular jibes" stressing that the national movement was deter-mined to remain in power even "if all its members were run over by British and American tanks." When Henderson raised his eyebrows, Mossadeq laughed heartily. Henderson "expressed sorrow at chain of events since his departure over two months ago." Mossadeq responded

---

[101] Mohammad Mossadeq, *Khaterat va Talefat* (Memoirs and Collected Works) (Tehran: Elmi Publications, 1986), 290. I would like to thank Ali Matin-Daftari for pointing out this citation. Mossadeq refers to his interpreter's notes which contain nothing about threats and instead focus on Henderson's interest in majles politics, destruction of statutes, and promise to keep political opponents out of the embassy. However, cabinet ministers waiting outside the meeting reported that Mossadeq had forthrightly dismissed the threats on the grounds that the Americans could not "do a damn thing." See Hussein Arabi, *Yadnameh-e Mohandes Hessabi* (Memoirs of Engineer Hessabi) (Tehran: Azer Publications, 1991), 124–5.

[102] *Ettela'at*, 18 August 1953. For a chronology of 15–19 August, see "Moment by Moment Steps towards 19 August," www.bbc.co.uk/persian/iran/2013/08/130815_28_mordad_timelive.

[103] Hussein Makki, *Kudeta-e Best-u-Haft-e Mordad* (The Coup of 19 August) (Tehran: Elmi Publication, 1999), 140.

[104] Henderson, Dispatch to the State Department (18 August 1953), *FRUS* (1989), 748–52.

with a "sarcastic smile." Henderson also expressed "concern" on the failure of the authorities to stop physical attacks on Americans, not just in the capital but also in the provinces. He added it might be necessary for the Americans to leave "en masse."

Henderson innocently inquired to know what had transpired during his absence. Mossadeq replied that Colonel Nasseri had been sent by the shah to arrest him on the night of 15 August. Although he had taken an oath of allegiance to the shah, this act had drastically changed the situation. Henderson further inquired if it was true that the shah had issued a *farman* replacing him with Zahedi. Mossadeq replied that the shah, as constitutional head of state, did not have such authority. The meeting ended, according to this version, with Henderson assuring Mossadeq that the embassy would not "harbor any political refugees."

Years later in an oral history project for Columbia University, Henderson provided a fuller account of the meeting.[105] He reminisced – without mentioning Roosevelt or the CIA – that the meeting focused on the "extremely serious problem" of Americans, including his naval attaché, being attacked by street "mobs" carrying red flags and shouting "Yankee Go Home." He narrated:

I told the Prime Minister that unless the Iranian police were prepared to stop Communist pillaging and attacks, it would be my duty to order all Americans, except those who were needed here, to leave the country at once. I added that I did not believe that he realized the extent to which the Communists were apparently being give a free hand to attack, destroy, and loot. The Prime Minister at this point called in one of his aides and asked if it was true the Communists were roaming the streets in gangs, pillaging, destroying, and attacking foreigners. When the answer was yes, in my presence, Mossadeq picked up the telephone, called the Chief of Police, and gave orders that the police be instructed immediately to restore order in the streets, to break up the roving gangs who were moving around engaging in violence. He said that persons marching under Communist banners or shouting Communist slogans should be treated with no more leniency than any other disturbers of peace. Apparently Mossadeq's orders were carried out with alacrity. When I returned to the Embassy an hour later, I saw the police breaking up the street gangs with what appeared to be joy.

---

[105] Don North, "Interview with Ambassador Loy Henderson (December 1970)," *Oral History Research Office* (New York: Columbia University, 1972).

Immediately after the coup, a similar account of the meeting was leaked to *Time*.[106] Since only three people had been present at the meeting – Henderson, Mossadeq, and the embassy interpreter, the source was probably Henderson himself. *Time* claimed that "things began to happen" soon after the ambassador questioned Mossadeq's legitimacy and demanded strong action against demonstrators. "Shaken," according to this account, "the old man went to the phone and ordered the army and police to drive the rioting Reds off the street. That call, turning the army loose on the most powerful street support he had, was Mossadegh's fatal mistake ... The next morning, the bruised and bitter Tudeh Central Committee proclaimed 'No more aid to Mossadegh'."

The US London embassy conveyed to the Foreign Office a similar account of the Henderson-Mossadeq meeting. It wrote that the crack down on the Tudeh on 18 August had initiated a "break" between Mossadeq and the communists, prompting the latter to withdraw support.[107] This, however, was probably a misinterpretation. Throughout these crucial three days, the Tudeh followed Mossadeq's lead and never declared "No more aid to Mossadeq." When, on 18 August, the prime minister requested people to stay off the streets, the Tudeh obliged. The demonstration on the evening of 18 August had been called by the youth section of the party probably without the endorsement of the Tudeh leadership. According to Wilber, the leadership had tried to persuade the demonstrators to disband before the evening crack down.[108] A later CIA history noted, "Tudeh leaders went into the streets to try to talk the demonstrators into going home."[109] The Tudeh, like the National Front, kept off the streets on these fateful final days not because of the police crack down but because Mossadeq had request them to do so. Mossadeq had full confidence in General Riyahi's ability to control the situation. The plea to stay off the streets was repeated on the morning of 19 August 19. The Tudeh as well as the National Front observed the plea.

Early in the morning of the 19th, Tayyeb, the main gang leader, gathered fellow thugs – Taher Hajj Rezayi, Ramazan Yakhi, Mahmud Masgar, Ismail Pour, and Biuk Saber – in the fruit and vegetable

---

[106] Anonymous, "The People Take Over," *Time*, 31 August 1953.
[107] Foreign Office, Notes on US Embassy Report (20 August 1953), *FO 371/Persia 1953/104570*.
[108] Wilber, *Overthrow of Premier Mossadeq*, 64.   [109] CIA, *Battle for Iran*, 65.

markets. They came armed with heavy batons and long clubs. Eyewitness accounts describe the crowd as a "grotesque procession of wrestlers, weightlifters, body builders," as well as other hired men from the southern part of the city.[110] Sha'aban Brainless, who had been imprisoned since the February Crisis, did not join until midday when he was released from jail. Kenneth Love of the *New York Times* later wrote that the USA channeled through Behbehani "large amounts of American currency" to gangs in southern Tehran.[111]

This crowd was soon augmented with peasants trucked from Veramin and Larak – villages belonging to the royal family and General Arfa. In his personal report to Churchill, Roosevelt reveals that a few days earlier the American embassy had "handed over large sums of money" to Ayatollah Behbehani to hire trucks and spend in southern Tehran.[112] This small paragraph was redacted in the earlier release of the same report. Cottam, the CIA analyst at the time, writes this money became known as "Behbehani dollars."[113] A CIA operative later reminisced so many dollars had flooded the country that its black market value had fallen from 100 to 50 rials.[114] Roosevelt mentions "large number of lorries were hired to provide free transport for demonstrators." He adds that the crowd totaled 3,000; that it contained "unemployed" as well as "hired well-known hooligans"; and that General Modabber, the police chief and fellow conspirator, had instructed his men not to interfere with the demonstration. Although Wilber credits the Boscoes with the street crowd, the Rashidians of MI6 had more substantial links with the *lutis* and *zurkhanehs*.

The motely crowd grew larger as it moved north into the heart of the city. It drew in policemen, Imperial Guards in civilian clothes, and activists from anti-government organizations – especially from the Toilers Party, Arya, Sumka, and Fedayan-e Islam. The crowd soon released inmates from the main jail – these included Sumka leaders, Sha'aban, Nasseri, and Batmanqalech. It also beat up pro-Mossadeq

---

[110] Stella Margold, "The Streets of Tehran," *The Reporter*, 10 November 1953; Richard and Gladys Harkness, "The Mysterious Doings of the CIA," *Saturday Evening Post*, 6 November 1954.

[111] Love, "The American Role in the Pahlavi Restoration," 40.

[112] Anonymous, British Memorandum, 780–8. See especially paragraph 11.

[113] Richard Cottam, *Nationalism in Iran* (Pittsburgh: University of Pittsburgh, 1962), 226.

[114] Mark Gasiorowski, "The 1953 Coup d'Etat in Iran," *International Journal of Middle East Studies*, Vol. 19, No. 3 (August 1987), 285.

newsagents; closed down shops; and ransacked buildings associated with the government – the Foreign Ministry, Iran Party, Pan-Iranist Party, Third Force, *Bakhtar-e Emruz*, and the satirical magazines *Shuresh*, *Hajji Baba*, and *Towfiq*. Not surprisingly, it also targeted buildings associated with the Tudeh – the famous Saedi Theatre, Palace Cinema, and the printing houses of *Shahbaz* and *Besuyeh-e Ayandeh*. It even ransacked the offices of *Ettela'at*.

A CIA analyst later noted that once the riot got going, the role of the "mob" diminished and that of the armed forces became "paramount."[115] A US air force adviser remembers seeing on the north Shemiran road ten trucks each loaded with forty tribesmen.[116] They wore tribal headgear and carried swords as well as truncheons. These men – not mentioned in official reports – most likely came from the Turkic-speaking Zolfaqari tribe outside Zanjan. The two Zolfaqari deputies, who had recently formed the royalist Zolfaqari Club, had probably rushed their men into Tehran.

The crowd totaled at most 3,000 – nothing like the 50,000–100,000 recently mustered by the Tudeh and National Front. Western papers reporting on the coup published mostly close-up photos of pro-shah men jammed into jeeps and onto tanks. Long-shot photos preserved in *Ettela'at* archives show mostly empty streets. The main function of this crowd was not to overthrow the government; it was to give acoustic cover for the military coup and to create mayhem that would provide the pretext for tanks to come into the city.

During the first half of the day, as many as twenty-four tanks, including Shermans, were dispatched into Tehran from Saltanatabad, Qasr, Jamshidieh, and Eshratabad. We still do not know who – if anyone in high command – gave orders to dispatch these tanks into Tehran. At Qasr and Eshratabad, royalist officers had replaced brigade commanders Nowzari and Ashrafi. At Jamshidieh, Lt. Colonel Zand Karimi – a Akhavi nominee – had replaced Colonel Momtaz who was guarding Mossadeq's home. At Saltanatabad, one account claims Captain Hamid Jahanbani, a relative of the royal family, had seized control during the early hours of the morning. Another claims "unnamed colonels" came early in the morning with instructions to take command of eight

---

[115] CIA Station, Memorandum to the CIA (28 August 1953), *FRUS* (2017), 725.
[116] Stephen Langlie, Personal Communications, 4 September 2013.

Shermans.[117] Another claims these instructions came directly from General Riyahi, the chief of staff himself.[118] Yet another claims they may have come from General Daftari, who, late in the morning, had been appointed both chief of police and military governor with instruction to break up the rowdy crowd.[119] According to a laudatory article written immediately after the coup, "patriotic and heroic" officers saved the country by driving as many as forty tanks into central Tehran.[120] The US air force adviser observed that the "CIA street mobs from south Tehran were a catalyst – nothing more," and that the military, especially the tanks, were the "key element in the coup's success."[121]

The supposed instructions to the tank commanders were to restore order in downtown Tehran. But, of course, once they entered the city they headed straight for the strategic points – the staff headquarters, the telephone-telegraph office, the radio station, and, most important, the prime minister's residence. The two light Czech tanks defending the residence were no match for heavy Shermans. By 6.30 p.m., Sha'aban and his thugs were busy looting the ruins of the bombed-residence. During the bombardment, National Front leaders in person and Tudeh leaders by phone beseeched Mossadeq to rally supporters, distribute arms, and bring troops in from barracks still loyal to the government.[122] Mossadeq refused – probably because he wanted to avoid further bloodshed and a possible civil war. He told one adviser that "he didn't want to pour more fuel into the fire."[123] Some advisers

---

[117] Mohammad Jafar Mohammadi, *Raz-e Pirouz-ye Kudeta-ye Bist-u-Hashteh-e Mordad* (The Secret of the Victory of the Coup d'Etat of 19 August) (Cologne: Forough Press, 2005).

[118] Jalel Bozorgmehr, *Doktor Mohammad Mossadeq va Resideg-e Farjam dar Divan-e Keshvar* (Dr. Mohammad Mossadeq and Final Investigation in the Supreme Court) (Tehran: Sahami Publications, 1988), 56; See also Mashallah Varqa, *Chan-u-Chun-e Fururiz-ye Dowlat-e Mossadeq* (Some Thoughts on the Fall of Mossadeq's Government) (n.p.: Ruzbeh Publication, 2006), 75.

[119] Varqa, *Some Thoughts*; See also Makki, *The Coup of 19th August*, 211.

[120] Anonymous, "From 15 to 19 August," *Salnameh-e Donya*, Vol. 10 (1954), 117–27.

[121] Langlie, Personal Communication, 4 September 2013.

[122] Iraj Davarpanah and Mehran Fesharki, "August 19," *Ettela'at*, 20 August 1979.

[123] Varqa, *Some Thoughts*, 50.

later described this refusal as a fatal mistake. He, together with some ministers, fled to neighboring homes.

Towards close of the day, Tehran radio announced that Zahedi was now prime minister – without, of course, using the word coup. The fighting left forty-one dead and seventy-five injured – rumors claimed over 300 killed.[124] The *New York Times* correspondent reported the day ended with a two-and-half hour pitch battle between tanks, especially Shermans, and 75 mm cannons, in the streets around the prime minister's home.[125] The paper described Zahedi as a "great nationalist." Zahedi himself described 19 August as *Ruz-e Jehad-e Melli* (Day of National Crusade). The radio praised it as a *Qeyam-e Melli* (National Uprising). Royalist papers hailed it as a glorious *inqelab* (revolution). The very first speakers on the radio included Zahedi, Baqai, Mir Ashrafi, Hamid Reza Pahlavi, Faramarzi, Qonatabadi, Tayyeb, Hussein Arab, Sha'aban Brainless, and one of Kashani's sons. Roosevelt concluded his confidential report on the coup:[126]

The success of the coup was due to the fact that it was well planned, that it was kept secret, and that plenty of money was made available to carry in out ... There was general agreement that, were it not for American's assistance and guidance, its financial contribution, and its encouragement to the Shah to withstand further humiliation, the plan for the overthrowing of Mussaddiq's government could not have succeeded.

Not to take chances, Zahedi and Batmanqalech rushed to Tehran five battalions from Rasht, Isfahan, Kerman, Tabriz, and Khorramabad.

When Roosevelt reported on the mission to 10 Downing Street, he quoted the shah as saying he owned his throne in part to God and Roosevelt. Churchill reportedly praised the venture as the "finest operations since the end of the War" and wished he had had been young enough to participate.[127] Allen Dulles quoted Eisenhower as saying the Roosevelt report read like a "a dime novel." Later Roosevelt wrote his

---

[124]   Ali Rahnema, "Blow by Blow Account of the Coup Day," *Andisheh-e Poya* (November–December 2004), 50–68; *Ettela'at*, 22 August 1953. The latter numbered the dead at forty-two and the injured at eighty-seven.
[125]   Kenneth Love, "Royalists oust Mossadegh: 300 Die in Iranian Fighting," *New York Times*, 20 August 1953.
[126]   Anonymous, British Memorandum, 787.
[127]   Louis, *Ends of British Imperialism*, 787.

book *Countercoup* in the style of Hardy Boys adventure stories –
a genre popular among teenagers of his class in America. The "adventure" story took on different flavor in the aftermath of the 1979 hostage
crisis.

Immediately after the coup, the State Department stressed that the
role of the "foreign hand had to be concealed." In a long memorandum
entitled "Measures which the US Government Might take in Support of
a Successor Government to Mosadeq," it emphasized:[128]

It would be literally fatal to any non-communist successor to Mosadeq if the
Iranian public gained an impression that the new premier was a "foreign
tool." The US Government should confine any comment upon a change in
government in Iran to a repetition of our traditional unwillingness to interfere in the internal affairs of a free country, and our willingness to work with
the government in power. The UK government should give no indication that
it considers a successor to Mossadeq to be ready to serve UK interests or that
the British had a hand in bringing him to power. Naturally, there should be
no expression of regret that Mossadeq has departed from the political scene.
The US Government should avoid any statement that the oil question is
involved in a change of government in Iran. It is important that neither the
US nor UK Governments should rejoice publicly over expectations of a more
reasonable Iranian attitude towards solution of the oil problem.

In his private diary Eisenhower echoes these same concerns. "Another
recent development," he wrote, "that we helped bring about was the
restoration of the Shah to power in Iran and the elimination of
Mossadegh. The things we did were 'covert.' If knowledge of them became
public, we would not only be embarrassed in the region, but our chances to
do anything of like nature in the future would almost totally
disappear."[129]

Wilber ends his own report with the startling claim the CIA "did not
spend one cent in the purchase of officers."[130] This is somewhat disin-
genuous. In a number of separate places, he admits that the CIA passed on
considerable amounts: some $1 million in April 1953; $11,000 per week
in May 1953; $60, 000 to Zahedi in the summer of 1953, and another
$150,000 for publicity; and $75,000 to the "military secretariat" in
Tehran. These figures do not include the substantial sums both the CIA

---

128 State Department, Memorandum, *FRUS* (2017), 645.
129 Eisenhower, Diary for 8 October 1953, *Declassified MR 2009–60*1/*
      10 May 2010.
130 Wilber, *Overthrow of Premier Mossadeq*, Appendix E, 22.

and MI6 spent separately in the previous two years. The CIA, in an "eyes only" document dated April 1951, explicitly approved "subsidies" – unspecified and not requiring receipts – to be passed to a "task force" assigned to "confound" oil nationalization advocates.[131] For its part, the MI6 man responsible for handing money describes the sums as "vast" and estimates over £700,000 was spent on the actual coup itself.[132] One impeccable source estimates that by the early 1950s MI6 was providing the Rashidians with as much as £10,000 *per month* to spend to the on the press and the bazaar.[133] Another impeccable source estimates the CIA spent as much as $1 million a year on its on-going operations supposedly against the Tudeh.[134] Immediately after the coup, the USA handed over $5 million in cash to Zahedi – probably to reward his immediate associates. In a final summary entitled "Campaign to Install Pro-Western Government in Iran," the CIA estimated the venture cost the USA a grand total of $5,330,000. But the actual sums spent from mid-May 1953 until 19 August 1953 remain classified to this very day.[135]

Money did not move in only one direction. Swiss bank documents leaked later to the *Nation* claim that the shah was exceedingly generous towards his American friends, especially Henderson, Allen Dulles, and Warne. Each supposedly received $1 million.[136] Roosevelt followed up his success by serving on a number of oil company boards; and, in the mid-1970s selling arms to Iran for Northrop – he received annually $75,000 plus expenses.[137] In 1979, he lobbied hard – lawyering up and mobilizing even the Rockefellers – to get CIA permission to publish his coup memoirs. The State Department surmised he had eyes on a Hollywood contract.[138] The mission to save Iran and the shah had proved to be highly lucrative.

[131] Wisner, Memo to Allen Dulles (23 April), *FRUS* (2017), 69.
[132] Granada TV, "Interview with Darbyshire," *End of Empire*, Channel 4 (UK)
       (1985). This part of the interview was not televised.
[133] Louis, *Ends of British Imperialism*, 742; See also Roger Louis, "How
       Mussadeq Was Ousted," *Times Literary Supplement*, 29 June 2001.
[134] Gasiorowski, "The 1953 Coup d'Etat in Iran," 286.
[135] CIA, Campaign to Install Pro-Western Government in Iran (8 March 1954),
       FRUS (2017), 910–12.
[136] Fred Cook, "The Billion-Dollar Mystery," *The Nation*, 12 April 1965, 380–97.
[137] Eric Pace, "Northrop Rebate Reported in Iran," *New York Times*,
       23 February 1976.
[138] National Security Archive, "Iran 1953: The Strange Odyssey of Kermit
       Roosevelt's *Countercoup*," www2.gwu/edu~narchiv/NSAEBB/NSAEBB468/.

5 | *Memory Revised*

Obsolescence is the unavoidable fate of a historian.

Eric Hobsbawm

In the realm of scholarship we all know that everything we've done and are doing will be obsolete in ten or twenty or fifty years. That is the destiny of such work – what's more, this is the *point* of such work. In a specific sense, scholarship, unlike any other cultural endeavor, is subjected to – dedicated – to its own obsolescence. Every scholarship work that "accomplishes" its goal produces new questions; it *wants* to be "surpassed" and left behind.

Max Weber

History Repressed

At the height of the 1978–9 revolution, a member of the British House of Commons informed the Foreign Office that an Iranian visitor at the annual Labour Party conference was circulating a pamphlet that accused the UK of having engineered the 1953 overthrow of Mossadeq. The MP was curious to know if there was any truth in this.[1] The Foreign Office assigned a young intern to search the archives. A few weeks later the intern reported back that the files contained no such information and only two cursory mentions of the overthrow: Peter Avery's well-known book *Modern Iran*; and a short biography of Mossadeq in the regular file on Leading Personalities in Iran. The Foreign Office Research Department, however, soon came out with a memorandum on "The Mossadegh Period" – this became the stock answer to any such future inquiries.[2] It argued Mossadeq

---

[1] H. Miers, Pamphlet by Ahmad Ghotbi circulated at the Labour Party Conference (15 October 1978), *FCO 8/3187–8*.

[2] Frances Grier, The Mossadegh Period (13 October 1978), *FCO 8/3187*. This was written by the Middle East Section of the Research Department at the request of the head of the Middle East Department.

had "come to power in a wave of nationalism," but had been "ousted by a military coup led by General Zahedi" because his "obduracy," "ineptitude," and "unconstitutional behavior" had sabotaged oil negotiations, deteriorated the economy, alienated former allies, and even led to a break with the communists.

The young intern, in the search into the files, somehow had overlooked numerous opaque mentions of the coup. Over the years, officials had meticulously avoided direct references to British – and even American – involvement in the actual coup. But they had occasionally dropped side remarks about the "events of 1953," "Zahedi's success," the shah's "counter-revolution," Mossadeq's "difficulties with his Majlis," or his erratic policies causing his own "demise." Soon after the coup, one diplomat even cryptically remarked: "The Shah seems to be living in a dream world. He seems to think that his restoration was due entirely to his popularity with his people and resents suggestion that any particular groups assisted in the process."[3]

Moreover, a senior Foreign Office official, in a note handwritten immediately after the coup, had advised colleagues interested in knowing what had happened to read a series of articles in the *Times of India*.[4] He explained that the author, G. Reddy, although an "unscrupulous socialist not very well disposed to us," was "astute" enough to have produced articles "well worth reading." Middleton, the previous chargé d'affaires, added that the articles were "very objective by local standards." Reddy had clearly kept his eyes and ears open while staying with his friend the Indian ambassador. The Foreign Office transmitted photocopies of the articles to appropriate embassies in the Commonwealth.

These articles drew an accurate outline of events leading up to the coup – Eisenhower's loan refusal, Dulles' bypassing Iran during his Middle East tour, Schwarzkopf and Princess Ashraf's sudden visits, Zahedi's meetings with mysterious foreigners, and Henderson's questioning of Mossadeq's legality.[5] They noted "a good many people in Iran, especially the middle class intelligentsia seem to believe that the

---

[3] Foreign Office, Conversations with the Shah (14 September 1953), *FO 371/ 104571*.

[4] Christopher Grady, Articles in the *Times of India*, FO 371/104568.

[5] G. Reddy, "Iran's Royalist Coup," *Times of India*, 16–17 September 1953. Handwritten note by Middleton, *FO 371/104568*. See also *FO 371/104571 & 104568*.

recent royalist coup d'état was largely inspired, if not actually engineered, by foreign elements, notably the United States." They stressed that the oil blockade had failed to cripple the economy; that Britain had rejected the Iranian definition of "fair compensation"; that many saw Point IV as "a cover for spies"; and that the USA had three different military missions and over 1,000 citizens residing in Iran – more than in any other Middle East country.[6] "Mossadeq's supporters," the articles concluded, "have put forward a book full of circumstantial evidence to prove their accusation that the US actively backed the recent coup ... Iranians are wondering whether, after all, Dr. Mossadeq's frequent accusations that the royalist 'plots' against him were inspired by foreign elements is without justification."

The Avery book mentioned by the intern contains a chapter on the oil crisis with the title "What One Man Can Do." It rehashes the stereotypical depiction of Mossadeq ending with him pulling a sheet over his head and laughing "Look what I have done!" as tanks were bombarding his house.[7] The biography ends with this assessment of Mossadeq:[8]

In his day he was a clever political manipulator and demagogue with considerable historic talent. His reputation for honesty stood him in good stead with the Iranian people. He worked on Persian xenophobia and popular discontent to make himself a national hero and by skillful intimidation secured the mastery of the 16th Majlis and later the country. He had no positive programme and no understanding of practical problems but kept going by creating one excitement after another. In the end he overreached himself but he very nearly succeeded in forcing the Shah off the throne.

On rare occasions when the Foreign Office mentioned Mossadeq's overthrow, it scrupulously avoided the word "coup" – not to mention the British role. "On 19 August," it typically declared after the 1979 revolution, "a sudden uprising overthrew Mosaddiq."[9] On the whole, it tended to dismiss – at least, in public – any such role as the inevitable product of the Iranian predisposition towards foreign plots and conspiratorial theories. It insisted the shah had won because the armed forces and the public had rallied behind him whereas the Tudeh "mob"

---

[6] G. Reddy, "The Economic Crisis," *Times of India*, 3 June 1953; "Iranian Round-Up," *Times of India*, 1–3 June 1953.
[7] Avery, *Modern Iran*, 417.
[8] British Embassy, Internal Affairs of Iran, FCO 8/3188.
[9] Foreign Office, Leading Personalities in Iran (1979), FCO 8/3349.

had "turned against the prime minister." Its quarterly report published immediately after the coup declared, "a surprising outburst of popular emotion swept away Dr. Musaddiq himself and the Shah regained, in one day, a degree of influence he had hardly enjoyed even from 1951."[10] One British diplomat reported – but in private – that the "CIA role in the overthrow of Mossadeq is regularly over dramatized."[11] In preparing the Foreign Secretary for a press interview, the Foreign Office advised him not to use the term "coup" – but if used to apply it exclusively to the dangers of a "Tudeh coup."[12] He was advised to stress that "our information comes chiefly from monitored broadcasts, agency tapes and press sources, and thus we had no prior knowledge and were surprised at the strength of Royalist feelings." The Foreign Office, in its annual printed report on Iran, spelled out its official account of August 1953:[13]

In 1953 Persia was at last relieved of the burden of Dr. Musaddiq. For seven months he clung to power steadily increasing the number of his enemies and sustained only by his own tenacity and an increasing reliance on the Tudeh. He rejected a further generous offer by HMG and the US government for the settlement of the oil dispute and thus accelerated the progress of Persian finances into bankruptcy. The Shah summoned up enough courage to dismiss him. The arrangements to enforce this dismissal miscarried but a popular uprising and the devoted efforts of some loyal officers swept away Dr. Musaddiq and returned the Shah with greater prestige than he previously enjoyed or then deserves.

The Butler postmortem on the crisis was equally circumspect even though written ten years later and circulated to a select few.[14] Titled significantly "British Policy Relinquishing Abadan in 1951," it began with the nationalization law, rushed through August 1953, and ended with the oil agreement in 1954. It placed the main onus for the whole crisis on the "erratic old man" and the "Persian character," and attributed his eventual fall mainly to "internal politics."

---

[10] Foreign Office, Quarterly Political Report: Political Events in Persia, July–September 1953, *FO 416/106.*

[11] Miers, Pamphlet by Ahmad Ghotbi, *FCO 8/3187.*

[12] Foreign Office, Memo Prepared for Lord Salisbury (28 August 1953), *FO 371/104577.*

[13] Foreign Office, Annual Report for Persia in 1953, *FO 416/107.*

[14] Butler, *British Policy in Relinquishing Abadan in 1951.*

The British embassy, however, remained surprisingly candid about the shah's continued unpopularity after the coup. On the first anniversary of the coup, the government orchestrated a major "carnival" with jeeps, buses, and trucks full of demagogues and "perspiring hooligans" to celebrate the National Uprising. But, according to the embassy, the show was clearly "contrived." One bystander told an embassy official "this has to been with the eyes, not with the heart." And a well-connected merchant confided:

It is hard to find a man in the street who was not dissatisfied and embittered ... The deception of the people for political purposes had become a fine art, but the people were now deeply cynical. The new element in the present situation is that the Crown itself is the singular object of internal resentment and external enmity, and the Head of State is now protected by no ministerial or parliamentary responsibility.[15]

Professor Lambton, who had urged Mossadeq's overthrow, seconded this view. After an extensive tour she readily admitted she was "amazed how unpopular the Shah was throughout the country" and how deluded he was to imagine he enjoyed public support.[16] She explained that Mossadeq's land reform, despite its shortcomings, had "brought home to the peasants that reform might become a practical possibility." She admitted the "labouring classes remained still discontented and supportive of Musaddiq":

During whole period of my stay I did not hear a single Persian, from highly placed official down to labourers and peasants, say anything in Shah's favour. All classes believe that he was personally running the administration of the country. Almost all the blame was place on him. ... Many speak of him with resentment, and some with contempt ... Britain is blamed on ground we are responsible for the Shah and therefore for the ills of the country ... To sum up, I would suggest that however satisfactory the situation may appear on the surface, it is in fact far from stable and the people are profoundly discontented.

The Foreign Office played down Lambton's report arguing she had no concrete remedies to offer and her views reflected the "seamier side of Persian life." It was comforted by the remark that anti-Americanism

---

[15] A. Keller, Letter to the Foreign Office (20 August 1954), *FO 371/140789*.
[16] British Embassy, Miss Lambton's Tour of Iran (Summer 1956), *FO 371/120714*.

now overshadowed anti-British sentiments. The Foreign Office, however, advertently admitted "Musaddiq's tremendous surviving appeal would make him a good figure head for a potential coup d'etat."[17] Once Mossadeq was exiled to his estate, the embassy speculated:

Musaddiq tucked away in his village presents no problem to the Government. But there is no doubt that were he allowed out and given a measure of political freedom, he would command considerable support – old and deaf as he is. Many Iranians will always regard him as a great national hero. He is certainly of a stature that has no peer in Persia today.[18]

The embassy biographies in 1957 described him as "still a name to conjure with in spite of all that has happened ... He was dismissed by the Shah but did not obey until forced out by a popular uprising on August 19, 1953, which followed General Zahedi's more or less abortive coup d'etat."[19]

The British government's reticence about its role in the coup has persisted well into the present. Desmond Harney – the MI6 man in Tehran during the 1979 revolution – mentions in passing that the shah was able to "take over" because Mossadeq faced difficulties in the majles.[20] This was certainly a creative way of explaining the coup. Anthony Parsons, the British ambassador during the revolution, in exploring the regime's many shortcoming in *The Pride and the Fall*, has only this to say about the coup: "This (1979) was the most sensational year in the recent history of Iran, certainly in the twenty-year period since the Shah re-established his leadership after the fall of Dr. Mossadegh in 1953."[21] Similarly, Browne – in his postmortem on the revolution – claims: "In the early 1950s the Shah was upstaged by Muhammad Mossadeq who nationalized Iran's oil fields and embarked on a long dispute with the West. Eventually Mossadeq's popularity waned and the Shah was able after a brief period of exile to contrive his dismissal and impeachment." He continues: "By mid-1954 [sic] Mossadeq's support was falling away. In August, after a short crisis

[17] Foreign Office, Talk with Professor Lambton, *FO 371/140787*.
[18] British Embassy, Letter (20 December 1956), *FO 371/120714*.
[19] British Embassy, Leading Personalities in Iran (1957), *FO371/127072*.
[20] Desmond Harney, *The Priest and the King* (London: Tauris, 1999), 57.
[21] Anthony Parsons, *The Pride and the Fall: Iran 1974–1979* (London: Butler and Tanner, 1984), 11.

in which he left the country, the Shah was able to regain control with the help of street demonstrations in his favour."[22]

These official accounts rarely mention the military coup – and never the MI6 and CIA. The reticence is caused not just by political correctness. The British Official Secrets Act threatens dire penalties for any public servant with access to confidential documents who openly contradicts government accounts of important issues – especially sensitive recent events. Since the British government – as of 2021 – has not admitted participating in the coup any statement claiming otherwise could technically violate the Official Secrets Act. Jack Straw, the Foreign Secretary during the invasion of Iraq, is the very first senior official – but retired one – to have publicly admitted to the British role in the coup. In testifying before the House of Commons in 2006, he stated:[23]

Serving Foreign Secretaries have no right to see any records from previous administrations. I saw none relating to the coup. However, by the time I took office in 2001, a huge amount of material had already been published about it, including an autobiography by SIS's head of station Monty Woodhouse, and account by the CIA leader of the coup, Kermit Roosevelt, and much more. Previously highly classified internal documents from the CIA were becoming available, which included chapter and verse on SIS's role. Despite the continuing official British line (neither confirm nor deny) on this subject, I thought it would be wholly risible to parrot this line when everyone knew that our intelligence services had been involved. So, giving evidence to the House of Commons Foreign Affairs Select Committee in February 2006, I said elements of British intelligence and the CIA *forced* a perfectly democratic Prime Minister Mossadeq, from Office.

The official transcript of Straw's testimony replaced *forced* with "stopped" – making the sentence meaningless. Straw's memoirs also mention that coup plans had been laid even before Eisenhower's election and that the intelligence services had "purchased" enough deputies to prevent the prime minister from being able to dissolve the majles.

The USA has its own version of the Official Secrets Act – the draconian 1917 Espionage Act. Officials with access to confidential information vow to "never divulge, publish, nor reveal classified information."

[22] Browne, *British Policy in Iran, 1974–78*, 40.
[23] Jack Straw, *The English Job: Understanding Iran* (London: Biteback Publications, 2019), 144–5.

Violators risk twenty-year prison sentences.[24] In a major address immediately after the coup, President Eisenhower set the standard explanation for the events of August 1953. He claimed that the shah had been saved in the nick of time by a spontaneous "groundswell" prompted by public fear of communism and by the loyalty of the armed forces.[25] The State Department followed this script in both public and confidential documents. Henderson – without irony – cabled Washington:[26]

Unfortunately impression becoming rather widespread that in some way or other this Embassy or at least US Government has contributed with funds and technical assistance to overthrow Mosadeq and establish Zahedi Government. Iranians unable to believe any important political development can take place in country without foreigners being involved. Intensive propaganda in Tudeh newspapers prior to their disappearance and over Soviet Radio that US Embassy working for Shah and Zahedi against Mosadeq has helped create this impression. Public, therefore, in general interpret various incidents or remarks as evidence American intervention ... We do not believe it would serve any useful purpose as far as Iran is concerned for department to deny US intervention unless it receives inquiries of character which would render such denial desirable. It might be useful, however, if spokesmen for Department could find suitable occasion stress in factual way spontaneity of the movement in Iran in favor of new Government, touching upon some factors which according to reports received from various sources responsible for what has happened ... We sincerely hope means will be found either through US Government channels or through private American news dissemination channels for American and world public to understand that (the) victory of Shah was (the) result (of the) will Iranian people.

Two months later, the NSC circulated a detailed "explanation" for Mossadeq's "downfall."[27] This remained classified until 2012. It offered a number of explanations: Mossadeq's "erratic, imperious

24 Karen Paget, *Patriotic Betrayal: The Inside Story of the CIA's Secret Campaign to Enroll American Students in the Crusade Against Communism* (New Haven: Yale University Press, 2015).
25 Eisenhower, "Speech Given to National Governor's Conference," in Yohan Alexander and Allan Nanes, *The United States and Iran: A Documentary History* (Maryland: University Publications of America, 1980), 257–8.
26 Henderson, Cable to State Department (21 August 1953), *FRUS* (1989), 759–80.
27 NSC, Contribution to NIE-102: Probable Developments in Iran: Causes of Mossadeq's Downfall (5 October 1953), Declassified 2012/09/20 CIA-RDP79R01012A003200030025-8.

and stubborn personality"; his "piece by piece" destruction of democracy and constitutional government; the economic blockade; the printing of paper money; the failure to obtain American aid; the alienation of powerful tribes; the personal attacks on the shah; and the disputes with Kashani, Baqai, and Makki over martial law, electoral reform, plenary powers, senate closing, military reorganizing, and the supposed "mass arrests." These difficulties supposedly had provided Zahedi with the opportunity to pull off the "completely spontaneous" uprising.

The State Department faithfully kept to this script for the next half century. It avoided mentioning the CIA, and only occasionally conceded that "Iranians hold America responsible for Mossadeq's fall."[28] Like the United Kingdom, the USA talked in generalities about the "events of 1953," the "riots of 19th August," the "spontaneous uprising," or just the "fall" of Mossadeq. The preferred line was to ignore the whole unsavory subject. For example, on 7 December 1953 – just after the coup – three students were killed in Tehran University only a stone's throw away from the US embassy. They were protesting the coup and Vice-President Nixon's visit. December 7 became the unofficial student national day. The American embassy, reporting on the vice president's visit, boasted "it was particularly gratifying that in spite of the delicate situation prevailing there had not been a single disagreeable incident."[29] Similarly, at the end of the 1950s, when psychology had become a fad, the State Department tried to explain urban middle-class "extremism," "radicalism," and "Mossadeq nostalgia," as well as "aggression" towards the ruling elite and the West, by resorting to a litany of "deep-seated" personality and cultural issues such as "anger," "frustration," "insecurity," "humiliation," "inadequacy," "maladjustment," "social confusion," and the Zoroastrian tendency to see the world in terms of absolute good or evil.[30] The 1953 coup was never mentioned.

In the quarter century after the coup, American and British reports from their embassies invariably portrayed the regime in glowing light

[28] NSC, *Probable Developments in Iran through 1955* (7 December 1954), www.cia.gov/library/readingroom/search/site/Iran.

[29] Henderson, *Memorandum on Conversation* (22 December 1953), *FRUS* (2017), 861–6.

[30] State Department, "Political Characteristics of the Iranian Urban Middle Class," in Alexander, *The United States and Iran*, 322–9.

with occasional footnotes mentioning such problems as "rampant corruption," "income inequality," "lack of political participation," "revolution of rising expectations," and shortcoming of the White Revolution. These dispatches continued to conspicuously avoid the impolite subject of 1953. The official postmortems on 1979 plead that the embassy dispatches did at times point out the reasons why the regime was unpopular. But these postmortems, as well as the dispatches, never mention the coup. Even the official US postmortem on the postmortems contains nothing on Mossadeq and the coup.[31] Similarly, Edward Luttwak, former adviser to the CIA, NSC and White House, in his well-known book *Coup D'Etat: A Practical Handbook* lists over 300 successful putsches, but somehow manages to overlook August 1953.[32] In short, official histories had successfully shredded the role of the CIA and MI6 from the history of Iran. Orwell would not have been surprised.

One State Department officer after intense training in Persian language and Iranian history was taken aback in 1960 to hear from an Iranian that the CIA had been involved in the coup:[33]

Over the remaining two years of my assignment in Mashed I came to make close friendships with several Iranians who, even while holding important Iranian government positions, had an underlying loyalty to Mossadeq and held us responsible for removing him. Looking back, now that our role in overthrowing Mosaddeq is so well known, it seems amazing to me that this knowledge was kept from someone like me assigned to an important US government post in Iran. But my case seems to have been the usual one, not the exception. A few years later, in 1963 or 1964, when I was Assistant Iran Desk Officer at the State Department, a message came to the Desk from our newly assigned Political Counselor at the embassy in Tehran describing how an Iranian he had come to know had said that the US was responsible for Mosaddeq's removal. Was there any truth in this? He asked.

Similarly, a senior diplomat reminisces that while in Tehran studying Persian with a wealthy aristocratic family he was surprised when he asked her who was the most popular Iranian. She replied without hesitation "Mossadeq." But, he replied, he has been gone for many

[31] Robert Jervis, *Why Intelligence Fails: Lessons from the Iranian Revolution and the Iraq War* (London: Cornell University Press, 2010).

[32] Edward Luttwak, *Coup D'Etat: A Practical Handbook* (Cambridge: Harvard University Press, 2016).

[33] Personal Communication, email on 25 April 2010.

years. "Yes," she retorted, "you Americans took him away from us."
"If this privileged woman feels that way," he wondered, "what must
the rest of the country think."[34] When Mossadeq died in March 1967,
the *New York Times* obituary described him as an "intensely emotional" and "extremely nationalistic" politician who wore "pink pajamas" [sic] and was "overthrown in riotous street fighting in 1953." It
added that "reportedly" the CIA had played a role.[35]

This repressed history – especially in official circles – created a wide
disconnect between how Americans and Iranians perceived 1953. For
Iranians, the USA had changed the course of their history. They saw
historical time as divided between before and after 1953. But for the
American elite, not to mention the general public, the USA had merely
cheered on an event that carried little, if any, significance in the larger
framework of global history. When, during the 1980 hostage crisis,
President Carter was asked about the coup he dismissed the subject as
"ancient history."[36] This memory vacuum has opened the way for
revisionist historians to present their interpretations of the coup –
interpretations that deny the significant role played both by the CIA
and by MI6.

History Revised

Condoleezza Rice, President Bush's Secretary of State, famously dismissed critics of the invasion of Iraq and skeptics of the notion that
Saddam Hussein had weapons of mass destruction as "revisionist
historians." President Bush quickly echoed Rice.[37] Since Rice and
Bush were not historians they probably deemed the term "revisionist"
to be derogatory; they were probably confusing the term with "history deniers" – as in Holocaust Deniers. Historians, of course, consider the past as something in constant need of revision once new facts
and new ways of seeing emerge. They consider and respect the process
of revising history is an integral part and parcel of writing about the
past.

---

[34] Anonymous, "What Memories Teach," email 22 April 2010.
[35] Anonymous, Obituary of Dr. Mossadeq, *New York Times*, 6 March 1967.
[36] President Carter, "News Conference (13 February 1980)," *Public Papers of the Presidents of the United States, Jimmy Carter*, Book 10, 1 January to 23 May 1980 (Washington, DC: US Government Printing Office, 1981), 307.
[37] Alex Keyssar, "Revisionist Historians," *Washington Post*, 24 June 2003.

The recent outpouring of revisionist writings on the coup should therefore be welcomed as fresh thinking. Reams of articles have poured out in the last decade – often on the anniversary of the coup – with such suggestive titles as "28 Mordad: The Myth that Haunts Iran"; "The Great Satan Myth"; "Six Myths about the Coup against Iran's Mossadegh"; "Iran: The Truth about the CIA and the Shah"; "The Myths of 1953"; "The Myth of an American Coup"; and "The 1953 Coup and the Mossadegh Myth."[38] These articles have appeared mostly in think-tank publications such as the *National Review, National Interest, The New Republic, Weekly Standard,* and *Campus Watch.* They have also been supplemented by two full books: Ardasher Zahedi's memoirs, and Darioush Bayandor's *Iran and the CIA: The Fall of Mosaddeq Revisited.* Zahedi dismisses earlier works, especially by Wilber and Roosevelt, as pure CIA propaganda, and claims – probably with a straight face – his father never talked with any Americans. He argues if the CIA could pull off such stunts they would have done so in Cuba and elsewhere.[39] Bayandor's book cover declares:[40]

On 19th August 1953, Mosaddeq was removed from office in a series of events that changed the course of Iranian history and still haunts the nation and its people today. For over a century, popular wisdom has attributed these dramatic events to foul play by the CIA and its British allies, creating a myth of CIA power and success that has mesmerized opinion ever since and cast a shadow over Iran's continuing troubled relations with the USA.

This pathbreaking study unearths compelling evidence to suggest a different version of events, revealing that Mosaddeq's fall actually took

---

[38] Amir Taheri, "28 Mordad: The Myth that Haunts Iran," *Kayhan International,* 22 August 2018 and https://kayhanlife.com/views/opinion-28-mordad-the-myth-that-haunts-iran/; Abbas Milani, "The Great Satan Myth," *New Republic,* 8 December 2009; Morgan Carlston, "Six Myths about the Coup against Iran's Mossadegh," *National Interest,* 2 September 2014; Josh Gelernter, "Iran: The Truth about the CIA and the Shah," *National Review,* 24 July 2015; Ray Takeyh, "The Myths of 1953," *Weekly Standard,* 24 July 2017; Ray Takeyh, "The Myths of an American Coup," *Weekly Standard,* 17 June 2013; Arash Azizi, "The 1953 Coup and the Mossadegh Myth," https://iranwire.com/en/features/4798; and A. J. Caschetta, "In Death, Morsi Becomes Mossadeq," *Campus Watch,* 3 July 2019. For an evaluation of such articles see Gregory Brew, "Misreading the 1953 Coup," https://lobelog .com/misreading-the-1953-coup/.

[39] Zahedi, *Memoirs of Ardasher Zahedi,* 261–76.

[40] Darioush Bayandor, *Iran and the CIA: The Fall of Mosaddeq Revisited* (New York: Palgrave, 2010).

Washington and London by complete surprise. Britain and the US did indeed collaborate in a plot to remove Mosaddeq but when they put their plan into action, it failed to ignite. Three days later, however, Mossadeq was ousted, a victim less of external agitation than of internal Iranian politics and the actions of prominent clerics, most notably the then grand Shi'i Maja, Ayatollah Boroujerdi.

The revisionists rarely engage directly with the many academic books on the subject – books such as Mark Gasiorowski and Malcolm Bryne's *Mohammad Mosaddeq and the Coup in Iran*; Stephen Kinzer's *All the Shah's Men: The Hidden Story of the CIA's Coup in Iran*; James Bill and Roger Louis's *Musaddiq, Iranian Nationalism, and Oil*; Fakhreddin Azimi's *Iran: The Crisis of Democracy*; Christopher Bellaigue's *Patriot of Persia: Muhammad Mossadegh and a Tragic Anglo-American Coup*; and Ali Rahnema's recent *Behind the 1953 Coup in Iran: Thugs, Turncoats, Soldiers and Spooks*. One revisionist dismisses these academic books as "phantasmagorical accounts."[41] Another claims the old "scholarship runs in circles around the same names" and that "younger scholars feel intimidated to question the narrative put in place by their elders 40, 50 years ago."[42]

Instead of engaging with these academic works, revisionists hammer away on two major points: that the CIA role has been much exaggerated at the expense of the indigenous forces; and that these indigenous forces were not the military but royalist "protestors" led by the clergy. The overall effect, according to some academics, is to tone down the role of the CIA-MI6 role, highlight that of the clergy, and "weaponize" Mossadeq's popularity against the present Islamic Republic.[43] In developing their new interpretation, revisionists rely heavily – but selectively – upon the two recently declassified CIA documents: *The Battle for Iran*, and *"Zendebad Shah!": The Central Intelligence Agency and the Fall of Iranian Prime Minister Mohammed Mossadeq, August 1953*.[44]

---

[41] Darioush Bayandor, "The Fall of Mosaddeq, August 1953: Institutional Narrative, Professor Mark Gasiorowski and My Study," *Iranian Studies*, Vol. 45, No 5 (September 2012), 679–91.

[42] Arash Azizi, Interview with Andrew Cooper, http://iranwire.com/en/features/4798.

[43] Roham Alvandi and Mark Gasiorowski, "The United States Overthrew Iran's Last Democratic Leader," *Foreign Affairs*, 30 October 2019.

[44] CIA History Staff, *Battle for Iran* (Washington, DC: Working Paper, n.d.). This was released in 2014 and made public by the National Security Archive at www2.gwu.edu~nsarchiv/NSAEBB/NAAEBB4/NSAEBB476/. Scott Koch,

At first glance the revisionist account could appear persuasive. According to the account, Mossadeq, by "obstinately" rejecting "innumerable" fair offers, prompted the British to impose the drastic economic embargo. This embargo inevitably led to a serious financial "meltdown," which, in turn, sharply deepened economic, social, and political discontent. "As the strains of the oil-less economy began to trickle down to ordinary folks," writes one revisionist, "things began to go sour on the home front." Mossadeq's main supporters, the intelligentsia and the professionals, began to "abandon him." This strengthened the opposition and increased Mossadeq's unpopularity. The clergy then channeled this unpopularity into their *Qeyam-e Melli* (National Uprising). "No military units," insists one prominent royalist, "were involved" in the popular overthrow.[45] This certainly would have been news to the participants – both victors and victims. These revisionists rarely give credit to the military for Mossadeq's overthrow. They prefer to point their fingers at the clergy.

According to an old saying, success has many heirs but failure only orphans. The coup contradicts this saying. Few were willing to take credit for the success. General Daftari told an oral history project he had been completely unaware of CIA activities, and that on the morning of 19 August had been minding his own business walking in the streets when he heard out of the blue that he had been appointed chief of police.[46] He was surprised to hear later that the CIA had passed money to Behbehani to hire a crowd. Princess Ashraf placed a paid announcement in the *New York Times* after the 1979 revolution claiming she had absolutely nothing to do with the coup because when she arrived in Tehran to talk to her brother, the latter had categorically refused to see her. "My brother," she claims, "ordered me to leave as soon as he learned of my arrival because he did not wish to overrule his Prime Minister."[47]

"Zendebad Shah!": The Central Intelligence Agency and the Fall of Iranian Prime Minister Mohammed Mossadeq, August 1953 (Washington, DC: CIA, 1998). This was released first in 2000, then in 2017, and a more complete version in 2018. The more complete version was posted by the National Security Archive at www2/gwu.edu/~nsarchiv/NSAEBB/NASEBB435/.

45   Amir Taheri, "28 Mordad: The Myth that Haunts Iran," *Kayhan International*, 22 August 2018.

46   Habib Ladjevardi, Interview with General Mohammad Daftari, *Iranian Oral History Collection* (Cambridge: Harvard University, 1993).

47   Princess Ashraf, "In Memory of My Brother Mohammad Reza Pahlavi," *New York Times*, 27 July 2013.

Sha'aban Brainless, in his post-1979 California exile, insisted he could not have possibly participated in the coup since he had been locked up in prison. General Hussein Fardoust, the shah's childhood friend and at the time a major in the Imperial Guards, in his memoirs claims he was far away in Paris during the coup.[48] Of course, many of the forty tank officers, the real "heroes," remained very much in the background.[49] They were soon eased out and became non-persons. As far as the shah was concerned, officers who had worked with the CIA to save him could well in future work with the same CIA to overthrow him.

Revised History Revisited

The revisionist narrative may sound persuasive. But is it supported by hard facts – by actual events and new documents such as *Zendebad Shah!* and *The Battle for Iran*? These two recently released documents have serious shortcomings. They – unlike the Wilber report – are not primary sources. The first was written in 1998 by an unknown Scott Koch; the second in the 1970s by an unnamed committee. They both rely heavily instead on secondary sources. This author was surprised to find his own work used as a source. They are long on generalities about Iran, Islam, and the Cold War, including George Kennan's "Long Telegram," but remarkably short on August 1953. They also remain heavily redacted. The latest released version of *Zendebad Shah!* totals ninety-three pages, but fifty-nine pages remain classified. The most recent version of *The Battle for Iran* leaves 43 pages out of 149 totally blank. What is more, the two reports contain numerous factual mistakes. For example, one claims the shah appointed Qavam prime minister in 1946; it was the majles that elected him. The National Security Archive, which lobbied for their declassification, explained the CIA had released them because the media, relying heavily on the Wilber report, had drawn a misleading picture of 1953. The CIA

---

[48] Hussein Fardoust, *Khaterat* (Memoirs) (Tehran: Kayhan Press, 1991). A government investigation compiled in August 1953 identifies him as one of the Imperial Guards involved in the failed coup. See "Dr. 'Elmieh's Affidavit," in Mohammad Jafa'ar Mohammadi, *Raz Pirouz-ye Kudeta-ye Bust-u-hashteh-e Mordad* (The Secret of the Success of the 19th August Coup) (Cologne: Forough Press, 2005), 225.

[49] Homs Sarshar, *Sha'aban Ja'fari* (Beverly Hills: Naab Press, 2002), 161.

claimed Wilber had failed to provide an "objective" analysis because he supposedly had "axes" to grind.[50]

The two new documents, moreover, do not bolster the revisionists. On the contrary, they tend to reinforce the Wilber report. The *Battle for Iran* categorically declares: "The military coup that overthrow Mossadeq was carried out under CIA direction as an act of US foreign policy, conceived and approved at the highest level of government." It repeats Roosevelt's explanation he had broken contact with the outside world after the failed coup so as to be able to implement the rest of the plan. It even describes 19 August as the "second, winning, phase of the operation." It admits that attempts to win over senior Qom clerics "produced no definite results"; that "truckloads of solders began driving through the streets" on 19 August; and "many of the people in the street were paid" – but with no mention of Kashani. In releasing the documents, the National Security Archive even billed them as "CIA Confirms Role in 1953 Iran Coup."[51]

"*Zendebad Shah!*" begins admitting the document was commissioned to answer two questions troubling historians: "Why did the USA act against Mosaddeq?" and "Would the Mosaddeq government have fallen if the USA had done nothing?" Speculations about imagined futures are invariably loaded as Richard Evans has shown in his *Altered Pasts: Counterfactuals in History*.[52] For Evans, "History does not conjugate in conditionals, it speaks of what is and what was, not what would be and would have been." "*Zendebad Shah!*" reveals – for the first time – the surprising information that the CIA briefly discussed whether Kashani or Zahedi would be a more preferable choice to bring to power. It also reinforces the account of Washington "writing off" the whole venture after the 15 August fiasco, but Roosevelt in Tehran persevering with the knowledge that the military component of the plans remained intact. The two documents further admit that the Rashidian brothers as well as unnamed "mullas" organized the "electrifying" *zurkhaneh* crowd; and that by noon the army had trucked in additional soldiers shouting "*Zendebad Shah!*"

[50] National Security Archive, "CIA declassifies more of 'Zendebad Shah!,'" https:// nsarchiv.gwu.edu/riefing-book/iran/2018-02-12.

[51] National Security Archive, "CIA Confirms Role in 1953 Coup," www2 .gwu.edu/~nsarchiv/NSAEBB/NSAEBB435.

[52] Richard Evans, *Altered Pasts: Counterfactuals in History* (Waltham: Brandeis University Press, 2013).

Unfortunately, much of the details on 19 August remain classified. The CIA concluded that TPAJAX had succeeded because of Roosevelt's "initiative, quick-thinking, calm analysis, and ability to recognize turning points and act decisively upon them." The document ends with the resounding declaration:

The fall of Mossadeq was a watershed in demonstrating civilian clandestine operational expertise and in putting a civilian intelligence agency at the forefront of planning and executing covert operations. After TPAJAX, the military could not argue as it did in Congressional Hearings of the Security Act of 1947, that civilians did not have the background, training, or experience for clandestine activity.

This runs counter to the revisionist claim that the CIA was a mere side observer of the 1953 coup.

What is more, the overall picture did not fit into the revisionist framework. The claim the British embargo caused an "economic free-fall" is a wide exaggeration. Even before the embargo was launched, the Foreign Office cautioned that such action would have little effect on an economy that was still predominantly agrarian. Iran was not yet a "rentier state" and the oil income formed less than 11 percent of government revenues – in 1950 it totaled no more than £16 million. The Foreign Office, as well as the US NIEs, conceded that the government dealt well with the embargo, that "loss of oil revenues did not seriously damage the economy," and that the "oil crisis had not had notable effect on the standard of living."[53] Harvests were "excellent" and exports of rugs and agricultural exports – especially of rice and barley – were doing well. The CIA admitted in late October 1952 that loss of oil revenues "had not done serious or lasting damage to the economy."[54]

Avery – no great admirer of Mossadeq – begrudgingly conceded that economic difficulties did not produce political discontent and the "majority of ordinary citizens continued to life their lives as always."[55] Iranians, he writes, were "resilient," those employed

---

[53] NSC, Prospect for Survival of Mossadeq Regime in Iran (14 October 1952), *FRUS* (2017), 367–70; NIE-75, Developments through 1953 (13 November 1952), *FRUS* (2017), 407–17; Middleton, Memorandum to the State Department (12 August 1953), *FRUS* (1989), 743; NIE-46, Probable Developments for Iran in 1952 (4 February 1953), *FRUS* (2017), 175–82.

[54] CIA, Prospects for Survival of Mossadeq's Regime (30 October 1952), CIA Electronic Library, www.cia.gov/library/readingroom/search/site/Iran.

[55] Avery, *Modern Iran*, 433–4.

continued to be paid, and those in need were helped by neighbors and local shopkeepers. Besides, he adds, "He [Mossadeq] was much loved by a very large number of people – an unusual phenomenon where Iranian Prime Ministers are concerned."

The government also took effective countermeasures. It restricted luxury imports, devaluated the currency, curtailed capital expenditures, issued bonds, drew on gold and foreign reserves, sold government stock, trimmed the military budget, and resorted to deficit financing to pay oil workers and state employees. Surprisingly, this did not trigger off runaway inflation. The CIA report issued on the very eve of the coup concluded that the government was not yet under "serious challenge" because the harvests continued to be excellent and "uncontrolled inflation was not imminent."[56] In fact, one of the many CIA schemes to destabilize the government was to flood the country with counterfeit paper money. Inflation became an issue only after 1953 when the succeeding government resorted to drastic deficit financing. After the coup, the US and UK embassies were surprised to discover that the government had not only run the oil industry efficiently but also regularly paid its employees, including military personnel.[57]

The economy in the summer of 1953 held some hope of improvement. Small oil companies, including from the US, were "restless" to get into the Iranian market.[58] Italian and Japanese courts had ruled that private companies could import oil from Iran. Argentine, Brazil, Formosa, Belgium, Spain, Finland, and Yugoslavia were showing similar interest.[59] *Ettela'at* claimed in May that fourteen tankers were at Abadan ready to load oil. Clearly, the government hoped to find ways of breaking the British embargo, and circumventing the monopoly the major oil companies had over the world tanker fleet.

What is more, Iran in the summer of 1953 initiated talks with the Soviet Union. The talks involved sale of oil and barter trade as well as settling of financial accounts from World War II. The Soviet Union had

[56] Sherman Kent, Current Outlook in Iran (13 August 1953), www.cia.gov/library/readingroom/search/site/Iran.

[57] For military personnel see NSC, Contributions to NIE-102 (5 October 1953), Declassified on 2012/09/20. For oil refinery see Wright, Letter to Eden (15 February 1954), FO 416/107.

[58] NIE-75, Political Developments in Iran through 1953 (9 January 1953), FRUS (2017), 436.

[59] Stutesman, General Situation, FRUS (2017), 341–51.

impounded 11.8 tons of Iranian gold in 1942; Iran had billed the Soviet Union $21 million for goods and services provided in 1941–5.[60] Some politicians made hay of the long delay in resolving these wartime accounts. But CIA documents released recently reveal that the USA and Iran were haggling over similar accounts even as late as the mid-1970s. In initiating talks with Moscow, Mossadeq assured the *New York Times* that President Eisenhower's refusal to a loan would not affect US-Iran relations. He also remarked Iran was now "obliged to develop greater trade with Eastern and European countries."[61] One can conclude that the coup did not come as a result of a disintegrating economy. On the contrary, it may have come because it was not disintegrating. As Mossadeq claimed at his trial, the coup had been engineered because the economy was improving.[62]

The economic discontent that existed did not flow into royalist channels. In the summer of 1953 there was only one major industrial strike – in the brick kilns outside Tehran. Citing the Social Stability Law, the government declared it illegal, arrested five ringleaders, and blamed the Tudeh. At no time did strikers express sympathy for the royalist opposition. The Toilers Party, despite its populist rhetoric, remained conspicuously absent. The anti-government parties all failed to make any inroads into the trade unions and the urban working class.

The claim that Mossadeq had lost popularity to the shah is grossly exaggerated. The British in their 1953 annual report admitted that Mossadeq could still hold "large public demonstrations," and arouse the "rabble more effectively than any other of his opponents."[63] Dennis Wright, the British chargé d'affaires appointed soon after the coup, reported:[64]

There seems little doubt that there is still much latent support for Musaddiq throughout the country. No Persian government in foreseeable future can afford to ignore the nationalism which he stirred up. Abadan marks a turning-point for many Persians, who would I believe rather do without

---

[60] CIA, Soviet Union Offers to Settle Iran's Financial Claims (22 July 1953), *FRUS* (2017), 633–5.

[61] *New York Times*, 23 July 1953.

[62] Katouzian, "Oil Boycott and the Political Economy," in *Musaddiq, Iranian Nationalism, and Oil* (ed. James Bill and Wm. Roger Louis) (Austin: Texas University Press, 1988), 203–27.

[63] Foreign Office, Annual Report for Persia in 1953, *FO 471/107*.

[64] Dennis Wright, Letter to Foreign Secretary (7 January 1954), *FO 416/107*.

an oil agreement than allow a government to bring back what they however wrongly, conceive to be a foreign exploiter. The present government appears to be well in control, but they lack popular support.

Wright added that Mossadeq's trial threatened to return to the fore his deep popularity:[65]

For two years he had been for them [the public] a symbol of national aspirations. By propaganda, and particularly by speeches he himself made over the radio, he had brought himself into contact with the masses in a way which had never been experienced before in this country. And his disregard, if not contempt, for those members of the governing classes who would not cooperate with him has not passed unheeded by the long-suffering majority of the population ... .The majority of the people probably still favour Dr. Musaddiq.

The *Times of India* – which happened to be well disposed towards the shah – admitted after the coup that many continued to "sympathize" with Mossadeq, retain "deep faith" in him, and respect him as a "national hero" and "symbol of the patriotism." They suspected "foreign influence" in the post-Mossadeq government. "Half the army," the paper noted, "keeps an eye on the tribes. The other half on the city population ... In some ways the picture is darker now than before the coup."[66] Meanwhile, the reopened British embassy slipped in the following unexpected admission: "The majority of people – leaving aside the Tudeh – probably still favour Dr. Mosaddiq, in spite of his policies or lack of them."[67] The British postmortem on 1979 reminded readers that the Mossadeq "myth held strong" long after 1953.[68]

Similarly, the US embassy reported after the coup that reliable advisers were unanimous in warning that a public trial for Mossadeq could be fraught with dangers.[69] The country still "wove around him a favorable myth," associated him with the "national movement," and respected him as a patriotic "symbol." "All shades of opinion," it continued, "stubbornly clung to the belief that he was a sincere

[65] Wright, Letter to Foreign Secretary (16 February 1954), FO 416/107.
[66] G. Reddy, "Iran's Royalist Coup," *Times of India*, 16–18 September 1953.
[67] British Embassy, Report on Political Situation (12 February 1954), FO 371/109986.
[68] Browne, *British Policy in Iran, 1974–78*, 9.
[69] Melbourne, Aspects of the Political Environment of the Zahedi Government (26 September 1953), *FRUS* (2017), 769–77.

patriot." It added that the campaign to "nullify his favorable image" had failed in part because the succeeding government was seen as having "come to power because of the US." "Mosadeq," the embassy stressed, "should not be allowed to put his histrionic abilities to work in a public trial."

The American embassy and the shah ignored Zahedi's and Imami's clamor for Mossadeq's execution.[70] They had no desire to make him into a national martyr. The CIA reported the "large following" Mossadeq still enjoyed undoubtedly deterred the shah from executing him.[71] The NIE for 1954 declared: "Mossadeq remains a problem. So long as he is alive he will be a potential leader for extremist opposition to the government. On the other hand, if he were to be executed the resultant disturbances would be serious."[72] A follow-up report explained: "The fall of Mosadeq and subsequent attempts to discredit him and his close followers have not changed the general Iranian belief that nationalization of the oil industry was an important and necessary step for Iran."[73] The CIA, in a late 1953 report, repeated the warning that exile or imprisonment could create serious dangers.[74] The special report drafted for Churchill included this enigmatic note:[75]

The future popularity of the Shah was generally agreed to be dependent on whether he acted as a strict constitutional monarch, or whether he resorted to his previous practices, which made him so unpopular in recent years. It should not be forgotten that measures adopted by Dr. Musaddiq to restrict the Shah's interference in the army had the universal support of the people, and that any future infringement of the Constitution by the Shah would be met by the opposition of all progressive elements in the country.

Throughout the 1950s, the CIA continued to be skeptical of the regime's chances of survival. It described the shah as having an "almost pathological fear of the opposition" – especially of the National

---

[70] CIS, Information Report (4 October 1953), *FRUS* (2017), 782–5.
[71] CIA, Political Developments, CIA Electronic Library, www.cia.gov/library/rea dingroom/search/site/Iran.
[72] NIE, Probable Developments in Iran through 1954 (16 November 1953), *FRUS* (2017), 833–45.
[73] NSC, Certain Problems Relating to Iran, *FRUS* (2017), 875–94.
[74] CIA, Immediate Prospects in Iran (12 November 1953), CIA Electronic Library, www.cia.gov/library/readingroom/search/site/Iran.
[75] Foreign Office, British Memorandum: Political Review of the Recent Crisis (2 September 1953), *FRUS* (1989), 786.

Front.[76] It admitted the shah "has not been successful in developing a solid basis of popular support, and, in fact, has actually lost ground since the events of 1953."[77] It warned: "He appears to be completely unaware of the growing dissatisfaction and political frustration which could threaten the very existence of his regime."[78] It conceded – without, of course, getting into embarrassing explanations – that the "Iranian public considers the Shah's regime to be US sponsored."[79] Even at the end of the decade, the CIA admitted "prospects of stability have not improved."[80] In a long 1958 analysis – printed to give it a wide internal circulation – the CIA provided an extensive list of reasons why the regime was unstable and the shah unpopular. But again the list did not mention the 1953 coup.[81] This reticence continued well into the 1979 revolution. In a long NIE drafted in 1976 and printed for internal circulation, the CIA enumerated all the possible sources of potential difficulties, but never mentioned the old issue of 1953.[82] Nor did the lengthy discussion that followed the NIE. Any such mention would have been deemed inappropriate.

In dealing with the events of 19 August, the revisionists exaggerate the role of the clergy in general and of Kashani in particular. The Wilber plans instructed the Tehran station to persuade the senior clergy – notably Grand Ayatollah Boroujerdi in Qom and the leading mojtaheds in Najaf-Karbala – to issue a formal fatwa against the Tudeh and circulars against Mossadeq.[83] They all remained conspicuously silent. The most Boroujerdi issued was a one curt telegram welcoming the shah home on 25 August. Revisionists have added a sentence of

---

[76] CIA, Report on Situation in Iran (9 December 1957), www/cia.gov/library/readingroom/search/site/Iran.

[77] CIA, NIE for Iran for 1957 (22 January 1957), www.cia.gov/readingroom/search/site/Iran.

[78] CIA, Iranian Political Stability Threatened (6 August 1957), www.cia.gov/readingroom/search/site/Iran.

[79] CIA, Background on Iran (5 February 1957), www.cia.gov/readingroom/search/site/Iran.

[80] CIA, Background Piece on Iran (9 September 1958), www.cia.gov/readingroom/search/site/Iran.

[81] CIA, Outlook for the Shah (15 August 1958), www.cia.gov/readingroom/search/site/Iran.

[82] NSC, NIE for Iran for 1976, Declassified on 2010/07/20: LOC-HAK-152-7-49-2.

[83] CIA, Telegram (19 August 1953), *FRUS* (2017), 699.

their own to this telegram.[84] Senior clerics followed Boroujerdi's long-held ruling that they should scrupulously avoid mundane politics. Ayatollah Behbehani, a prominent exception, was deemed more of a *darbari* (courtier) than a venerable man of the cloth. He was soon eased out of the court for lobbying to get his son appointed finance minister.[85] Zahedi and the shah – probably at the advice of the USA – were willing to give him money but not the important ministry. The Foreign Office described Behbehani as "corrupt" and "unscrupulous." It added that having played an "important role in the events which led to Mosaddiq's overthrow he expects and usually receives payments for his services, in particularly from the Shah."[86]

Cottam, the CIA's main analyst on the religious wing of the National Front, later conceded that Kashani himself lost much support when he broke with Mossadeq.[87] He writes:

The mistake of each of the three men [Kashani, Baqai, and Makki] was the failure to understand that this opponent was not just an Iranian politician by the name of Mohammad Mossadeq, but a man around whom a vital, intense, popular movement had crystallized. Since his followers were convinced that Mossadeq's crusade was mainly directed against foreign imperialism, the logical conclusion was that anyone who turned against him was in league with the imperialists. Thus Makki, Baqai, and Kashani were not only shorn of support, but were regarded by any of their former supporters as having sold out to the foreign enemy.

Coming from a CIA analyst this speaks volumes. The turbaned deputies from Tabriz elected on Kashani's ticket – Morteza Shabestari, Mohammad Ali Angechi, Javad Ganjehi, and Ibrahim Milani – all sided with Mossadeq and voted for the referendum dissolving the majles. Qonatabadi, who sided with Kashani, soon discarded the turban and entered the business world.[88] Many clerics who had supported Mossadeq in the past continued to do so well beyond the coup – clerics such as Hojjat al-Islams (later Ayatollahs) Mahmud Taleqani, Reza Zanjani, Abul al-Fazel Zanjani, Baqi Rasuli, Hussein Ali Rashed, and

[84] Fakhreddin Azimi, "The Overthrow of the Government of Mosaddeq Reconsidered," *Iranian Studies*, Vol. 45, No. 5 (September 2012), 693–712.

[85] CIA, Information Report (4 October 1953), *FRUS* (2017), 782.

[86] Foreign Office, Leading Personalities in Iran (1957), *FO 371/127072*.

[87] Cottam, *Nationalism in Iran*, 279.

[88] Naqrehkar, *Zendegiha-ye Gowd Godrat: Naqsh-e Siyasi va 'Ejetema-ye Jahaha va Latha dar Tarekh-e M'oser-e Iran*, 96.

Morteza Pasandideh. The latter was Khomeini's elder brother. Jalali-Mousavi, often lead spokesman at government rallies, was an eloquent pulpit preacher and a turbaned majles deputy.

Even in the Tehran bazaar, Kashani's supposed base of support, many influential merchants – such as Ali Shamshiri, Qassem Labaschi, and Mohammad Maniyan – remained on Mossadeq's side. British reports on the bazaar compiled in late 1953 admit that much of the commercial community continued to support Mossadeq despite Zahedi's and Kashani's attempts to create their own Merchants Union.[89] Ayatollah Khomeini himself years later commiserated that Kashani had become the butt of jokes, even among fellow clerics.[90] Khomeini did not explain if this was due to Kashani's defection from Mossadeq or his naivety in being taken in by Zahedi and the Americans.

It is clear that Zahedi, as well as the Americans and the British, used Kashani to undermine Mossadeq – especially in trying to remove him through parliamentary means. But it is not clear they actually used him on 19 August. The blow-by-blow account sent immediately to the Foreign Office mentions by name Behbehani but not Kashani. A full paragraph – that remained classified until 2001 – describes how on 10 August the "American embassy handed over large sums to Behbehani." The account adds, "Only the military commanders, the Chief of Police, and Ayatollah Behbehani who was responsible for organizing demonstrations, knew of the plan ... It is widely believed that the success of the coup was due to the fact that it was well planned, that it was kept secret, and that plenty of money was made available to carry it out."[91] The CIA-MI6 probably kept Kashani out of the loop because they did not trust him – not because he was unwilling to participate. Soon after the coup, Zahedi and the shah quietly visited Kashani. But this was probably to thank him for his previous activities. Of course, they never intended to give him the promised ministries.

[89] British Embassy, Report on the Significance of the Tehran Bazaar
       (19 December 1953); Report on the Majlis Elections (11 January 1954), Report
       on the Political Situation (12 February 1954), *FO 371/109986.*
[90] Ayatollah Khomeini, "Campaign against Ayatollah Kashani," *Iran Times,*
       6 January 1984.
[91] State Department, Persia: Political Review of the Recent Crisis
       (2 September 1953), Declassified Authority 832934, 6 April 2001. A redacted
       version was published in State Department, British Memorandum: Political
       Review of the Recent Crisis (2 September 1953), *FRUS* (1989), 780–8.

Zahedi had assured Henderson he had no intention of working with Kashani, Baqai, or Makki. The only way, he assured Henderson, any of them would regain influence would be if the shah himself "appointed them to the Senate."[92]

In consolidating power, the shah and Zahedi scrupulously avoided calling the coup by its true name. They heralded it as a *Qeyam-e Melli* (National Uprising); placed trusted politicians in key posts; initially promoted officers who had taken part in the overthrow; and raised across the board military salaries by as much as 60 percent. They declined to reconvene the 17th Majles; kept the capital under martial law; closed down journals, newspapers, as well as social centers such as clubs, theatres, and cinemas; and imprisoned Mossadeq, his advisers, as well as thousands of National Front and Tudeh supporters. In the first month alone, they arrested 1,300 activists and dismissed over 3,000 government employees.

The USA, for its part, rushed in $45 million in emergency aid – more came in the following year; delivered three battalions of Patton tanks; actively helped select a new cabinet; and urged mass imprisonment in Khark, a desolate island in the Persian Gulf. Executions and systematic prison torture came later. The US political attaché questioned the liberal "notion" that poverty creates communism and that economic improvement could resolve the problem.[93] He argued that since communists came from the ranks of the literate and *employed* (emphasis in the original) workers as well as from frustrated middle-class intellectuals, they should be treated as "dangerous, virtually incurable, criminals." He recommended tough treatment and creation of a new centralized security police – this later became known as SAVAK. He also recommended a concerted ideological campaign that would include translating the works of Max Eastman, Arthur Koestler, Bertrand Russell, and Benedetto Croce.

The USA wasted no time assigning Hoover, the veteran oilman, to negotiate with Iran to form a consortium with the major oil companies. The companies included AIOC (now renamed BP) as well as Shell, Exxon, Gulf, Texaco, and Standard Oil of California. Hoover was instructed to meet their four basic requirements: "effective control

---

92 Henderson, Letter to the State Department (7 January 1954), *FRUS* (2017), 897.

93 US Embassy, Suggestions for Combatting Communism (9 October 1953), *FRUS* (2017), 793–8.

over management, production and refining": control over "all export-
able oil"; 50/50 sharing of the profits; and a concession lasting at least
forty years.[94] The CIA reported, "Consortium feels that a clear-cut
grant of effective management control is imperative."[95]

The final agreement thus conformed to McGhee's original proposal.
The industry was declared nationalized in name, but actual management remained safely in Western hands. The Foreign Office was
informed that participating companies demanded "the exclusive right
to explore for, drill for, and produce and refine, and the right to
transport and export oil and gas together with the right of effective
control and management of these operations."[96] Wright, the British
negotiator, put it succinctly: "A formula was found that satisfied the
Persian government's idea of sovereignty while giving the consortium
the control they considered essential over the operations."[97] The
Iranian negotiator confided to his British counterpart, "All the
Persian Government wanted really was a 'decent window
dressing.'"[98] The Butler postmortem was equally blunt: "The 1954
Agreement camouflaged from Persian public opinion the reality that
effective control of the oil industry remained outside Iranian hands."[99]
Iran was generously conceded "full control" over the company's
schools, medical clinics, clubs, swimming pools, and one golf course.
Royalists worked hard to convince themselves that the oil industry had
remained nationalized.

To facilitate the public acceptance of the oil concession, the CIA
"gave extensive financial and material" guidance to the shah and
Zahedi through publications, broadcasts, films, and even lyrics.[100]
And to help the passage of the concession through the majles, the
CIA, in its own words, took: "Very active interest in influencing the
composition of the government slate [2 lines not declassified].
Headquarters has begun a systematic analysis of all election

[94] NSC, Briefing (12 April 1954), www.cia.gov/readingroom/search/site/Iran.
[95] CIA, Status of Oil Negotiations (1 June 1954), www.cia.gov/readingroom/sea
rch/site/Iran.
[96] Sir Roger Stevens, Telegram to Foreign Office and State Department
(14 April 1953), *FO 371/11006*.
[97] Dennis Wright, Annual for Events in Persia in 1954, *FO 371/114805*.
[98] British Ambassador, Letter to the Foreign Office (27 March 1954), *FO 371/
110060*.
[99] Butler, *British Policy in Relinquishing Abadan in 1951*.
[100] CIA, Quarterly Report (8 July 1954), *FRUS* (2017), 926.

information with intent of providing Station with maximum support and guidance during the electoral phase [2 lines not declassified]."[101] In a further study on majles elections, the CIA elaborated:[102]

The information has been gathered in order to give us the proper operational intelligence needed to draw up an electoral program of our own. It is obvious from this study that we cannot hope to change the methods of operations for the 18th Majlis, but instead we must resort to the same methods, through the government and the Shah for the election of a Majlis favorable to our purposes in Iran. We already have a list of declared candidates for the 18th Majlis. We are initiating electoral talks with the government on 14 November. We already have a list of declared candidates and we are ready to do what we can to assist the [Name not declassified] in this matter.

The USA remained involved in the 18th Majles elections as it has been in the 17th Majles. One embassy official cautioned that such interference was "knotty" even though circumstances had somehow produced such a situation.[103] Another noted that the British had placed "great reliance upon such measures but the success of these measures has not been very impressive."[104] He warned against "free-wheeling" and advised "pulling in our horns" to avoid "running the grave risk of becoming known as an intriguing power."

Even though many in London and Washington touted the fall of Mossadeq as a great victory for the West – to compensate for the stalemate in Korea – the Foreign Office was not so sanguine about the future. A former embassy official reiterated his long-held jaundiced view of Iran:[105]

The Persians are a volatile people, manufacturing crises of confidence at will and frequently for no very apparent reason. They respond to strong direction; but they positively rejoice at an opportunity to make confusion more confounded. What they undoubtedly need is a benevolent dictator on the pattern of Dr. Salazar; even Reza Shah Pahlavi managed to reduce the country to some kind of order, though he did virtually nothing for its

101 CIA, Monthly Report (December 1953), *FRUS* (2017), 866–7.
102 CIA, A Study of Electoral Methods in Iran (13 November 1953), *FRUS* (2017), 333–7.
103 US Embassy, Letter of First Secretary to the State Department (30 November 1953), *FRUS* (2017), 851–2.
104 John Stutesman, Letter to Melbourne (6 November 1953), *FRUS* (2017), 829–311.
105 L. Fry, Foreign Office Note (16 June 1955), *FO 371/114810*.

economic well-being. The present Shah unfortunately has the virtues of neither of his father nor of a Dr. Salazar, and, that being so, the only hope is that he will appoint a really good Prime Minister (if such a person exists).

This official obviously harbored no illusions about the coup saving Iran for democracy.

The revisionist argument that has gained most currency is the contention that previous historians have "much exaggerated the role of the US in the overthrow of Mossadeq." This would have some validity if any historian had made the absurd claim the tanks rolling into the city were manned by US officers or the crowd from southern Tehran was full of Americans masquerading as *zurkhaneh* bodybuilders. The new documents firmly reinforce the standard view that the coup would not have occurred without the active participation of the Americans – especially the CIA and the embassy. Without US pressure, including ultimatum, the shah would not have taken part. Without US direction, Zahedi, with few assets, could not have pulled off a military coup. Without CIA coordination, Akhavi's list of officers would have remained just a roster of names. Without embassy influence, parliamentary business would not have ground to a complete halt. Without Henderson's intervention, the streets would not have been empty of Mossadeq supporters on fateful morning of 19 August. Without Roosevelt, the enterprise would have been abandoned after the failure of its first component. And without "Behbehani dollars," the rowdy crowd would not have materialized. The only people who can justly complain the US role had been exaggerated – at their expense – would be the operatives from MI6.

History Returns

The shah had been perceptive enough to realize that if he opposed Mossadeq and oil nationalization he would undermine the legitimacy of the monarchy in general and of his throne in particular. This explains his reluctance to participate in the coup. His concerns were well founded. The coup was perceived by the public as having replanted the national hero with a ruler beholden not just to any foreign power but also to Britain, Iran's traditional imperial master, as well as to America, the new emerging world power. If oil nationalization had been Iran's declaration of independence from imperialism, the

Consortium Agreement was seen as the relinquishing of national sovereignty and the shameful return of colonialism. If Mossadeq embodied patriotism, the shah – by overthrowing him – epitomized the exact opposite. In short, the events of 1953 delegitimized the monarchy, and, thereby, inadvertently paved the way for the eventual 1979 revolution. The coup became the regime's original sin.

The shah continued to be haunted by Mossadeq for the rest of his life even though he did his best to make him into a non-person, banning mention of his name in public. Asadollah Alam, the royal confidant, in his diaries admitted as much even into the heyday of the 1970's oil boom.[106] Dr. Abdol Madjidi, long-time director of the Plan and Budget Organization, argued that the shah deemed Mossadeq to be his "nemesis" and was haunted by his "ghost."[107] Similarly, during the 1973 oil crisis, *The Economist* noted the shah remained "haunted by Mossadeq's ghost."[108] Andrew Cooper, who has interviewed members of the royal family and tends to see the revolution through their eyes, quotes extensively from *The Economist*: "Even after 20 years, the ghost of Mossadegh, the politician who laid claim to the mantle of Iranian nationalism and outbid the Arabs in challenging the West, still haunts the Shah."[109] The British ambassador in 1979 noted the shah continued to be "obsessed" by the fear of another Mossadeq long after the latter's death.[110] Desmond Harney, the MI6 man in Tehran during the 1979 revolution, told an interviewer that the shah continued to suffer from "inferiority complex about Mossadeq."[111] Tony Benn, the British Secretary of State, in a private audience with the shah in 1976, tried to butter him up by asking him where he had got his "great ideas." The shah began with generalities about "Swiss peasants," but then, without apparent logic, leaped into a long tirade against Mossadeq. "That mad man," he exclaimed, "came to power and caused a great deal of

---

[106] Asadollah Alam, *The Shah and I: The Confidential Diary of Iran's Royal Court* (ed. Alinaghi Alikhani) (New York: St. Martin's Press, 1991), 318.

[107] Cyrus Kadivar, *Farewell Shiraz: An Iranian Memoir of Revolution and Exile* (New York: American University of Cairo, 2019), 267.

[108] Special Reporter, "The Shah Goes to the Brink," *The Economist*, 29 December 1973.

[109] Andrew Cooper, *The Oil Kings* (New York: Simon and Shuster, 2011), 147.

[110] British Embassy, Leading Personalities in Iran (1979), FCO 8/3349.

[111] Ladjevardi, Interview with Desmond Harney, *The Iranian Oral History Project* (Cambridge: Harvard University, 1994).

harm."[112] One does not have to be a psychologist to understand this unexpected leap.

Losing national credibility, the shah searched desperately for substitutes. He took on the mantle of Two Thousand Years of Iranian History – especially of the supposed long line of Imperial Monarchy. He adopted the aura of a Bismarckian radical launching from above with much fanfare the White Revolution that soon became the Shah-People's Revolution. This was supposed to create a deep-seated "dialectical relationship" between himself and his loyal subjects. He tried to project the image of a militant "hawk" leading OPEC's campaign to raise oil prices. He also tried to project the image of himself as a powerful national leader building the largest and best-equipped army, navy, and air force in the region – in the Persian Gulf and even into the Indian Ocean.

These measures had unintended and unfortunate consequences. The resort to ancient Iran was seen by the religious-minded as an insidious scheme to undermine their Shi'i Islam. The White Revolution, instead of winning new supporters, sharply undercut old ones – notably the landlords and tribal chiefs, who, with their peasants and tribesmen, had in the past served as the monarch's main bulwark. His "hawkish" period inside OPEC lasted a mere three months and failed to cut much ice with the general public. What is more, the well-publicized bid to become the major power in the region reinforced the suspicion that the Americans had installed him in 1953 so that he would serve as their main policeman in the Persian Gulf.

In the midst of the ostentatious celebrations for the 2,500-year monarchy, Anthony Parson, the British ambassador, noted that despite all the "pomp," "bombast," and "majesty," the shah "knows that the fabric of the state is still fragile."[113] The ambassador suspected that although the shah had regional pretensions his main concern was internal security, and that the show of world dignitaries bearing "tribute" and treating him as "center of the universe" was designed primarily for internal considerations and to impress his own people. In other words, the shah was trying to create some form of legitimacy. Parsons, not surprisingly, shied away from delving into why the state was

---

[112] FCO, Memorandum (28 April 1976), *FCO 96/535*.
[113] Parsons, "Ten Page Report on Persepolis," cited in Browne, *British Policy in Iran*.

a "fragile state" despite all the oil money and impregnable-looking institutions. Such an inquiry would have led him back to 1953.

The lack of legitimacy proved fatal in 1977–8 when the shah found himself unexpectedly facing two relatively minor difficulties: a slight dip in the still substantial oil revenues; and pressure from the international press, backed by the Carter administration, to improve human rights – especially prison conditions. A regime with a semblance of legitimacy could have weathered such minor difficulties. The shah's regime could not. As protests grew from scattered demonstrations to mass rallies and million-strong processions, and eventually to a nationwide general strike, the shah discovered there was no one he could negotiate with. The British postmortem on the 1979 revolution mentions, but only in passing, that the "Mossadeq myth" remained strong into the 1970s.[114] Harney of MI6 writes:[115]

> The truth of twenty-five years is coming out – and the people (all of us) are fascinated. The Persian democratic tradition has been preserved and is alive and well, *alhamdolellah*. And we are hearing real Persian spoken again, not the pompous, stuffy rubbish of the old order, but free, humorous, satirical, anecdotal, and fierce.
>
> ... The hatred and passion and discontent in the people is terrifying – not just the typically radical students. It is easy to forget of course, that most of the middle or junior officials one meets were students abroad themselves a few years back when they were radicalized for a time. That process has gone on for twenty years or more – and they are to be found at every level.

John Stemple, the de facto head American representative during the revolution, admits the shah had difficulty finding opposition leaders to negotiate with simply because they all considered him illegitimate.[116] Stemple, probably inhibited by secrecy laws, does not admit this illegitimacy came from 1953. William Polk, however, veteran of the State Department from the early 1950s and a close observer of Iran in the following decades, felt free in 2009 – after Albright's admission – to explicitly draw a direct line between 1953 and 1979. His book *Understanding Iran* ends with the categorical statement that the coup had made the shah appear "in the eyes of most Iranians as a puppet of

---

[114] Browne, *British Policy in Iran, 1974–78*, chapter 3, 9.

[115] Harney, *The Priest and the King*, 22, 76.

[116] John Stemple, *Inside the Iranian Revolution* (Bloomingdale: Indiana University Press, 1981), 320.

America." This, he concludes, was so deeply "seared" into public memory that "to understand subsequent events, right to the present, one must understand the coup."[117] Similarly, Straw, the Foreign Secretary, draws "a direct line from the 1953 coup through the Islamic Republic of 1979 to the present."[118] He adds Mossadeq became the "standard bearer and iconic figure of Iran's national struggle against foreign powers," and his overthrow was one of the "defining moments that explain the abiding suspicion, not to say paranoia, about foreign interference in Iran." Finally, Shaul Bakhash, the highly respected historian of modern Iran, in analyzing the 1979 revolution writes: "This [1953 coup] was a seminal event in the modern history of Iran. The involvement of the CIA and British intelligence in a coup that overthrew a properly elected and very popular PM has remained seared into the Iranian historical imagination and has colored the US-Iranian relationship."[119] Malcolm X would have said: "Chickens have come to roost."

[117] William Polk, *Understanding Iran* (New York: Palgrave, 2009), 114, 179.
[118] Straw, *The English Job*, 156.
[119] Shaul Bakhash, "The US and Iran in Historical Perspective," *Foreign Policy*, 25 September 2009.

Selected Bibliography

Documents

The US government documents are in State Department, *Foreign Relations of the United States, 1952–54, Vol. X, Iran, 1951–54* (ed. William Slany) (Washington, DC: US Government Printing Office, 1989); and State Department, *Foreign Relations of the United States, 1952–54, Iran, 1951–54* (ed. William Van Hook) (Washington, DC: US Government Printing House, 2017). They can be found at history@state.gov.

The CIA has drafted three major studies on the coup:

1. Donald Wilber, *Overthrow of Premier Mossadeq of Iran, November 1952–August 1953* (Washington, DC: CIA Historical Division, 1954). This was posted – with some names removed – at http://cryptome.org/cia-iran-all.htm. It was also published – again with some names erased – as *Regime Change in Iran: Overthrow of Premier Mossadeq of Iran* (London: Russell Press, 2006).
2. Scott Koch, *"Zendebad Shah!": The CIA and the Fall of the Iranian Prime Minister Mohammad Mossadeq, August 1953* (Washington, DC: History Staff, 1963). This was posted by the National Security Archive at www2.gwu.edu/~nsarchiv/NSAEBB4/NSAEBB435. See also https://bit.ly/2Jjh1pm.
3. History Staff, *The Battle for Iran* (Washington, DC: Near East Division, n.d.). This was declassified in 2014 and released by the National Security Archive at
www2.gwu.edu/~narchive/NSAEBB/NSAEBB435.

The CIA has also posted occasional documents at

www.cia.gov/library/readingroom/search/site/iran.

The Foreign Office documents are in London at the British National Archives (formerly the Public Record Office). They are filed mostly under FO 371/Persia/82306–82385/91448–91575/91521–91543/91601–91616/98595–98732/104561–104576/109988–110093/114805–114813.

The British postmortem on the oil crisis written by Rohan Butler and entitled *British Policy in the Relinquishing of Abadan in 1951* is in FO 370/2694.

The British postmortem on the 1979 revolution written by Nicholas Browne and entitled *British Policy in Iran, 1974–78* is in FCO 8/3601.

Selected Works

Abrahamian, Ervand. *The Coup: 1953, The CIA, and the Roots of Modern US-Iranian Relations* (New York: New Press, 2013).

Acheson, Dean. *Present at Creation* (New York: Norton, 1969).

Afshar, Iraj. *Toqrerat-e Mossadeq dar Zendan* (Mossadeq's Comments in Prison) (Tehran: Sazman-e Ketab Publications, 1980).

Ahmadi, Hamid. *Asrar-e Kudeta* (Coup Secrets) (Tehran: Ney Publications, 2001).

Alam, Asadollah. *The Shah and I: The Confidential Diary of Iran's Royal Court* (ed. Alinaghi Alikhani) (New York: St. Martin's Press, 1991).

Ansari, Ali. *Modern Iran Since 1921* (London: Longman, 2003).

Arsanjani, Hassan. *Yaddashtha-ye Seyasi-e Man: Seyum-e Tir* (My Political Memoirs: July 21st) (Tehran: Atesh Press, 1956).

Atesh. *Qeyam dar Rah-e Saltanat* (Revolt for the Monarchy) (Tehran: Majles Publications, 1954).

Avery, Peter. *Modern Iran* (London: Benn, 1965).

Azimi, Fakhreddin. *The Crisis of Democracy* (London: Tauris, 2009).

"The Overthrow of the Government of Mosaddeq Reconsidered," *Iranian Studies*, Vol. 45, No. 5 (September 2012), 693–712.

"A Rejoinder to Mr. Darioush Bayandor," *Iranian Studies*, Vol. 46, No. 3 (May 2013), 477–80.

Bayandor, Darioush. *Iran and the CIA: The Fall of Mosaddeq Revisited* (New York: Palgrave, 2010).

Bellaigue, Christopher de. *Patriot of Persia: Muhammad Mossadegh and a Tragic Anglo-American Coup* (New York: HarperCollins, 2012).

Bill, James. *The Eagle and the Lion: The Tragedy of American-Iranian Relations* (New Haven: Yale University Press, 1988).

Bill, James & Louis, Wm. R. *Mussadiq, Iranian Nationalism, and Oil* (London: Tauris, 1988).

CIA. *A Study of Assassinations: The Secret Assassination Manual* (Beckley, WV: Shadow Warrior Publications, 2019).

Cook, Fred. "The Billion Dollar Mystery," *The Nation*, 12 April 1965.

Cooper, Andrew. *The Oil Kings* (New York: Simon & Schuster, 2011).

The Fall of Heaven (New York: Henry Holt, 2016).

Bozorgmehr, Jalel. *Mohammad Mossadeq dar Mahakemeh-e Nezami* (Mohammad Mossadeq in Military Court) (Tehran: Jahan Publications, 1984).

Doktor Mohammad Mossadeq va Residegi-ye Farjam dar Divan-e Keshvar (Dr. Mossadeq and Final Investigation in the Supreme Court) (Tehran: Sahami Publications, 1988).

Copeland, Miles. *The Game Player: Confessions of the CIA's Original Political Operative* (London: Aurum Press, 1989).

Cottam, Richard. *Nationalism in Iran* (Pittsburgh, PA: University of Pittsburgh Press, 1967).

Dahnowi, Mohammad. *Majmu'ah-e az Maktubat, Sukhanraniha va Paymanha-ye Ayatollah Kashani* (Collection of Ayatollah Kashani's Teachings, Speeches and Messages) (Tehran: Ashna Publications, 1982), Vols. I–III.

Dorril, Stephen. *MI6: Inside the Covert World of Her Majesty's Secret Service* (New York: Free Press, 2000).

Ebrahimi, Mansoureh. *The British Role in Iranian Domestic Politics (1951–1953)* (Malaysia: Springer, 2016).

Elm, Mostafa. *Oil, Power and Principle: Iran's Oil Nationalization and Its Aftermath* (Syracuse: Syracuse University Press, 1992).

Elwell-Sutton, L. P. *Persian Oil: A Study in Power Politics* (London: Lawrence and Wishart, 1955).

Falle, Sam. *My Lucky Life* (London: Book Guild, 1996).

Fardoust, Hussein. *Khaterat* (Memoirs) (Tehran: Ettela'at Publications, 1982).

Fateh, Mustafa. *Panjah Sal-e Naft* (Fifty Years of Oil) (Tehran: Kavesh Publications, 1955).

Gasiorowski, Mark. "The 1953 Coup d'Etat in Iran," *International Journal of Middle East Studies*, Vol. 19, No. 3 (August 1987), 261–86.

   "The Causes of Iran's 1953 Coup: A Critique of Darioush Bayandor's Iran and the CIA," *Iranian Studies*, Vol. 45, No. 5 (September 2012), 669–78.

Gasiorowski, Mark & Malcolm Byrne. *Mohammad Mosaddeq and the 1953 Coup in Iran* (Syracuse: Syracuse University Press, 2004).

Goode, James. *The United States and Iran: In the Shadow of Musaddiq* (New York: St. Martin's Press, 1997).

Harney, Desmond. *The Priest and the King* (London: Tauris, 1999).

Iskandari, Iraj. *Yadnameh-ha va Yaddasht-ha-ye Parakandeh* (Scattered Notes and Reminiscences) (Germany: Marde Emruz Publication, 1986).

Kadivar, Cyrus. *Farewell Shiraz: An Iranian Memoir of Revolution and Exile* (New York: University of Cairo Press, 1019).

Kaplan, Morton. *The Communist Coup in Czechoslovakia* (Princeton, NJ: Princeton University Press, 1960).

Kashani, Morteza. *Khaterat* (Memoirs) (Tehran: Islamic Revolution Publications, 2011).

Katouzian, Homa. *Khalil Maleki: The Human Face of Iranian Socialism* (London: Oneworld Academic Press, 2018).
Musaddiq and the Struggle for Power in Iran (London: Tauris, 1999).
Keshavarz, Mohammad (ed.). *Asnad-e Enteqabat-e Majles-e Shura-ye Melli dar Dowreh-e Pahlavi-e Aval* (Documents of Parliamentary Elections during the Reign of Pahlavi I) (Tehran: Ministry of Culture, 1999).
Kianouri, Nuraldin. *Khaterat* (Memoirs) (Tehran: Ettela'at Publications, 1992).
Kinzer, Stephen. *All the King's Men: An American Coup and the Roots of Middle East Terror* (Hoboken, NJ: Wiley, 2008).
Ladjevardi, Habib. *Iranian Oral History Project* (Cambridge: Harvard University, 1993).
Louis, Roger Wm. *Ends of British Imperialism: The Scramble for Empire, Suez and Decolonization* (London: Tauris, 2006).
Majles. *Muzakerat-e Majles-e Shura-ye Melli* (Majles Debates) (Tehran: Majles Printing House, 1953), 17th Majles.
Makki, Hussein. *Vaqa-ye Seyum-e Tir* (The Events of 21 July) (Tehran: Elm Publications, 1999).
Marsh, Steve. "The United States, Iran and Operation 'Ajax': Inverting Interpretative Orthodoxy," *Middle Eastern Studies*, Vol. 39, No. 3 (July 2003), 1–37.
May, Ernest (ed.). *American Cold War Strategy: Interpreting NSC 68* (New York: St. Martin's Press, 1993).
McGhee, George. *Envoy to the Middle East* (New York: Harper and Row, 1983).
Mohammadi, Mohammad Jafar. *Raz-e Pirouz-e Kudeta-ye Best-u-Hasht-e Mordad* (The Secret of the victory of the Coup d'État of 19 August) (Cologne: Forough Press, 2005).
Mokhtari, Fariborz. "Iran's 1953 Coup Revisited: Internal Dynamics versus External Intrigue," *Middle East Journal*, Vol. 62, No. 3 (Summer 2008), 462–88.
Mossadeq, Mohammad. *Khaterat va Ta'alumat* (Memories and Sorrows) (Tehran: Elm Publications, 2007).
Movahhed, Mohammad. *Khavb-e Ashufeteh-e Naft* (The Oil Nightmare) (Tehran: Karnameh Publications, 1999), Vols. I–II.
Noqrehkar, Masoud. *Zendegiha-ye Gowd Godrat: Naqsh-e Seyasi va 'Ejetema-ye Jahaha va Latha dar Tarekh-e Mo'ser-e Iran* (Lives from the Exercise Arena: The Political and Social Role of Lutis in Contemporary Iran) (Cologne: Forough Press, 2016).
Paget, Karen. *Patriotic Betrayal: The Inside Story of the CIA's Secret Campaign to Enroll American Students in the Crusade Against Communism* (New Haven, CT: Yale University Press, 2015).

Painter, David. *Oil and the American Century* (London: Johns Hopkins University Press, 1986).

Parsons, Anthony. *The Pride and the Fall* (London: Jonathan Cape, 1984).

Polk, William. *Understanding Iran* (New York: Palgrave, 2009).

Rahnema, Ali. *Neruha-ye Mazhabi* (Religious Forces) (Tehran: Gam-e Now Press, 1985).

"Overthrowing Mosaddeq in Iran," *Iranian Studies*, Vol. 45, No. 5 (September 2012), 661–91.

Behind the 1953 Coup in Iran (Cambridge: Cambridge University Press, 2015).

Roosevelt, Kermit. *Countercoup: The Struggle for the Control of Iran* (New York: McGraw Hill, 1970).

Ruehsen, Moyara De Moraes. "Operation Ajax Revisited: Iran, 1953," *Middle Eastern Studies*, Vol. 29, No. 3 (July 1993), 467–86.

Sadre, Mahmoud (ed.). *A Profile in Courage: Dr. Mohammad Mossadegh in Military Court* (Costa Mesa: Mazda Publications, 2019).

Saleh, Allahyar. *Gozaresh-e Seyas-ye Vashington* (Political Events in Washington) (Tehran: Sukhan Publications, 2010).

Senate. *Muzakerat-e Majles-e Sena* (Senate Debates) (Tehran: Senate Printing House, 1953), 1st Senate.

Shayegan, Ahmad. *Sayyed Ali Shayegan* (Tehran: Ney Publications, 2004), Vols. I–II.

Stempel, John. *Inside the Iranian Revolution* (Bloomington: Indiana University Press, 1981).

Straw, Jack. *The English Job: Understanding Iran* (London: Biteback Publications, 2019).

Tatari, Ali (ed.). *Negah beh Majles-e Shura-ye Melli* (Look at the National Assembly) (Tehran: Ministry of Culture, 2015).

Upton, Joseph. *The History of Modern Iran: An Interpretation* (Cambridge, MA: Harvard University Middle East Monographs, 1960).

Wilber, Donald. *Adventures in the Middle East* (Princeton, NJ: Darwin Press, 1986).

Woodhouse, C. M. *Something Ventured* (London: Granada, 1982).

Young, Cuyler T. "The Social Support of Current Iranian Policy," *Middle East Journal*, Vol. 6, No. 2 (Spring 1952), 125–43.

"Iran in Continuing Crisis," *Foreign Affairs*, Vol. 40, No. 2 (January 1962), 275–92.

Zabih, Sepehr. *The Mossadegh Era: Roots of the Iranian Revolution* (Chicago, IL: Lake View Press, 1982).

Index